Lost & Found
in Latin America

All About Brazil's World Cup Soccer,

the Argentine Pope & Mariachi

John Wright

Dave and Deana—

Your friendship is a
lasting treasure and your
encouragement was central
to this project.

Jeb
April 2014

Rainy City Publishing
P.O. Box 82813
Kenmore, Washington
Copyright © 2014 Authored By John Wright
All rights reserved.

ISBN: 0615952100
ISBN 13: 9780615952109
Library of Congress Control Number: 2014900619
Rainy City Publishing, Kenmore, WA

To B. James Wright, my uncle, mentor, traveling companion, confidante and inspiration

Acknowledgments

My parents, Richard and Helen, stimulated my imagination from a young age, always allowing me to search and discover. Before I entered kindergarten, Grandma Mert and Aunt Hazel patiently read my stories about a peripatetic cat named Mr. Someo and urged me to write more.

Jules Waldman, Clem Cohen and Sally Weeks gave me a home at *The Daily Journal* in Caracas. Jean-François van de Walle became my roommate and one of my closest lifelong friends. Numerous people generously taught me the ways of Venezuela, including Tibor Somlo, Irving Jordan, Peter Greiff, Kay Pinckney, Madelyn Farr, Moira Tamayo, Ana Maria Hernandez, Teddy Phocas, Lucrecia Añez, Stuart Fricke, Julia Martinez, and Ev Bauman. Walter (Dago) and Maria Rosa Muller included me in their joyous family life.

Flavio Aloe changed the course of my life by generously inviting me to visit him in Brazil.

Tom Kent and Dave Minthorn brought me to The Associated Press, my next step overseas. My colleagues at AP, including Carmen Valdivieso Hulbert, Mario Schizman, David Smyth, Frank Perez, Arthur Allen, Andrew Selsky, Dan Harker, and Mary Sedor, broadened and deepened my knowledge about Latin America. Eloy Aguilar, Joe Frazier, Anita Snow, Jim Anderson, Nick Levi, Sergio "El Puma" Carrasco, Candice Hughes and Chris Angelo tutored me all about Mexico. John Hitchcock, Jim Furlong and Hammad Jawdat trusted me to open the Dow Jones office in Brazil. There I had the good fortune to work with Stan Lehman, Jonathan Wheatley, John Kolodziejski,

Adam Brown, Emily Schwartz, Veronica Goyzueta, Mara Lemos, Any Cabrera, Michael Astor, Harold Olmos, and Maria Jose Miranda.

Gonzalo Berrocal Brenes and his wonderful family make me feel at home every time in Costa Rica. Hiram, Lilian, and Jarito Laws, and Marlene Sanchez, piqued my curiosity about Panama decades before I went there.

My literary agent, Alison Picard, tirelessly promoted this book to numerous publishers. Dave Carpenter offered valuable feedback and inspiration at multiple points; Jeff Donn performed crucial research; and Peter Muello took a flabby manuscript, painstakingly whipped it into shape, and made it sing.

Maria is the love of my life who gave me the greatest joy, Juliana and Joseph. I am proud to count Lia, Marcella and Bruna as part of my family. I cherish my brothers Rick and Stephan, my sisters Roxane and Cathy, and their spouses, Rhonda, Sharmon, Casey and Craig. Uncles Jack, Chuck and Bill and Aunt Helene have been supportive of my endeavors my entire life. My mother-in-law, Juliana, is an example of how to live; my late father-in-law José was one of the great influences on my life. Annie Skipper works hard so that others can rest, and Maharishi taught me how to find a peaceful, quiet place inside.

Contents

CONTENTS

"Surrealism comes from the reality of Latin America"

– Gabriel Garcia Marquez

Author's Note

Thank you for joining me on this three-decade journey around Latin America; I am honored that you are willing to spend your time reading my book. Without readers, a writer would have no *Raison d'être*. I hope you can laugh and cry with me, poke fun at my frequent pratfalls and missteps, and perhaps learn something new about our Latin neighbors.

From the start, I need to explain an important premise. I take no literary license whatsoever. As a journalist for nearly forty years, my only commitment is to the truth, and so I have attempted to lay out all the facts as I see them, without embellishment. Every person mentioned in this book is somebody I really met, and their names are real. There are no fictional characters or composites. Each event is something I really did or saw or partook in. I visited all the places I describe. I have scoured my memory for the most accurate representation of people, places and events. I have reviewed my travel diaries, letters sent to family members, and news articles I wrote at the time. I have used reference books, maps, Internet searches and conversations with people I knew at the time to fill in gaps. I accept sole responsibility for any eventual inaccuracy.

Some memoirs are vehicles to settle scores or exact revenge for past insults and slights. This book, however, would not be sidetracked by personal pettiness.

For readers who try to follow my travels on a map, I apologize that the narratives are not always in continuous chronological order. Because I visited many places multiple times, I organized chapters thematically to make them easier to read. Thus, two trips through Andean countries got rolled into a single continuous narrative, and two journeys through the Amazon were compressed into one. Vignettes about Brazil, Venezuela, and Mexico combine the times I lived there with travels before or afterward. Likewise, the chapter on Central America involves both journalistic work in the region and separate travel for pleasure.

Thus, the story thread occasionally may yo-yo back and forth through time and space, at the risk of causing literary whiplash, but I seek to make the gist of these narratives easier to grasp.

The journalist in me has devoted years to overcoming my individual opinions and writing about events as objectively as possible. This book, however, is my own personal memoir, and the author in me knows that the only way to tell it accurately is through the subjective first person. Above all, I hope you get something of value out of reading this.

John Wright
Darien, Panama
December 2013

The Great National Tragedy

What was the great national tragedy? Ask any American, and everyone will answer the same thing: the deadly September 11 terrorist attacks. A Brazilian will offer a different response. Brazil's great "National Tragedy" occurred July 16, 1950 in front of two hundred thousand stunned fans at Maracanã Stadium in Rio de Janeiro, the nation's most revered temple to its unofficial national religion, when Brazil's "unbeatable" team was toppled at home in the World Cup final.

This same stadium, after a billion-dollar facelift, was the scene of Brazil's 2013 Confederations Cup victory over Spain and will hold seventy-nine thousand exuberant shouting spectators to watch the final showdown in the 2014 World Cup.

In 1950, the upset of historic proportions occurred when tiny Uruguay, smaller than the southernmost state it borders in Brazil, defeated the cocky Brazilians by two to one. Sure, the Brazilians were humiliated, but to carry a grudge sixty-four years? How many of the people who watched that game in 1950 are even alive today? Yet, the memory is seared in the national consciousness.

Brazil enters the 2014 World Cup as the only nation to have won the world's most prestigious soccer tournament five times. Yet somehow it remains a painful memory to have been felled by the cheeky upstart neighbors who have won only twice. For perspective, imagine the combined American and National League All-Stars crushed by a motley bunch of semi-pro baseball players from Bulgaria.

It's not as if Brazil lacks genuine tragedies. Uncounted children who roam the streets have been butchered by off-duty police officers or wannabe cops. Floods and landslides routinely bury entire towns and kill dozens. Fires sweep through slums and incinerate everything in their path. Countless landless peasants have been slaughtered by vigilantes hired by ruthless land owners. Military dictators ruled with an iron fist for two decades and tortured suspected opponents, including Dilma Rousseff, who is now president. And, untold numbers of ordinary citizens have been snuffed out by violent bandits who prowl Brazil's streets. The overall death toll in these Brazilian tragedies vastly outnumbers the lives snuffed out by Osama bin Laden's henchmen on September 11. And yet, the World Cup loss is still called Brazil's national tragedy, even if somewhat hyperbolically.

What does the World Cup mean to Brazil? Take the World Series, Super Bowl, Stanley Cup, NBA finals, NCAA Final Four, Indy 500, and Kentucky Derby, roll them all into a single event with the enthusiasm generated by a rock music festival and the emotional intensity of a Billy Graham crusade, and you get the rough equivalent of how Brazilians are captivated by the World Cup. The peerless Edson Arantes do Nascimento, better known as Pelé, has been Brazil's undisputed national hero – surpassing all politicians, entertainers and other athletes – since the 1960s.

When I worked as the Brazil bureau chief for Dow Jones in São Paulo, our office overlooked Avenida 9 de Julho, the main highway slicing through the center of a city of eleven million residents. Day and night, cars backed up and horns blared. We often shut our windows to avoid choking on the poisonous fumes pouring from stopped cars, trucks and buses. But, when Brazil plays in the World Cup, even a preliminary qualifying match against nobodies without a prayer of winning, all of Brazil comes to a halt. The always-crowded highway was vacant. A random taxi or emergency vehicle breezed through occasionally, but the whole country was at a standstill. Bars and restaurants with televisions overflow with everybody glued to the game. Another year, I saw the same thing in the remote small town where my wife grew up in Minas Gerais state. You don't need to watch the game to follow it. Even a blind person could keep up by hearing all the TVs in the neighborhood. Every time Brazil scores, the announcers breathlessly shout "g-o-o-o-o-o-o-o-o-o-o-o-l!" which is drowned out by non-stop cheering and hoots of "Brasil! Brasil!" Each goal scored against the Brazilian players is loudly cursed. If Brazil wins the game, everybody pours into the street to dance and scream, or pile into a car to drive around aimlessly for an hour honking and screaming in ecstasy.

When Argentina won the World Cup, for the second time in 1986, I was living in New York City and saw Argentines equally excited, jamming the streets with blasting horns and waving the blue-and-white striped Argentine flag. Even though my Brooklyn neighborhood was inhabited predominantly by Orthodox Jews, the whole city seemed to be overrun by joyous, boisterous Argentines. Among the millions of Argentines celebrating that same night back at home was a priest named Jorge Mario Bergoglio. Should it surprise anyone that Pope Francis, the first pontiff from Latin America, is a devoted soccer fan?

And if you think Brazilians and Argentines are soccer fanatics, consider Honduras and El Salvador. They went to war for four days in 1969, triggered by a dispute over qualifying matches for the 1970 World Cup. After riots in which fans were injured, Honduras severed diplomatic ties. El Salvador invaded, and thousands of civilians perished.

Enthusiasm by American sports fans shrivels by comparison. I lived in Seattle when the SuperSonics won the NBA finals and when the Seahawks dominated the Super Bowl. I lived in Los Angeles when the Dodgers triumphed in the World Series and in New York when the Yankees and Mets won different World Series. The depth and breadth of support, while lively, falls short of the emotional intensity of the World Cup in Latin America.

No team sport other than soccer even registers throughout most of Latin America, with a few exceptions. Venezuelans and Dominicans are rabid fans of *béisbol*, cheering every *jonrón* by their countrymen in the U.S. big leagues as well as farm clubs. Baseball is also popular in Cuba and Mexico, along with parts of Central America and Colombia. Brazil has a professional basketball league, but attendance is sparse. Brazilians play aggressive volleyball at the beach, and the nation sends powerful teams to the Olympics. Formula One racer Ayrton Senna, who died in a crash in the 1994 San Marino Grand Prix, was a beloved icon.

But soccer is the undisputed national passion. Brazilians are divided by income levels, social class, race, politics, and religion – evangelicals are winning over vast numbers of converts among the world's biggest population of Roman Catholics – but soccer brings them all together.

And it's not just soccer that unites Brazilians from the steamy equatorial Amazon to the windy pampas of the South and everywhere in-between. Once a year, the country is subsumed by Carnival fever. For four consecutive days, rich and poor don ornate sequined and feathered costumes, dance all night, and belt out catchy samba tunes which juxtapose the sacred and profane. Some dancers, wearing nothing but a birthday suit, elaborately paint their bodies head to toe. From Friday night through noon Ash Wednesday, Carnival rules the country. Don't bother going to a bank or the post office. They are all shut.

The big news at the 1994 Rio Carnival involved photos of a festive President Itamar Franco, unwittingly, in the company of his younger date wearing a short skirt with no panties. Even mainstream publications showed the woman full monte.

The humblest of people devote a huge percentage of their meager wages to elaborate costumes – called *fantasias* – and spend months rehearsing their marches, dances and songs. The day after the Carnival confetti, booze bottles, and every sort of debris are swept off the streets, planning begins for next year. Too bad they can't hose off the whole country to eradicate the overpowering stench of urine, vomit and alcohol. Some folks jaded from too many noisy Carnival blowouts seek refuge in the countryside.

Despite, or because of, all the Carnival revelry, the death toll rises. Infidelity by those who get carried away by the passion of the moment leads to violence, as does over-consumption of alcohol.

Other countries have their own versions of Carnival. People in Trinidad and Tobago and other Caribbean island nations also sport elaborate costumes, dance, march and sing, but the tunes are bouncy calypso and soca rather than samba. In Potosi, Bolivia, off-key brass bands parade in the streets. Sucre, Bolivia is overtaken by joyous water balloon battles, in which everyone, including the Carnival parade dancers, gets soaked head to toe amid the exploding firecrackers. In

Oruro, Bolivia, people march in parades wearing masks and feather caps. Venezuelans tend to get drunk, become obnoxious and play nasty tricks for a cheap laugh.

When I lived in Caracas, during Carnival I made the mistake of walking down typical middle-class residential streets, veritable canyons squeezed between the surrounding skyscrapers. Without warning, I was struck by a cascading waterfall, smacking me to the sidewalk and punching the wind out of me. Stunned, I didn't know what had hit me until I realized my entire body was soaked and supine on the ground. Then I heard ripples of roaring laughter echoing off the buildings. Dizzy, I looked up and saw a knot of people on a balcony, a couple of them holding a fifty-gallon plastic trash can upside-down. These miscreants – fully-grown adults, not teenagers – had filled the garbage can with water and dumped it down on me.

Most residents of Caracas, who call themselves *caraqueños*, keep a trash can full of water in their house or apartment because shutoffs for several days at a time are frequent. That way, they can scoop out water for cooking, washing dishes, flushing toilets and bathing. Brazilians deal with water interruptions by putting auxiliary water tanks on the roof to supply the household when the taps stop flowing.

Latin America is a lot more than soccer and Carnival. The region is home to profound cultural heritage; complex societies; fast-growing economies; diverse scenery; two of the world's three most-gargantuan metropolises, Mexico City and São Paulo; and spellbinding ancient ruins bequeathed by Incas, Mayas, and Aztecs. Fifty-two million Hispanics, or 16.7 percent of the total population, reside in the United States, which shares a nearly two-thousand-mile border with Mexico. Yet, stereotypes abound, with little true understanding about Latin America by most North Americans.

Lost & Found in Latin America: All About Brazil's World Cup Soccer, the Argentine Pope & Mariachi intends to serve as a prism to reflect the diversity and richness of the people, nations and cultures of Latin America. I describe everyday life as well as the temples of political and economic power between the muddy Rio Grande along the Texas border and Rio Grande on Tierra del Fuego.

One more thing: Uruguay's official name is República Oriental del Uruguay. Lest you think that means it's in Asia, the name is derived from the fact that South America's second-smallest nation lies East (*Oriente* in Spanish) of the Uruguay River.

If you read this book with an open mind, you might gain a much greater appreciation of your Latin America neighbors. When we understand and value others, we are more inclined to view them as individuals and treat them with dignity. Then, *naturalmente*, they will have a better impression of us.

Because most Americans have never been to Paraguay, El Salvador or the Dominican Republic, their views about Latin America often are based on Mexico. It might be from a trip to Tijuana or Cancún, or their impressions, positive or negative, of Mexicans (or perhaps Puerto Ricans) living in the United States.

Boiling down impressions into a few words evokes cartoonish caricatures: nice, hard-working, lazy, dirty, dishonest, thrifty, shiftless. But we shouldn't judge a whole region based on sketchy knowledge of a few people; furthermore, individuals and societies are too complex to be boiled down to a few brief words or impressions.

Most of what we think we know about Latin America is painfully wrong, either stereotypes or innuendo with little bearing on reality. Consider the frequent portrayal of Hispanics in news reports, TV shows and movies: East Los Angeles gang members, Puerto Rican muggers in crumbling slums, Colombian drug kingpins, Mexican gunrunners, steroid-injecting pro athletes, corrupt cops, and guerrillas who terrorize their own fellow citizens. We are bombarded with those depressing images *ad nauseam*.

That's nothing new. An enduring example from yesteryear is *The Alamo*, the 1960 film which pitted John Wayne as a heroic leader against uncouth Mexicans (ironic, considering that we stole their territory, not vice-versa). Little has changed since then.

It's not just anecdotal. Academic studies show Hispanics are usually typecast in TV and films as negative clichés, most often criminals or uneducated, rather than well-rounded characters.

And stereotypes, of course, rub both ways. Think of how many people in Latin America view the United States and Americans: rich, arrogant, aggressive, impatient, rude, exploitive, pushy. Ouch. Do those descriptions accurately represent all of us?

Sadly, as recently as 2013, Alaska's Don Young, a powerful, senior member of the U.S. Congress, referred to Mexicans as "wetbacks" (a slur which refers to crossing the Rio Grande illegally) – and then failed to comprehend why people found the degrading term so offensive. Some political leaders, fortunately, get it right. President George W. Bush invited Mexican-Americans to the White House in 2005, telling them, *"Mi casa es su casa."* In fact, Bush's brother Jeb married a woman born in Mexico. In 2013, Barack Obama went to Mexico, calling for an end to "old stereotypes." I agree wholeheartedly with such efforts. That's precisely why I wrote this book, to topple preconceptions and misconceptions about Latin America.

A Strange Hodgepodge

Most reference books – encyclopedias, dictionaries, almanacs and the like – describe Latin America as encompassing all Spanish-speaking countries in the Americas, plus Portuguese-language Brazil. This includes nations in North, Central and South America, along with a smattering of Caribbean islands. It's difficult to grasp because the region consists of some nations that are not contiguous while excising others sharing land borders.

Few maps, in fact, even depict Latin America. A map of the region would look like Thomas Jefferson's Bible, with a lot of cutting and pasting to achieve the final result. Latin America, simply put, is undeniably a strange and mysterious hodgepodge.

South of the Rio Grande lies Mexico, plus Guatemala, El Salvador, Honduras and Costa Rica in Central America but not Belize, formerly known as British Honduras, which abuts Guatemala and Mexico, but strangely, considering its former name, not Honduras. Belize is considered part of the Caribbean and is bunched together with other English-speakers, such as Jamaica and Guyana, not Latin America.

Then, there's Panama, a curious little world that used to be separated by a narrow American territory astride the canal before it was ceded back to the Panamanians in 1999. Some geographical purists snidely consider Panama part of South America, rather than Central America, because it was formerly owned by Colombia. When Colombians balked at the scheme to excavate a waterway across their northern province, insurrectionists formed an independent nation that welcomed the project, along with the largesse flowing from Uncle

Sam's wallet. Still, it seems silly to place Panama in South America: it is a narrow isthmus like the rest of Central America. Using snooty geographer logic, you'd be forced to call Guam part of North America rather than the South Pacific because it is U.S. territory.

Panama has more surprises. *Capitalinos,* as Panama City residents call themselves, see the sun rise out of the Pacific Ocean. You could swim in the Caribbean Sea, which adjoins the Atlantic Ocean, in the morning, then head eastward to surf in the Pacific Ocean after lunch. East? If someone wants to bet you on this proposition, your compass could help you win some money. While the Pacific Ocean lies west of the Atlantic, a portion of Panama hooks around sinuously and perhaps sneakily back on itself.

Most countries in South America are Latin American. That would encompass Spanish-speaking Venezuela, Colombia, Ecuador, Peru, Chile, Argentina, Bolivia, Uruguay and Paraguay. Most geographers lump Portuguese-speaking Brazil in the same category, which not all Brazilians accept. Some believe Latin America is the western part of their continent and see themselves unique and apart. "You mean *cucarachas over there* in Latin America, not *here,*" some Brazilians sneer, using the Spanish language word for cockroach. (Yes, the centuries-old rivalry of Spain and Portugal lives on in the New World between their former colonies).

President Ronald Reagan, during a 1982 visit to Brazil, infamously toasted "the people of Bolivia." While his innocent gaffe was obviously a slip of the tongue by a jet-lagged septuagenarian, it reinforced the resentment felt by many Latins that outsiders don't care enough about them to get facts straight.

Three South American countries that conclusively are not Latin American by any standard definition are English-speaking Guyana, Dutch-speaking Suriname and French Guiana, though a case could be argued for French Guiana because Latin was every bit the progenitor to the French language that it was to Spanish and Portuguese. Let's be thankful the Italians and Romanians, who speak the two other major Romance languages, did not colonize the Americas – except, of course, for Italian Christopher Columbus at the behest of the Spanish crown – or the struggle to define Latin America would get even more muddled and elusive.

Guyana shares closer ties to nearby English-speaking Trinidad and Tobago than to Venezuela, Brazil and Suriname along its land borders. Nearby Trinidadians, by the way, call Venezuelans *Spanyolies* because they speak *español*, a language little understood on Trinidad, barely seven miles away.

Likewise, residents of Suriname, once a colony called Dutch Guiana, feel closer to the Netherlands Antilles islands of Curaçao, Aruba and Bonaire than to their contiguous neighbors.

While Guyana and Suriname have been independent for decades, French Guiana remains tethered to France, the same way Hawaii is an American state, so its residents enjoy full French citizenship. *Guyane*, as it is called locally, is culturally close to Caribbean islands such as Guadeloupe and Martinique but has little in common with bordering Suriname or Brazil.

Latin America also embraces the Spanish-speaking Caribbean. Cuba is part of the region, as is U.S. commonwealth Puerto Rico (which many Americans confuse with Costa Rica and think is a foreign country). Dominican Republic, the eastern half of Hispaniola island, is also part of the region. But the western half of the island, French-speaking Haiti, is not.

Even though Cuba lies near Jamaica, it has much more in common culturally with faraway Uruguay than with its English-speaking neighbor. While Cuba has been isolated politically since Fidel Castro took power, it maintains friendly ties with many Spanish-speaking nations in the region, even those which sharply disagree with Havana's Communist government.

That doesn't mean they get along. Many countries have border disputes. Maps printed in Venezuela show sixty percent of Guyana, called the Essequibo, as part of its territory; the Guyanese disagree. Maps in landlocked Bolivia show most northerly Chile, along the Pacific Coast, as its "reclamation zone." Ecuador and Peru fought wars in 1981 and 1995 over Amazon rain forest that was once considered to have little economic value. Now, it is believed to hold crude oil, making it valuable.

Suriname disagrees on its borders with both Guyana and French Guyana; even some Brazilian states contest their state lines. Whew!

Modern Paraguay, a contradiction in terms, is only a wisp of its former self. The devastating Chaco War in the nineteenth century reduced the nation to half its previous size, with Bolivia and Brazil engorging themselves by gobbling up former Paraguayan territory. That wasn't Brazil's only expansion; it grew westward as surely as the United States muscled its manifest destiny on everybody in its way. In 1493, the pope drew a vertical line on the map to demarcate Spain's and Portugal's claims. If Brazil had observed those confines, it would comprise little more than half its present size, and numerous neighbors would be much larger.

What about other far-flung pinpricks of land on the periphery?

The Falkland Islands lie in the South Atlantic, three-hundred miles off the southern reaches of Patagonia. Residents briskly dismiss even remote consideration that they are part of Latin America, especially after going to war in 1982 to remain tied to Mother England when Argentines, who had claimed the islands since their independence from Spain, followed jingoistic military dictators to occupy the provincial capital, Stanley. The mighty British Armada resolutely steamed down to storm the tiny islands and seized them back within days.

On the opposite side of the continent, Ecuador owns the Galapagos Islands – a thousand miles off the Pacific coast – where Charles Darwin stumbled upon curious life forms that laid the foundation for his revolutionary theory of evolution. Though this solitary wayside has more Blue-footed Boobies and Magnificent Frigatebirds than people, the few towns on those islands culturally are undeniably Ecuadoran.

Easter Island, famous for the immense monolithic stone heads erected by mysterious ancestors, even father afield at two-thousand four-hundred miles out in the Pacific, is legally part of Chile. But the island's distinct customs and language have more in common with Hawaii and other Pacific islands than with Chile.

All but one nation in Latin America speak Spanish. They share a common mother country, Spain, and language brought by the Spanish explorers and *conquistadores,* along with Roman Catholicism, but the distinctions and differences are wider than most outsiders think. First and foremost, consider that many Americans think Brazilians speak Spanish rather than Portuguese.

Accents change dramatically from one country to another. Ponder the following: Does an Ozark hillbilly speak the same language as the Scottish highlander or Australian Aborigine? Technically yes. But if you put them all in the same room, would they understand each other? Maybe. Ecuadorans munch on *mani* (peanuts), which Central Americans call *cacahuates*. The Peruvian writes with a *lapicera*, while Argentines sign checks with a *birome*. When chatting with a Venezuelan you are *charlando*, but in Mexico *platicando*.

I learned over and over again that a word or mannerism I had picked up in Venezuela or Colombia might not be transferable to Guatemala or Paraguay. Sometimes a simple word can be embarrassing. *Concha*, a vulgar expression for the female sex organ in Argentina, is an innocent description of a seashell elsewhere. Chile's most popular wine is *Concha y Toro,* which leads to endless jokes in neighboring countries.

When it comes to Brazil, forget what you learned in Spanish-speaking countries. It's a totally different world, and a lot of words can trip you.

Mexicans munch on *tacos* and *tamales*. Argentines prefer a grilled *parillada*, while Venezuelans can't get enough *arepas*. A mistake most Americans make is assuming that their interpretation of Latin American culture – brought northward by Mexican immigrants – represents the rest of the region.

The region also has a wide variety of climates, not just tropical jungles and deserts. Mexico City, Bogotá, Quito and La Paz all lie in mountain valleys or plateaus a mile or more above sea level and have cooler climates than you might expect. Sweaters are common in these cities. Yet, within a couple of hours, you can get to lower-elevation, warmer areas where highlanders relax on weekends.

Argentina and Chile are mostly outside the Tropic of Capricorn, and none of Uruguay is tropical. Southern Argentina and Chile get regular winter snowfall, as do the high Andes and some higher-elevation areas of northern Mexico near the U.S. border. A few mountain towns in southern Brazil get snow on occasion. Many residents of Buenos Aires and Santiago grab their skis and hit the slopes – in June, July and August – in the nearby Andes.

Below the equator, the reversed seasons take some getting used to. In Brazil, the beach is the most popular destination during the week between Christmas and New Year, the hottest time of the year (although poor Santa, or *Papai Noel* as Brazilians call him, still swelters in his white beard and red suit in the shopping malls). Come winter, people in Rio and São Paulo bundle up in nearby mountain towns where nights sometimes hit freezing and central heating is rare.

One more thing: many people think South America is directly south of North America. Not really. The westernmost tip of South America in Ecuador is the same longitude as Miami. The farthest point east in Brazil is only 1,000 miles west of westernmost Africa. That's why Brazil's major cities are six hours ahead of the U.S. West Coast during their summer (when Brazil is on daylight savings time) in the dead of winter way up north.

Contrary to popular belief, water does not drain counter-clockwise south of the equator. Where did that crazy one ever get started?

Now that you are thoroughly perplexed about how to define Latin America, you are in the ideal frame of mind to wander with me through a region that is a collection of massive contradictions, perpetual mazes, surprising contrasts, chilling convolutions and, most of all, amazing discoveries.

Chapter 1

A Lifelong Dream Fulfilled,
but in the Wrong Place

Since I was a child, I fantasized about traveling and living overseas. Growing into adulthood, I seemed destined to become a foreign correspondent. I envisioned working for the *International Herald Tribune* in Paris or the *Daily American* in Rome and sipping wine at sidewalk cafes with European bohemians. It never dawned on me that I would wind up instead in the bedlam of Latin America, dodging open sewers and bandits. When a job offer came from *The Daily Journal*, it was in disorderly Caracas, not romantic Europe. Take it or leave it.

In my twenties, I was looking for adventure – a spicy interlude of a few years – never imagining that I would live more than a decade in that vast, bewildering region and remain tethered by family ties the rest of my life. By the time I moved back to the United States years later, I had lived in three countries – Brazil, Mexico and Venezuela – fluently spoke two intriguing romance languages – Spanish and Portuguese – and felt at home in Latin America. After setting foot in nearly every nation in the region, I returned with a Brazilian wife and two dual-national, bilingual kids in tow.

I went nearly everywhere, from scorched deserts to icy Tierra del Fuego, buffeted by treacherous winds from Antarctica. In-between these extremes, I encountered vast, sprawling slums; perpetual twilight in dense jungles; soothing tropical beaches; deforested wastelands; deformed beggars; and indigenous people in secluded places who babbled in only traditional tongues.

The job offer grew into a dilemma of truly epic proportions. I was of two minds – perhaps a tad schizophrenic – about what I wanted to do. I did not want to leave my beloved Seattle, with gorgeous vistas, cleansing rain, cool temperatures, funky alternative lifestyle, and access to mossy forests and snow-domed mountains.

Plus, I was captivated by the classy, gorgeous Sheri. At odds with our nascent romance was something gnawing my insides like a wild beast determined to escape the jaws of a steel trap. Some animals will chew off a body part to escape. Similarly, I was willing to sacrifice romantic love for another kind of romance, the call of the wild.

I had already visited all fifty states, lived in numerous places and seen my share of the good, the bad and the ugly. I had spent a summer on the Eurail Pass/youth hostel backpack circuit, seen numerous Canadian provinces, and sojourned several places across the Mexican border. Still, it wasn't enough. A voice inside me shouted loudly, clearly and insistently – rattling me if I refused to listen – that I could not be satisfied until I unlocked a mystery that lay on the other side of the world.

At that time, I wrote for a newspaper in the nearby city of Everett about school boards, city councils and planning commissions, the basic elements toward becoming a seasoned journalist. I yearned to tackle the "big story" that would be my breakthrough. I had no idea that I would eventually interview heads of state, write about overseas conflicts, and even feel the *frisson* of danger on occasion.

Submerging and losing myself in a totally alien environment would give me the opportunity to chase big stories in my path. I would let myself be transformed by unseen experiences and events as a stranger in a strange land. I could not fathom how lost and isolated a person can feel without having any of the accustomed cultural touchstones to lean on.

Only a year earlier, I had returned from a half-year, cross-country trip to research a book about ferryboats. To my indignity and displeasure, the publisher who earlier had seemed so enthusiastic about the project wallowed in hesitancy. "It's neither fish nor fowl," he quacked at me, nipping on my heels. That was that. No other publisher was interested. I had no alternative, so I could either view it as time wasted on a dead-end project or see it as the chance of a lifetime to skim across the bayous, behold the Manhattan skyline from the Staten Island ferry, traverse the Great Lakes over choppy waves, and stumble upon quotidian ferries in the strangest-sounding places, such as Toad Suck, Arkansas.

The most memorable route was the Los Ebanos ferry, a hand-pulled steel plate barge which plies the murky Rio Grande between Los Ebanos, Texas and Ciudad Diaz Ordaz, Mexico. Today it is the only ferry linking the two nations as well as the sole hand-drawn ferry remaining in the United States, a century after others became motorized or were replaced by bridges. Ferry tenders, wearing thick leather gloves, grip a rope and propel the craft hand-over-hand for the few minutes it takes to traverse two hundred feet. The workers chat in Spanish at machine gun clip, *ranchera* music blasting from a portable radio's tinny speakers. The custom-made vessel – which fits three vehicles and a handful of passengers – slides into the soft, muddy bank on the other side, and the ramp is dropped and hoisted by hand.

Returning to Seattle from my cross-country trip, I learned that a colleague had found a job in Hong Kong. That was my clarion call: If Patti could do it, I could too. I promptly sent away for an expensive guidebook, *Editor & Publisher Yearbook*, to get names and addresses and spent days and nights researching the seemingly endless possibilities. I found English-language dailies in exotic-sounding ports of call around the world: Tokyo, Hong Kong, Seoul, Manila, Nairobi, Johannesburg, Mexico City, São Paulo, Buenos Aires, Panama City, Paris, Rome. I sent letters to all those places and marveled at the colorful stamps on the letters I got in response. At the time, I was comfortable blabbing in French and barely conversant in Spanish, so I did what every ambitious job seeker does: I embellished my qualifications. Put it this way: The letter to Paris bragged that I was fluent in French, and the ones to Spanish-speaking countries said the half-truth that I spoke Spanish. Because I knew a handful of disjointed words in Portuguese and Italian, my letters said I spoke "a little" of these tongues.

A decade later, in an alumni publication at my alma mater, Humboldt State University in Northern California, an interviewer quoted me as saying I had "lied" about my language skills to get the job. I was amused by that article. Strangely, I had not recalled my letter as a deception, but in fact, it was. And, that exaggeration made me stumble on my first step.

Weeks after sending out my résumé and letter, I was startled to get a "Dear John" response of the best sort, an invitation to join *The Daily Journal* in Caracas. I immediately called and asked for the man who wrote to me, editor Clem Cohen. I don't remember our conversation until he abruptly switched from English to Spanish. Suddenly, a breezy conversation got thorny. Although he spoke slowly and enunciated clearly, I didn't understand enough of what he said to respond intelligently. Frustrated, I told him it was a bad connection and I could not hear clearly.

Clem persisted in quizzing me in Spanish, since that is the *lingua franca* of the country he was interviewing me to work in, and my responses were feeble. In frustration, I blurted out, *Coño, que mierda,*" learned from a Puerto Rican buddy who had taught me colorful Spanish obscenities. A pregnant silence occupied the other end of the line after this fragrant profanity; I worried I had offended him and felt my chances sinking into a black hole. I expected him to hang up in anger. Instead, his rolling cackle began to infect me four thousand miles away. Finally he said, "Well, John, you can handle yourself effectively where it counts. When can you start?"

We discussed the financial arrangements. The newspaper would pay for my hotel room at the start and reimburse my airfare, but only after I had worked for six months. Too many drifters went there for a lark on the company dime, only to turn around when culture shock set in after a few weeks or months.

Three weeks later, I was living in Caracas. During my first weekend, I befriended a teacher at the American school whose roommate would soon marry a shy Venezuelan woman. It struck me as peculiar, even beyond my comprehension, to marry someone from such a different background. My family on both sides is middle-class American going back to immigrants from the British Isles and northern France, in other words, Anglo Saxon. I could not have imagined I would one day have a wife born in rural Brazil and would enjoy staying with her family in the boondocks with no running water, electricity or telephone.

Venezuela was vibrant and chaotic, welcoming but frightful, crammed full of buildings that reached skyward yet at the same time tumbling down, joyful yet strangely tense, glitzy allure tinged with the vulgar and profane, energetic but lackadaisical. It first charmed me, then irritated and repelled me before finally winning me over again. I eventually embraced this bizarre world wholeheartedly as my own.

Even after settling back in Seattle, I have frequently returned to Latin America, mostly to Brazil to visit family, but also for work assignments in Venezuela and Mexico, and pleasure trips to other countries. When I go to Latin America, I feel at home. It does not feel foreign to me. Foreign would be Asia or Africa, where I have never been.

I'm glad I traveled when I was young and had the patience to tolerate the discomfort to swing sweatily from a hammock aboard a riverboat chugging along the Amazon, sprawl atop lumpy potato sacks piled on the back of a truck across Bolivia, bump along all night on a rickety bus over rutted dirt roads through the Colombian Andes, or sleep fitfully on a mattress made from a cloth-covered slab of plywood with no cushioning.

Older folks tell youth to embark on these wild adventures "to get it out of your system." Have I purged it from my system? Not a chance. I still yearn for more adventures in new frontiers.

Lost & Found in Latin America: All About Brazil's World Cup Soccer, the Argentine Pope & Mariachi is a collection of my own experiences, impressions and observations. These were snapshots in time, and much has changed since then. I have read numerous worthwhile volumes about the region's history, geography, economics, politics, social conditions, ethnography and development, as well as exceptional books profiling individual nations (see Appendix B). I have enjoyed some top-notch travel memoirs. But my own book is none of the above, or perhaps a cocktail blending them all. I have compiled reflections gathered from the road, family life, work experience, friends and acquaintances, and attempted to derive some coherence from my jumble of experiences. Along the way, I tried to keep my wits about me and a sense of humor, even when it would have been easier to pack it in and return to the security and comforts of home. Most of all, I seek to improve understanding about a surprisingly little-known, misunderstood world on our own doorstep.

Chapter 2

Toto, I Have a Feeling We're Not in Kansas Anymore

I only had a few weeks to prepare for my new life, with no way of knowing what to expect from Venezuela and no reference point in my personal life. I had never even met a Venezuelan. There was a hint of danger and anarchy as I recalled scenes of a Caracas mob attacking Richard Nixon when he was vice president. Recently, I had seen an intriguing film called *Bye Bye Brasil* about a traveling circus that found its small town audiences shriveled after the arrival of television. Unbeknownst to me, I would visit countless sleepy villages in Latin America that looked much the same: bright pastel adobe buildings on dusty roads.

During my remaining weeks at home, I recorded my favorite music on my cassette player and packed my favorite paperbacks. Add to that my clothes – minus winter coats – plus towels, washcloths, vitamins, and I was set. My suitcases were plaid fabric, zipped shut and folded in half. I kept stuffing one more thing after another, imagining that I might need another shirt or doo-dad. In the end, I could barely lift each bag.

My parents drove me to the airport on a cold, clear winter day and towed a small utility trailer with my belongings to store in the basement of the family farmhouse in Oregon. Sheri and a buddy also bade me farewell. It was wrenching, not knowing if I was throwing away the chance to marry the love of my life.

Flying cross-country during winter enabled me to marvel at snow-glossed mountain peaks on my way to the snowless tropics. In Miami, awaiting my bags at luggage claim, I noticed clothing strewn all over the carousel belt. I laughed at the poor sap whose belongings were falling on the floor, until the hollow realization struck me that they were mine. It was a flagrant case of overpacking; when my suitcase finally rolled down, it was ripped apart. A helpful airport employee found me a big thick plastic bag to collect the scattered items.

As I clutched my remaining suitcase and plastic bag, I realized how difficult it would be to get around, burdened by my possessions. With little money, I had to do this on the cheap. The Miami airport hotel was far beyond my means, so I took a bus heading downtown and asked the driver to let me off near some cheap hotels. The collective weight of my bags seemingly pulled my arms out of their sockets.

Cheap was right. My room cost about twenty dollars. A single dim flickering light bulb dangled from a frayed wire in the ceiling. The room stank of spoiled food, stale beer, human sweat, and urine; the street clatter and loud neighbors intruded. The bathroom was unsanitary. I had not even left the United States, and I was already in the Third World. This crazy lark was no longer exciting, and I began to sob.

There was no way back. I had to stick it out. I had already purchased my ticket and could not afford a flight back to Seattle. I barely slept that warm night in January, haunted by fears I was making the biggest mistake of my life. I had turned down job offers at newspapers in Boise and Walla Walla, which had sounded too mundane. Lying in bed as my eyes tracked a squeaky overhead fan, those jobs were suddenly appealing, safe and predictable, something I could no longer count on.

I spent much of the next day roaming around Miami. The shopping district, coincidentally, was full of Venezuelans. Signs on many shops read *Se aceptan bolivares*, the Venezuelan currency bearing a portrait of national hero Simón Bolivar. I needed a new suitcase but had little money, so I got a giant nylon duffel bag that would carry everything, and which still serves me today.

My Avensa flight departed three hours late. I had expected to view the sparkling Caribbean below me and arrive in Caracas by seven, but instead got in after ten. Inky darkness swallowed the Caribbean; occasional clusters of lights shone from mysterious islands below.

The airplane was filled with boisterous Venezuelans chattering loudly about their vacations in Miami. The flight crew did not seem to care that few people sat in their seats wearing seatbelts. Passengers wandered all over the airplane or turned around to converse with people behind them. Shortly before landing, the flight crew handed out cards to fill out, a customs declaration form for natives and tourist cards for everybody else. The flight attendants asked "*Bay-nay-so-lon-no* (Venezuelan)?" They had run out of tourist cards in English, so I had to make sense of one in Spanish and try to put the right information. Outside, the contours of the lights showed a jagged coastline and craggy mountains plunging into the sea.

When I got off the plane, Pedro, a man about my age who spoke English, greeted me at the gate. My new employer had sent him to get me through immigration and customs and to my hotel safely. This time there were no surprises as my bags rolled down the conveyor belt, and I had an extra hand to tote my burdensome luggage. Pedro ushered me through the crowd out to the curb. The night was hot and humid, the air heavy with the sweet fragrance of pungent tropical flowers. Pedro stashed my bags into the trunk of a taxi, paid the driver, and told him where to take me. The driver blabbed away rat-tat-tat, but I understood little. Crossing the coastal mountains to Caracas in an inland valley, I saw mile after mile of precarious slums climbing the steep hillsides.

After the final hill, Caracas spread out below, exactly as I had dreamed: buildings twenty to thirty stories high in all directions. Few people walked the streets at this hour, but cars were plentiful, zipping in and out like pinballs. We stopped in front of my appointed hotel, the Veroes.

My room was spartan but clean, opening out to a silent air shaft. Thankfully, it was an improvement over the Miami dump where I stayed.

I was facing the biggest learning curve of my life. In the coming days, weeks and months, I would have to assimilate myself into a language and culture about which I knew little. And from the start, there were other things to incorporate: the fact that you must throw toilet paper into a waste basket after use, not the toilet, because the sewer systems can't accommodate the paper. All the rules of conduct, in fact, go into the waste basket, and you start from scratch. As I lay in my bed that first night, I didn't have the vaguest notion of how my life would be transformed so dramatically.

Chapter 3

The Daily Journal

The first order of business after I awoke in noisy, bewildering Caracas was to find my new office. The address, Avenida Fuerzas Armadas entre Crucecita y San Ramon, was embossed on the envelope in my pocket.

The hotel clerk pointed me in the right direction; I was only about four blocks away. I stepped out onto noisy Avenida Urdaneta, already crammed with honking cars and the sidewalks, way above street level, bustling with pedestrians. I walked two blocks to an overpass where Fuerzas Armadas crossed over Urdaneta. I turned left and noticed immediately that street numbers were not sequential. Odd and even can be on the same side of the street. A typical numbering scheme might be 28, 57, 33, and so on randomly. Besides naming streets, Venezuelans also name corners. That way, I just had to find Crucecita (little cross) and San Ramon, and my destination would lie between those corners. Later I found corners with intriguing names such as Death, Little Angels, Danger, Deaf, Jesuits, and Veroes (a Basque name), the same as my hotel. I expected a tall building with the newspaper name proudly shining from an overhead neon sign, but instead it was in an unpretentious squat building with no sign.

I had to identify myself to be buzzed in. That was standard practice in offices and residential buildings in Caracas, a city with frightening crime levels, unlike laid-back Seattle. An office boy led me back to Clem Cohen's office, where I also met his deputy, Sally Weeks.

Clem, the *chivo grande* (big goat), was the offspring of a Canadian father and Salvadoran mother; twenty years earlier, he had come to Venezuela after graduating from Princeton, much as I was doing that day, and never left. He was an avid *Adeco,* a member of the *Acción Democrática* opposition party known as AD while the other major party controlled the levers of power. After writing for *The Daily Journal* in his twenties, he had worked at major newspapers and TV stations in Caracas before heading the government news agency Venpres during the presidency of Carlos Andres Perez. He recounted how Perez, known as CAP, womanized on a Kennedyesque scale and mind-boggling corruption. He described corruption in an offhand way, as an ordinary fact of life.

An unapologetic smoker, Clem always had a cigarette in his hand. He described Venezuelans as being more direct than Americans and Canadians. A Venezuelan will bluntly tell you the brutal truth, while *norteamericanos* can be overly polite and indirect. At the same time, Venezuelans are sworn enemies to punctuality. Someone might be a couple hours late or not show up, and no apologies would be in order. They view time as a wide range rather than something precise, so appointments are difficult to make. Once you accept that – and you really have no choice – it's less of a problem.

It didn't take long to start noticing local idiosyncrasies which might seem rude to outsiders. For instance, a Venezuelan trying to get your attention will hiss loudly. To point someone out, they purse their lips and point with the nose. And, like all Caribbean Latins, they use vulgarity nonchalantly, particularly about someone's mother.

Venezuelans love to deflate pomposity. *Chamo* is a slang expression meaning boy. A pressmen at the newspaper one day referred to me as *chamo,* to which I responded, *"No soy chamo. Soy adulto. Soy hombre."* All the other pressmen howled at my umbrage. Of course, an American would not call an adult "boy," but another meaning for *chamo* is "buddy." *Vale* also denotes "buddy." On the other hand, someone who wears a tie to work believes he is entitled to be called "doctor," whether or not he has earned an advanced degree in medicine or any other field.

I became acquainted with bureaucracy in both the public and private sectors right away. Getting my work visa, called *transeunte,* literally transient, took weeks of waiting in lines. Every time any foreign resident wants to leave the country, he must get an exit permit called a *solvencia,* proof that taxes are paid. Venezuelans admitted that most of their countrymen cheated on their taxes – my friends, of course, the exceptions – so the government prevented foreigners from leaving the country until they proved they were up to date in contributing their 25 percent of gross pay. I was also required to get a Venezuelan to co-sign the document, saying that if I did not pay my taxes, they would be legally responsible.

The good-natured, heavy-set general manager at the newspaper, Tibor Somlo, born in Hungary but naturalized Venezuelan, often signed this document for the reporters. Once your papers were signed, you headed to the Diex (Venezuela's immigration office) to get your documents stamped. Hundreds of people were always in line, requiring a wait of half a day, if not all day. Although there were about a dozen windows, it was rare if more than one was open at a time. The gum-smacking clerks at the other windows might be reading a magazine, filing fingernails, chatting with a colleague or doing anything other than his or her job.

While only one or two clerks assisted the public, numerous armed guards supervised the long lines. Their job was to impose proper line waiting etiquette: no smoking, no gum chewing, no leaning against the wall, no sitting on the floor, and certainly, no complaining about having to wait. It occurred to me that if all the clerks were working, there would be no need for guards to supervise the line because it would move quickly. I spent more time at the Diex than anywhere else outside my apartment or office in Venezuela.

The private sector banks were as bad as government departments. Cashing a check could take half a day, involving four long lines. First, a clerk would verify that your ID matched the name on the check. Then you would start all over again in a second line to confirm that the account upon which the check was drawn had sufficient funds. The next line would collect your check and give you a voucher for the amount of money you were getting. The fourth line dispensed money. Whew.

Well-to-do Venezuelans don't bother with such nonsense. They hire office boys to handle their government documents, banking and other chores which require long waits. *The Daily Journal* had messenger boys who waited in line for us. One thing I never understood was trusting a minimum wage employee to cash checks for numerous people that totaled years of salary at their pay scale. In our case, they might cash half a dozen paychecks at once. It also seemed to make them a target for the ever-present bandits.

And for tasks that an office boy was unable to perform, Venezuelans and most other Latins pay agencies to obtain a passport or driver's license, pay taxes or fines, and myriad other time-wasting chores. Thus, there is little incentive for businesses or bureaucrats to improve service because only the poor, who have no influence, wait in lines. Everybody else pays someone a pittance to do the waiting for them.

Venezuelans, in fact, use influence, called *palanca*, literally "leverage," every chance they get. I used my press card to get into buildings, and I got used to my own limited *palanca*. One night, when told that a movie was sold out, I showed my press card in hopes that they had set aside a few tickets in case somebody with *palanca* showed up, but the clerk explained, "Señor, it really is sold out. No tickets left."

Venezuela has a diverse mix of people: Africans, Indians, Caucasians, and every conceivable combination. Africans were brought in to work on sugar plantations along the coast. In the twentieth century, working-class Italians, Spaniards and Portuguese immigrated. The humble newcomers became a merchant class, leaving the Indians, blacks and mixed-race people at the bottom rung of the social and economic ladder. While whites were a minority of the populace, they occupied most of the managerial and government leadership posts. That remains true to this day throughout most of Latin America.

Clem had a medium complexion, slender build, gently contoured face, thinning gray hair and a gray goatee. Sally was slim and pale, revealing her Midwest WASP background. She outlined her plans for me and for the newspaper. Drifters had wandered in and out of the newsroom without making any contribution. Because the newspaper did not pay much, about a thousand dollars a month – and the cost of living in Caracas at the time was higher than in New York – they basically took anybody who spoke English and fancied him or herself as a journalist. I was the first of a new wave of experienced journalists who would replace the drifters as they wandered off. Sally wanted to remake the newspaper with the highest journalistic principles.

Sally had a tough act to follow; her popular predecessor had gone to Reuters. Sally seemed to move too far too fast, implementing rules that people didn't like. Not everyone had the skills to comply with her exacting demands, which often seemed arbitrary, and she was not an experienced manager at dealing with people effectively.

The other reporters welcomed me and briefed me on the ins and outs of Venezuela. Would I be covering riots, earthquakes, major crimes? The first day offered no clue. It was too soon to turn me loose; I needed to get acclimated first. After the introductions, I was handed my first assignment: a pile of stories from Venezuelan wire services. I had to sort them for newsworthiness and translate the ones we wanted to print. Most ended up in briefs columns. So this was the exciting life of a foreign correspondent, compiling and translating marginal stories? I grabbed a Spanish-English dictionary and got to work.

The turnover was rapid. It took no more than about six months for Sally to get her wishes and have a newsroom stocked with her hand-picked staff. *The Daily Journal* was a great training ground, and many of my contemporaries went on to work at major news organizations such as Reuters, The Associated Press, United Press International, *The Miami Herald* and *The Wall Street Journal.* A few years later, at the AP international news desk in New York, I worked with other *Daily Journal* alumni.

There were also misfits. As soon as I arrived, they buzzed me like flies, trying to win me over in the turf wars.

While most of the news staff was American or British, Irving was a native English speaker from the Caribbean island of Trinidad. He taught me local expressions and how to react when dissed in Spanish. He wrote about local politics with a flair based on years of knowledge. I enjoyed working and lunching with him even though he was twenty years my senior. It seemed tragic that at his age and with his talents he was stuck working alongside much greener reporters and probably earning about the same. Irving, who had toiled at the newspaper for a decade, coveted Sally's job – she had only been there a year or so – but believed he did not get it due to his race. He was fixated on racial matters.

Irving's long tenure came to an abrupt end. One day as people began arriving at the office, we found our desks moved all around. Sally decided that we needed a different arrangement, like a school-teacher's new mandatory seating chart.

Irving was furious that his desk was moved away from the middle of the newsroom to near the door. "I'm not going to work there," he told Sally, who began to explain her rationale. He was adamant and marched defiantly into Clem's office. Clem told him to calm down, but Irving grew more irate by the minute. "Everybody is going to think I'm the doorman," he yelled.

"That makes no sense. We have no doorman. You're a reporter," Clem responded calmly.

"Everybody will think that the black man by the door is the door-man," Irving countered.

He had a point. It was an economic fact of life that many low-paid, unskilled doormen and security guards were black.

For half an hour, Irving threatened to quit, and Clem kept trying to calm him down and persuade him to stay. Irving, however, was determined he would not sit by the door. He cleaned out his desk on the spot, threw his belongings into a cardboard box, and strode out the door. He soon took a job at UPI. I occasionally picked up AP, UPI and Reuters dispatches when printers or transmission equipment broke down. UPI was in a monstrosity high-rise on the twenty-something floor. Elevators always broke down, and blackouts were quite common. That meant a long hike up the stairs, amid legions of other panting, sweaty people trudging up and downstairs. Irving had no regrets. He was the UPI bureau chief, commensurate to his experience and talents, and nobody would ever confuse him for a doorman.

Irving was witty, and outside his racial fears, relatively calm. That was not the case with Nick, a Briton who was the copy editor. Nick befriended me quickly, as he did with all the new hires, because everyone else loathed him. The common fear was that he would explode any minute and go on a killing spree. He carried a hunting knife on his belt and loudly voiced his fantasies of killing people he did not like, which most people quickly surmised meant practically everybody. By his reckoning, everybody was incompetent, stupid, lazy and malicious. It was a classical paranoid personality. He belittled all the reporters about their stories. Having gone straight to a newspaper after high school, he berated college graduates with seething envy. Luckily, I rose to supervisory positions and quickly outranked him, so he stopped messing with my stories.

Nick had a sharp, pointed face, reddish-blond hair and a moustache drooping over his upper lip. While most of the young singles at the newspaper easily met companions, I never saw Nick with a romantic partner. I occasionally drank beer with him after work because I pitied him, but found him boorish. After I stopped at a couple, Nick would drink to oblivion and rebuked anyone as a wimp or sissy who did not imbibe to his level of excess. He offered a unique view on the world that I never heard from others.

One night after work, I asked him about why he had left England. He began describing a car accident, implying that it was the result of intoxication. While he never said so explicitly, I got the impression that he had been responsible for the death or serious injury of someone due to drunken driving. Then again, the tale might have been the product of a pathetic, twisted mind.

My work involved writing about frequent protest marches, a triple airplane hijacking, a nationwide census that halted the country, and oil. I interviewed ambassadors and notables. Distinguished Argentine author Jorge Luis Borges was nearly blind but still mentally lucid at eighty-two. Ella Fitzgerald told me that even after singing professionally for four decades, "I still have stage fright every time. Each audience is different and I wonder if the people will accept me ... You never know how long you're going to last in this business. I'm grateful to still be around." She also confessed to being a soap opera buff. Farrah Fawcett said it was "a little bit of a relief" when Bo Derek replaced her as the top sex symbol. "It took some of the heat off me."

I traveled to Yare, a village with an annual Corpus Christi festival which grew out of an exorcism ritual started in Spain in the Middle Ages. I saw the 222nd time it was held in Venezuela. A couple hundred participants wearing blood-red costumes and hand-painted, grotesque *papier-mâché* masks to depict the devil gyrated, shook maracas and pounded drums. Ten thousand spectators watched, including boys as agile as monkeys in treetops. Many Venezuelan festivals, religious or otherwise, were an excuse for people to get drunk and cause a commotion.

Everywhere in Caracas are slums, called *ranchos*. The poor built on any vacant lot and little by little made improvements as they could afford them. There was a collection of *ranchos* right behind my apartment near Plaza Altamira, a big open area with a tall obelisk. Residents of the *ranchos* tossed garbage on the cars in our parking lot and made a lot of noise. Venezuelans make a distinction between a house and a *rancho*. I once commented during a car ride to a girlfriend that a certain hillside was crammed full of houses. She abruptly corrected: "Why, those aren't houses, *querido*. They are *ranchos*."

When construction began on the Caracas subway line, the round-the-clock drilling next door made never-ending noise and unleashed swarms of mosquitoes through my screenless windows.

Peddlers roamed the streets selling food or trinkets; others offered plumbing, auto repair or locksmith services. My favorites were the cobblers, who wandered the streets singing out *zapatero, zapatero*.

Venezuela's national dishes are *arepas*, flattened, deep-fried or baked cornmeal patties stuffed with meat or cheese or beans, and *Pabellón criollo*, a montage of shredded beef with rice and beans. I was stricken with severe food sickness a few times, once from something as innocent as fresh, juicy plums. However, I loved the fresh seafood as well as the tropical fruit juices, many of which I had never tasted before: *parchita* (passion fruit) and *guanabana* (soursop), plus pineapple, papaya, and guava.

I wandered in the colorful open-air market called Guaicaipuro, which had juice stands and artisan crafts, redolent with the tangy scents of fresh red snapper, mangoes and exotic spices.

I began to get out of shape. I had jogged for miles every day for years, but I stopped the habit in Caracas because the smog made me cough. In Seattle, I had played tennis frequently at public parks and schools, but in Caracas the few places with courts were pricey country clubs, so I only played when I got the occasional invitation.

An unwelcome companion in the tropics – in mansions and tumbledown shacks – is the cockroach, *cucaracha* in Spanish and *barata* in Portuguese. They were a never-ending battle in my apartment. I wrote a letter home saying: "I just finished smashing cockroaches on the kitchen counter. Now my hand is full of squashed, icky guts of cockroaches. They are quite loveable little creatures. They get into food, leave little turds around, loads of fun." I captured one under an upturned ashtray. For a week it ran around in captivity. One day we saw little turds, but the next day they were mysteriously gone. We surmised that in captivity, the roach must have eaten them. After a week, it was still. I lifted the ashtray in victory, only to see it scamper off and disappear into a crack in the wall. My roommate, Jean-François, said no self-respecting cockroach would ever take us seriously again.

I finally arrived journalistically when I got invited to a press conference at *Miraflores*, the ornate presidential palace. I had attended events where President Luis Herrera Campins spoke, but never had the opportunity to ask him a question myself. Imagine the Pillsbury Doughboy with a graying Groucho Marx moustache and eyebrows, and you can envision the pudgy chief executive. Venezuelans considered him and his wife to be dimwits, but he was good natured and reasonably well liked. He came from the generation of Venezuelans who did not take democracy for granted after being jailed for opposing dictator Marcos Pérez Jiménez in the 1950s. They reveled in democracy to the very fullest: Herrera was pelted with constant barbs by opponents. I blamed Herrera for the rampant corruption and inefficiency, unaware that it was just as bad under the men who preceded and followed him in office. Later, I gained respect for Herrera when Venezuelan friends told me that he lived simply and rode public transportation during his post-presidential golden years. Compare that to U.S. ex-presidents, who, despite exceedingly generous pensions, still have the gall to exploit their reputations for big bucks. Herrera's modest retirement seemed to prove his honesty, because anyone who had looted the federal treasury would not live humbly. Herrera served a single five-year term long before megalomaniac Hugo Chavez maneuvered a way to be president for life and clung to power nearly fourteen years until his death from cancer in early 2013. Venezuelans – desperate to end the rampant crime, corruption and crony capitalism – found that crime and corruption worsened, as did stagflation, under Chavez's flagrant crony socialism.

Herrera's appointments included the usual big-mouth hacks, opportunists, cronies, buffoons and crooks, with a pair of innovative exceptions. Intelligence Minister Luis Alberto Machado, the world's first Cabinet minister devoted exclusively to the development of human intelligence, pushed wide-ranging initiatives including early childhood development, nutrition, and education. Swashbuckling Youth Minister Charles Brewer Carias earned comparisons to Indiana Jones by taking teens to explore the jungle, showing them a whole new world outside their wretched lives in the *ranchos*.

I talked frequently with Machado, a committed idealist. The last time I interviewed him was in his office, where I stood up and pointed at the *ranchos* outside the floor-to-ceiling window. Wasn't it far-fetched and utopian to tinker with experiments to raise intelligence when people needed to focus on the basics of life: food, shelter and health care? He corrected me: "That's what it's all about. If they raise their intelligence they will surpass their basic needs." Machado said it was time to "puncture myths," that "all knowledge should be passed to all people" and "a man who can think critically can never be exploited."

Today Venezuela is in far worse shape than it was when Machado and Brewer held their positions. It's tragic that their groundbreaking work was halted before it could achieve long-lasting effects.

Chapter 4

Culture Shock

The expression "culture shock" is hackneyed and misused. Only people who have lived in a culture different from their own know what it is. I had not encountered culture shock during an entire summer in Europe because I was on the move the whole time. Although many things had seemed strange and different, even bewildering, culture shock had never set in because I carried a return ticket in my backpack.

Seven years later, things were different. The culture shock began in Miami and kept slapping me in waves for months after that. So many things were hard to adapt to.

Public services were dreadful. The phone system, if you managed to get a dial tone, usually connected the wrong number. Blackouts were common, as were water shutoffs for days at a time. And since I left Venezuela, those conditions have only worsened.

Within days of my arrival, Clem noticed that my Spanish skills were not up to snuff. They were used to getting greenhorn gringos who needed to become fluent. The newest staff members often spent a couple of months stuck in the office translating briefs and covering events in the English-speaking community while getting acclimated to the local scene and improving language competency before venturing out into the rough-and-tumble streets. I started on the bottom rung.

That meant tailing the U.S. and British ambassadors, following American Chamber of Commerce functions, social organizations for expatriates and the like. As I improved my language skills, Clem put me in charge of remaking the community pages which were filled mostly with gossip columns and badly written pointless announcements. That was certainly part of coverage because many of our readers attended events organized by embassies, multinational companies, and expatriate social organizations. But I went to Venezuela to get a stab at covering "the big story," not social gatherings.

Some people flitted from one diplomatic soiree to another, from one shallow conversation to the next. Instead, I used these occasions to pepper diplomats with sharp questions about foreign policies. Friends and I entertained each other by guessing the identities of CIA plants among the U.S. Embassy staff. The diplomats were not amused. My favorite parties were those sponsored by the French Embassy and French companies. Why? They had the best food and drink. Fare at U.S. and British embassy shindigs, by comparison, was humdrum.

When I got there, *The Daily Journal* was in for some changes. Diplomatic parties were not the end-all and be-all of everybody's lives. I increased coverage of the schools and churches frequented by our readers, as well as philanthropic organizations. Some expatriates I met were involved in education, health care and other worthwhile projects, so they merited coverage too.

In the early 1980s, civil wars were exploding in Central America, as the United States and Soviet Union used proxies to carry out their dirty work. Venezuela was a major regional player trying to use its influence – it had been a stable democracy since 1959 with tremendous oil wealth after prices rocketed in the seventies – to seek peaceful solutions. I made valuable contacts at diplomatic events to expand coverage of regional issues.

I was not willing to be anything less than a full player at *The Daily Journal.* Some people who had arrived after me had gotten coveted assignments at the presidential palace or Congress because of their language skills. Especially proficient were Cuban refugees and Mexican-Americans who grew up bilingual in the United States. No matter how long I spoke Spanish, I would never achieve their adeptness. But I was determined not to lag behind or become someone like Nick, stuck in the office and unable to cover events in Spanish due to inadequate language skills or poor attitude.

Like others before me, I enrolled in intensive Spanish classes at the Centro Venezolano Americano. Outside the classroom, I immersed myself in the language. This was before cable and satellite became widely available, so fortunately, I did not have the temptation to watch TV in English. At home I had the TV or radio on all the time to hear Spanish. I spent free time reading Spanish, looking up words in a pocket dictionary I carried everywhere. Venezuelans speak at breakneck pace and, as is common in the Spanish-speaking Caribbean, swallow the ends of most words. Few cooperated when I beseeched *más despacio, por favor* (slower please).

Everything was new to me, like a child born into the world with full realization of its surroundings. The chaos was intriguing, even charming. Salsa music was lively. People were noisy, evocative and vibrant. Caracas was energetic. I felt as if on the stage of an elaborately choreographed play, absorbing my surroundings voraciously and heedless whether I belonged. Not only was I experiencing all these new sensations, but I was learning to make sense of them.

Some local customs, however, began to grate on me, especially the intense level of noise. People talked loudly; they played music nonstop. It seemed there was no quiet place to relax in silence, not even parks. Driving was so erratic that I nearly got run over by cars or buses several times while crossing streets with the green light in my favor. Everybody seemed to honk needlessly all the time; drivers rigged their car burglar alarms to use as ear-splitting horns.

Manhole covers were missing on many sidewalks and streets, and I met someone who was hospitalized after stumbling into a deep hole.

Taxi drivers overcharged anyone with a foreign accent, and I suspected shopkeepers would sometimes rip me off because of my nationality.

I even offended the barber on the corner, a Spaniard with greased back hair and a skimpy Hitler moustache. I told him to just snip a little off the sides and out of my face. I comb my hair down my forehead and sport a walrus-style full moustache. I was horrified when I looked in the mirror. He had cut my hair all wrong, slicked it back, and made my moustache look like his. He had remade a West Coast surfer dude into a Spanish Nationalist. I imagined him in a Spanish Army uniform, right arm outstretched in a fascist salute to General Francisco Franco. He greeted me every day in the street until the day I wore a new haircut by a rival. After that, he made scary, scornful expressions, making me wonder if he sympathized with Franco's Army with a mandate and license to kill anyone suspected of being an anti-fascist sympathizer.

I was embarrassed by uncouth macho catcalls to women. Some said these *piropos* were often imaginative, but what I heard were disgusting descriptions of female anatomy and sex acts. Many women ignored the rude comments or made dismissive gestures, but others seemed to find the attention enjoyable.

What had seemed charming became annoying. The intrigue and novelty had worn off. After a few months, I was experiencing exactly what Clem had warned about, the culture shock that so many people feel until they click their heels like Dorothy in the Land of Oz and head home away from this bizarre world.

Some days were so bleak that I seriously considered taking the job I had turned down in Walla Walla or Boise. At least those would be stepping stones to Seattle or Portland, eventually.

But the drive that took me overseas kept me there. By leaving precipitously, I would be a failure. I was determined to make it, to survive and grow from the experience, no matter how unpleasant.

It took about six months before I had my epiphany, which arrived like a thunderbolt from the heavens. One day, sitting on a *por puesto* mini-bus going to work, I was reading a newspaper and listening to the bouncy salsa. Suddenly I could follow the conversation of two women sitting at my side. I was not eavesdropping. Rather, it was a revelation that I had achieved fluency. It was no longer just bits and pieces, drips and drabs. I could keep up with the flow and knew exactly what they were saying. *¡Que maravilla!*

The process of discovery of new ideas was flowing furiously, gloriously, ferociously in me with incredible intensity – *¡Que chévere!* I marched into Clem's office and demanded to cover events that required Spanish fluency.

My skills in Spanish were not perfect at this point – in fact, they still are not – but I had reached the point that I could express nearly any thought and understand most of what I heard or read. Still, I had to endure insults, such as a colleague who snorted one day, "Aren't you ashamed of speaking Spanish so badly?"

I was tempted to respond the way Winston Churchill reputedly uttered when told he was drunk ("but tomorrow I shall be sober and you will still be disgustingly ugly"). Instead, I answered simply, "How else can you learn a language except by speaking and practicing it?" To this day, I offer the same vignette and advice to people who are learning a foreign language or to foreigners struggling with English. Mimic, pay attention to the way people speak, and don't be self-conscious about enunciation or grammar. Those come with time (if I corrected the poor grammar and pronunciation of every native English speaker I hear in daily life, I would be even more boring and pedantic). It is far more important to simply get into the swing of things. You can study a foreign language textbook for years and learn all about verb tenses, the subjunctive, and masculine and feminine nouns, but none of that means you'll be able to use a language properly. Moreover, language is but one vital element in adapting to a foreign land, where understanding cultural nuances and habits is equally important.

I had to integrate myself fully into Venezuelan life, and that meant having my mind and body in the same place, not scattered over the globe. A long-distance love affair was holding me back. My feelings for Sheri remained strong. If she had been in Venezuela, we might have stayed together. But she was attending the University of Washington; finishing college was best for her. I was giving up a lot, but I had changed. I mailed her my version of a "Dear John" letter at the worst possible time; she received it shortly before final exams and Christmas. I deserved the angry phone call I got from her. In the end, she managed her life just fine by staying in college and meeting other men. She certainly deserved better.

Shortly after that, I was completely acclimated. I began to flirt voraciously. Venezuelan women are so attractive, even though too many of them bathe in makeup and perfume.

I met Lucrecia, an untamed, free-spirited Venezuelan, with all the attributes for a compelling fictional character if I had not known her in real life. She had lived for a year in Santa Barbara and was the quintessential Latin American mixed-race beauty: dark hair looping down her shoulders loosely, clear copper skin, sultry features, curvy in tight jeans, a seductive smile. How could I resist? While most Venezuelan women try to look like fashion queens or Barbie dolls, Lucrecia impressed me as unconventional and brave enough to break the mold: entirely comfortable in her own skin. She wore colorful baggy Peruvian blouses, Mexican sweaters and exotic jewelry. A high school biology teacher, she had hitched her way around Peru, Ecuador and Colombia. When an acquaintance told us he came from a family of twelve, Lucrecia quipped: "If I had twelve children, I wouldn't be able to remember all their names."

When I called Lucrecia on the phone one time, her mother answered. I identified myself as John. Her mother did not understand me and responded: "Chong?" Because of my accent, she surmised that I was Chinese. After that, Lucrecia called me *chinito* (Chinese).

As Lucrecia and I were walking in the streets of Caracas arm in arm, a young man leaned out the window of a passing car and shouted, "*Catire!*" a term that refers to a fair-skinned person or foreigner. Another way to describe people of North European lineage is *misiu*, a bastardization of the French *monsieur* used derisively. I got used to hearing people yell out nonsensical words and phrases in English, often obscenities, in Venezuela and elsewhere, which was sometimes amusing but usually annoying.

Lucrecia and I never became serious, but I learned to see life through her eyes. We spent weekends traveling to beaches and small towns without encountering other foreigners. I came to accept the aspects of life in Venezuela that had irritated me so much. I could speak the language, eat the food, dance to salsa, albeit clumsily, and sing along with the music. I was no longer in a hurry to leave, and the original goal of one year faded unnoticed. As I surveyed a second year in Venezuela, my departure became open-ended. There was no reason to go home. In fact, it was becoming home. I even began to follow one of the insipid soap operas called *tele-novelas* because it gave me insight into Venezuelan slang and mannerisms. I also found the shapely young actresses irresistible, but the wretched acting and dialogue got tiring.

When seeing the histrionics of Venezuelan women dating fellow gringos, I wondered if life imitated art or vice-versa. It seemed that the girlfriends were always jealous about someone or something, always demanding more attention. Were they exhibiting these intense emotional dramatics because TV programs showed them how to act, or was this part of their nature reflected by the boob tube? That is a question I never answered.

After becoming accustomed to Venezuela, it was much easier to adapt to other countries. My ability to adjust to Latin America – a completely alien culture – was curious, considering that a few years earlier I had not blended into life in either Wyoming or Hawaii and left both places after less than a year. I surrendered myself to the surrealistic nature of life in Latin America, long before author Gabriel Garcia Marquez defined it that way to me.

A couple years after adapting to Venezuela, I was comfortable in Brazil and speaking Portuguese. While on the road, I had not used English regularly in months and met a gringo who lived in a small town for about fifteen years after marrying a local woman. He rarely used English. When talking with him, I noticed that he spoke his native English with a Portuguese cadence and rhythm. Then I realized that I had an identical lilt, after speaking Portuguese every day.

Expatriates use the term "gone native" to describe someone who fits in so well that he loses the attributes of his homeland. Gone native can be complimentary in terms of adaptability, or derisive in losing one's true nature akin to the madman Kurtz in Joseph Conrad's *Heart of Darkness*. I had already taken the first steps toward going native myself without realizing it.

Chapter 5

Oil Wealth: Petrodollars
Are Not a Panacea

Some believe oil is a menace that is destroying our planet with poisonous gases, pollution, and global warming. Others see petroleum as providing irreplaceable modern-day marvels: automobiles and jet travel, machines that keep us alive in the hospital, miracle drugs, and plastics.

Nobody disputes that oil is the world's most lucrative business. Arab sheiks buy whole countries and enjoy lifestyles befitting a reality show. While a handful of people become obscenely rich from petrodollars, oil distorts a national economy for everybody else. Despots seize power in backwards lands to milk the petro-cash cow. Some of the biggest oil producers are nearly feudal: Saudi Arabia, Iran, Kuwait, United Arab Emirates.

Economists can explain this phenomenon far better than I; books and doctoral dissertations dissect the pros and cons. All I offer are observations of a major producer at the peak – and crash – of its oil wealth. Oil prices reached then-unprecedented highs when I lived in Venezuela, so I saw tremendous benefits and drawbacks from dependency on oil-centered earnings.

If a government can be sustained by taxes on oil production, it can tax its own citizens less. Alaska does not collect a state income tax, and it shares annual royalties with all residents equally, usually a thousand-plus dollars. When it seems that everybody in Hawaii on winter vacation is from Alaska, those vacations are the result of generous

Permanent Fund Dividend payments. Alaska has numerous sources of income, such as military bases, tourism and extraction of minerals other than oil, so it is not wholly dependent on oil.

In Venezuela, oil income exceeds ninety percent of export revenues and comprises more than half of the federal budget. Revenues, like an oil well, sometimes gush, while at other times they sputter. Over the years, oil income funded everything from aluminum and steel mills to education, housing, vast hydroelectric dams, and health care.

Oil largesse brought outrageous prices. Why should an apartment be more expensive in Venezuela or Nigeria than in New York, Paris, or London? Could they possibly be more desirable? It's one more ugly side-effect of petro-dollar distortions.

In the coming years, Brazil has a major challenge to develop its vast pre-salt deepwater oil resources without repeating the blunders of neighboring Venezuela.

Because the United States for decades has consumed more oil than it produced, sympathies run in favor of buyers, while viewing oil producers and the OPEC cartel with suspicion. The tables have turned in recent years as the United States moves toward self-sufficiency in oil production, and at the same time has become a major exporter of gasoline and diesel. It will be interesting to see whether the consumer-producer dynamic changes in the American psyche.

Consumers everywhere gripe when food prices rise. Farmers, however, benefit. As a buyer, I love it when apples are on sale. But when my family owned a commercial orchard, I rooted for higher prices. Likewise, if you live in an oil-producing nation, you gradually begin to understand reality from their viewpoint.

When world oil prices peaked in 1980, this former South American backwater flexed its muscles, giving Venezuelans an unmistakable swagger. There was chatter aplenty about OPEC solidarity, Latin American unity, and Venezuela's role in the "non-aligned" movement. In the end, however, Venezuela reverted to just another unstable banana republic and an irritant to Western policy makers.

Venezuela's fortunes were never better than during the early eighties when I lived there. On the surface, things looked great when large numbers of Venezuelans owned condos in Miami and packed the flights to Europe. Still, all was not well. Oil wealth masked a witch's brew of smoldering troubles, unresolved during the gold rush years, that poked their ugly hydra heads back up later when oil income crumbled.

Petrodollars create illusions. People, by virtue of their birth, think they are Jed Clampett who hit a gusher, whether or not they contributed to the industry. During the Christmas season, Venezuelan bag boys at the grocery stick their hands in your face and demand *aguinaldos*, or holiday gifts. The mailman knocked on our door to claim his *aguinaldo*. Unless we forked over generously, he threatened to discard our mail.

A former manager at state-run Petroleos de Venezuela (PDVSA) explained that an unrealistic expectation of wealth permeates the mentality.

"The average Venezuelan thinks that this is a rich country, but they are poor. They think someone is taking their money," Ciro Izarra, the former manager for international marketing at PDVSA, told me. Opinion surveys show Venezuelans expect oil profits to support them, without working. "They think someone is robbing five thousand dollars a day from them, that it must be politicians or PDVSA management. Nobody here knows what PDVSA does."

Chaos and corruption often are a sad corollary to oil wealth. Petty bureaucrats earning modest salaries envision gold mines. Venezuelans traveling overseas carried back all sorts of goodies, usually electronic gadgets, and avoided import duties. Instead of filling out forms and making travelers pay fines, customs agents simply collected the "fine" themselves. The traveler could take his new stereo, computer or camera home, and the customs agent weaseled enough bribe money to start buying things like that. Venezuelans grumbled but treated small-time graft as a hidden tax.

Oil wealth discouraged work and investment in other sectors, such as food production. When semi-skilled jobs held by quasi-educated people in the oil industry paid huge wages (by Third World standards), there was little incentive for people to work on farms for far less money.

Venezuela has been a net food importer for decades, even native products like sugar. This works when oil prices are high and the dollars rain down like manna from heaven but leads to trouble when cyclical prices cave in. That leaves less foreign exchange available to buy wheat, beef, corn and other necessities even though Venezuela is blessed with fertile land and the ability, but not the will, to be a food exporter.

Venezuela's oil wealth in the late seventies and early eighties funded a building binge. It seemed that every week the president would dedicate a new skyscraper, public housing complex, school, hospital, highway or port facility. The buildings in Caracas glistened in the tropical sun. The skyline was imposing, and I would sometimes get a flashback, ultimately deceptive, to modern Los Angeles. A prime example was the modern Bolivar Towers, squatting atop a divided highway in central Caracas housing government offices. A closer look revealed broken windows in the twin towers and an open sewer percolating in the street below. Inside, half the elevators were perpetually broken, even when the buildings were only a few years old.

Buildings and highways were impressive and modern, but poorly maintained, what I call the *Applause Syndrome*. Politicians love the attention of snipping ribbons, but no fanfare accompanies basic upkeep, so maintenance gets the short shrift. As the nation's fortunes tumbled with less money available for new construction and none for upkeep, decay quickly set in.

In the early eighties, PDVSA maintained the same structure as the U.S. and European multinationals which built Venezuela's oil industry in the 1920s before nationalization in 1975. The government invested in the oil industry's future by devoting huge sums of money to scholarships. Venezuelans were encouraged to study geology, engineering and marketing to help the oil industry run as efficiently as possible. The top students flocked to Venezuela's leading universities as well as those in Texas and Oklahoma which have petroleum-related studies. The decision makers at PDVSA were top-notch pros who could have filled the same posts efficiently at any oil company in the world.

The catchphrase at the time was to diversify the economy so it would not be entirely dependent on oil. Guess what? Today, Venezuela is more dependent than ever on petrodollars. Aluminum and steel mills have sucked billions of dollars of government subsidies and fallen shamefully short of production targets. Scholarships paid off in the eighties as educated Venezuelans gradually replaced foreigners in the oil industry. After a general strike in 2002, however, many of the best-educated, hardest-working, and most-qualified professionals were fired or quit, causing an unprecedented brain drain and an irreplaceable loss for the country. Venezuela's best and brightest now work for oil companies in the United States, Canada, Colombia, Brazil, and Spain. The housing, schools and hospitals built with oil income are crumbling. Electricity supplies have been in a crisis for years: the power generated by dams is lost as the entire country suffers year after year of crippling rolling blackouts.

Government subsidies bestow upon Venezuela the lowest gasoline prices in the world, or nearly the lowest. When I lived there, drivers paid a nickel a gallon, and even today, it's still incredibly cheap. Inexpensive gasoline meant low transportation costs. A city bus cost a quarter and a *por puesto*, a van seating about a dozen passengers, half a dollar. Caracas looked like the United States a decade earlier when gas guzzlers ruled the road. After the oil shocks in the seventies, many Americans bought economical cars, but with nearly free gasoline, Venezuelans could afford to drive big Chevys and Fords. I don't recall seeing compact Toyotas or Hondas on Venezuelan roads in those days.

After I left, the government doubled gasoline prices to a dime in 1989. The reaction? The *Caracazo* riots, which left hundreds of people dead.

When Hugo Chavez took power in 1998, he transformed the industry. Political loyalty became the main criterion for employment, from top to bottom, disregarding professional competence. That directive accelerated after the 2002 strike that temporarily halted crude output, refining, and delivery of oil and refined products. PDVSA never fully recovered from that crippling walkout. Since then, crude oil production has plunged from pre-strike levels, refinery breakdowns have reached epidemic proportions, badly needed natural gas projects have been delayed a decade, and Venezuela has spent billions of dollars on oil subsides for Cuba. PDVSA steered away from deals with U.S. and European companies, as Chavez intended, but he also made the company subservient to China. By 2014, cash-strapped PDVSA owed more than forty billion dollars to China, and an increasing proportion of oil and refined product deliveries for years will go toward repaying loans instead of earning revenue. PDVSA's relationship with China resembles an exploitative company store: Venezuela is obligated to buy inferior Chinese products at inflated prices and sell its oil to China on the cheap.

I went back to Venezuela in 2003, nearly twenty years after I first left. Gasoline was still cheap, about a quarter a gallon, and big cars still ruled the mean streets. But the nearly free gasoline has a staggering hidden cost: billions of dollars in losses for PDVSA every year. When its own refineries break down, which is frequent, Venezuela imports gasoline from the United States at high world prices but sells at low local prices. PDVSA refuses to admit that refinery breakdowns result from its own poor planning, lack of maintenance, and incompetent staff. Instead, it borrows a strategy from Hitler and Stalin by blaming unidentified "saboteurs" for all the company's woes.

PDVSA was beset by troubles when I visited in 2003, and morale was at a low point after all the dismissals. At the Paraguana refining complex, the largest in the Western Hemisphere, I met Edgar Rasquin, the general manager, who soon would be replaced by a Chavez political hack. Everywhere we went in Punto Fijo, admiring refinery workers flocked to Edgar. When we encountered a woman in a broken-down car, Edgar insisted that we get out and push her car. After his dismissal, he went to Spain.

Upon my return to Caracas I visited PDVSA headquarters. Starkly symbolizing all these problems were two scruffy little stands outside the building: One sold communist literature, extolling the virtues of Cuba and decrying capitalist imperialism. Another offered a kaleidoscopic potpourri of T-shirts bearing the image of revolutionary folk hero Ernesto "Che" Guevara, red berets favored by Chavez, and buttons proclaiming "PDVSA belongs to the people."

In and of itself, the sale of such paraphernalia should hardly raise eyebrows in a tolerant, pluralistic society with freedom of expression and a press fiercely independent since the late fifties. What was troubling – as real estate agents say – was location, location, location.

Opponents of Chavez and his far-left rant decried the propaganda being shoved down their throats at PDVSA headquarters and what it represented. To them, it symbolized everything wrong at the company in particular, and in Venezuela as a whole.

The stands and what they embodied clearly made people uneasy. Workers tried to laugh it off with a nervous shrug, but none would say forthrightly that they opposed Chavez or the stands. Former employees could be bolder.

"It's really shameful," Izarra, who was fired for his participation in the walkout, told me. He explained that the sale of propaganda clearly drove home the message to employees that they must march lockstep with the government or their jobs were in jeopardy, that differing individual opinions were not tolerated.

The spot occupied by the stands, which formerly was home to a newsstand, had a curious history. When the anti-Chavez general strike began in early December 2002, up to ninety percent of employees companywide walked off their jobs: from the oil fields and pipelines to refinery workers, ship captains and crews, and administrative employees.

When he was in trouble, Chavez turned to thuggery. Unwilling to face a sea of angry, albeit peaceful, protesters, PDVSA President Ali Rodriguez, in a nationwide broadcast, called on the so-called "Bolivarian Circles" and "patriots" to defend the headquarters from strikers, who he labeled "coup-mongers." Strutting like roosters in their red berets, "Bolivarian Circles" occupied the entrance to the modern steel-and-glass high-rise headquarters and surrounding streets to harass strikers outside.

The National Guard, which is responsible for protection of all PDVSA facilities, stood back and allowed the ragtag hooligans, who are not part of any official security forces, to rough up strikers and run them off.

Days stretched into weeks and melted into months. The strike never officially ended. Some workers began to trickle back to their jobs, but the government fired eighteen thousand of the company's forty thousand employees.

The mobilization soon descended into an anarchic free-for-all. The Chavez goons, who had nothing better to do, refused to abandon their posts and even operated a makeshift brothel in a tent to relieve their revolutionary tedium.

After a while, the "Bolivarian Circles" – filching the name of Venezuela's hero of independence, Simón Bolivar – got restless. They blocked the company chief at the entrance, demanding permanent jobs and pay for "protecting" the edifice. Rodriguez told the motley lot that they did not have the skills necessary to serve the company and that no money had been authorized to pay for their "services." A similar scene occurred in eastern Venezuela, where Luis Marin, the regional head of PDVSA, was also barred from his office. The incident was seen as one of the reasons Marin left Venezuela to work as CEO of Citgo, the PDVSA subsidiary based in Tulsa before later moving to Houston.

After that, the mobs and their tent city disappeared quickly, leaving behind only the propaganda stands. It was unclear who owns the stands; workers there would not say.

Following the U.S. invasion of Iraq, a huge Iraqi flag was draped on the outside wall facing Avenida Libertador, one of the Venezuelan capital's main thoroughfares.

A bizarre tangle of beggars lounged near the entrance scant steps from the shiny new black Lincoln Town Cars – protected behind steel gates – that whisk around company bigwigs. On the other side of the building, beneath an overhang, lived a phalanx of homeless people using an outdoor electrical outlet to power a hot plate to cook meals.

Chavez always promised to help Venezuela's vast army of destitute citizens, which grew in numbers under his watch. So, in a very tangible way, some of them survived, just barely, off crumbs in the shadows of the source of the nation's squandered wealth. After Chavez died in 2013, his hand-picked successor, Nicolas Maduro, doubled down on Chavez policies at PDVSA as the company quickly crumbled.

Chapter 6

Living Where They Take Vacations Seriously, Very Seriously

The American idea of vacation tends to be frugal, bordering on masochistic, with many people taking only a week or two per year, and some take no time off at all. In fact, Americans have coined a word to describe when folks don't travel: the "staycation." No wonder Americans feel so stressful! The rest of the world takes relaxation much more seriously, with the enlightened view that vacation is essential to human well-being.

I first discovered this in Venezuela, where generous labor laws guarantee everybody a month vacation, plus time off for Carnival, Easter, Christmas and New Year. While Venezuela does not have the Mardi Gras celebrations of New Orleans or the colorful Carnival parades and festivities of Brazil, Venezuelans still get time off for the pre-Lenten bash from Friday night until Ash Wednesday. Most business close for the long holiday, and people head for the beach. Because newspapers publish during holidays, we had a skeleton staff, so I worked during Carnival my first year there. A couple of months later, I got five days off for Easter break and fled to the nearby island of Curaçao, a flight of less than an hour.

As if a month off and the generous holidays were not enough, many Venezuelans also made *puentes* (bridges), stretching out a random holiday that falls in the middle of the week to add the weekend before or after, or even both, into even more time off. If there was a holiday in the middle of the week, it was unlikely I would find anyone to interview for the entire week.

A great advantage about Venezuela's location is that while it is part of Latin America, it is on the cusp of the non-Latin world, and I could escape in just an hour to numerous destinations in the Caribbean.

I was exhausted by Easter break and was ready to get away from Venezuela. When I got to the airport on a sunny morning in April, I had to clear several hurdles. My *solvencia* was all right. My passport was fine. My Venezuelan visa was in order. Next step was customs. Anything to declare? I could not fathom why I had to clear customs to leave the country, but it was necessary. "*Nada a declarar*," I told the agent and showed him my documents.

His beady eyes locked on the stained camera bag strapped around my neck, and he ordered me to open it. The old Minolta single-lens reflex camera, wide-angle lens and telephoto lens were beaten up long before reaching Venezuela. During a backpacking trip in the Olympic Mountains a few years earlier, everything was soaked when we were swept away by the Queets River. This old, heavy mechanical camera had survived the ordeal which destroyed a brand new, expensive electronic camera. This same photographic ensemble had accompanied me on other wilderness excursions and my cross-country ferryboat journey. The camera worked fine but was dented and scratched.

"How do I know the camera was not stolen? How do I know you are not taking a stolen camera to Curaçao to sell it?" he said.

I explained that it was obvious the camera was old and badly punished, that thieves steal shiny, new fancy gadgets, not old battered hulks. To no avail. He said it was his "patriotic duty" to confiscate contraband to return to its rightful owner. He was "letting me off easy" by simply seizing my swag and not arresting me, which he made it clear he had a right to do. The guard emphasized that he was doing me a favor.

With his covetous eyes focused on my camera, I nervously checked my watch, worried that I would miss my flight. This was a reminder about why I really needed to get out of the country. This petty martinet knew he had me in a bind. My command of Spanish was poor, so it was a struggle just to communicate the basics.

But it occurred to me that press freedom was a potent weapon; Venezuelan newspapers hit hard on corruption with an unencumbered voice. Venezuelans had thrown out their last dictator nearly a quarter century earlier. Yes, it was devastatingly corrupt, but people had the right to complain, and they squealed loudly.

I pulled out my press ID card reading PRENSA in big, bold letters. I placed it in front of him, along with my business card and that of my boss. I was learning how to deal with machismo run amok in Venezuela. I had to be firm, but not threatening. If I humiliated him, it was curtains for me. But if I caved in, I was dead meat. I had to stand my ground but give him a dignified way out.

"Because I'm new in the country, could you please call my boss and tell him the law I have broken so he can explain it to me? I don't want to break the law," I said.

He grabbed my press card and compared the photo to verify that it was me. Next he picked up the business card of the managing editor at *The Daily Journal* and nervously tapped it edgewise on his desk. It was clear that I had *palanca* which I had waited judiciously before exercising.

"*Periodista?*" he said. "*Disculpe me, señor.*" He put the camera in the bag and handed it back to me. "*Buen viaje.*"

That was that. I had effectively weathered my first personal crisis involving corruption. As I walked through the terminal, I realized how lucky I was. Most other people, whether tourists, residents or citizens, had no recourse and would lose their camera and whatever else the customs agent wanted in a classic, sleazy shakedown.

My jaunt to Curaçao was a godsend, just the tonic I needed. Everything was clean and organized on a little speck in the Caribbean, without the agitation or crowds of Caracas. I suddenly had wide-open space around me again and sucked in pure air. I was feeling trapped in Caracas, an oppressive city of five million people crammed like cockroaches in a valley ten miles long by about four miles wide.

Curaçao was a curious place. People spoke English, Spanish, Dutch, and their own language, a curious *bouillabaisse* called Papiamento, a mixture of all three, with some melodious Portuguese words thrown in.

Travelers go to Curaçao to enjoy the beaches. Those were indeed beautiful, with amazingly clear water in a crisp blue sea. There were palms, and a lot of cactus. But what intrigued me even more was the Dutch culture. Every day I dined in restaurants looking at Dutch-style buildings reflected in a canal. At first glance, you could think you were in Amsterdam because the buildings were so authentic. The only give-away was the palm trees. I relaxed there, loved the scenery, the friendly people and was able to return to my new home in Venezuela truly refreshed after five days in a completely new world.

After that, it was only another five months before I left Venezuela again. This time, Sheri came from Seattle to visit for a few weeks before returning for college in September. I had gone to numerous Caribbean beaches in Venezuela but yearned to explore new islands. St. Vincent, a small English-speaking volcanic island, appeared to be among the least developed and virtually unspoiled.

I had not made room reservations because there were no resorts or chain hotels. I simply could not obtain information about accommodations, which suited me because it meant the place was not overrun. The tourist information counter at the airport gave us list of hotels. There were only a half dozen on the island, so we picked what looked right for us by pictures and prices. How could you go wrong at the Coconut Beach Inn? It was on the water, and the pictures were straight out of *Key Largo*.

The hotel cost twenty-five dollars a night, so we could afford this refuge, seemingly forgotten by the world. Our room matched every dream of a tropical paradise, overlooking Indian Bay Beach and Bequia Island, one of the tiny isles collectively called the Grenadines. Yachts were anchored off Bequia, an expensive resort we were told was frequented by Mick Jagger and other jet setters.

The walls were pastel seascapes. Our room resembled the Tiki Room at Disneyland, bright pink closets and tropical hardwood trim. We left our window open to the fresh tropical breeze blowing off the water. We swam right outside our door every day. Some days we rode a bus into Kingstown, the capital, to the open air market. We wandered near the harbor and bought juicy fresh oranges, guava, pineapple and papaya. We also experimented the local staple, breadfruit, but found it bitter. The two-lane road into town was winding and narrow, lined by brightly painted wood slat houses: blue, pink or yellow. The population was almost entirely black, their ancestors imported by the British from Africa to tend sugar plantations. Numerous sugar mills on the island were rusted, broken down hulks.

We were content to swim and lounge around the hotel most of the week. But we needed a car to do one thing I had always dreamed of doing: witnessing the sun lift out of the ocean, then later see it fall into the sea on the other side of the island. I had seen the sun rise from Atlantic beaches and set into the Pacific many times but had never experienced both on the same day, despite having lived in Honolulu. The hotel owner said we should also visit the *La Soufrière* (sulfurer) volcano and the petroglyph, a rock carved by prehistoric people. Both sights required strenuous hiking and a guide because trails were unmarked.

We rented a car the day before, a little Toyota with a stick shift. I had never driven on the "wrong side" before, and it seemed out of place to sit on the right side of the car, shifting with my left hand and driving on the left side of the road.

We arose in the dark and followed our map to the windward side, past coconut palms and through sleepy little villages. We found an empty black sand beach beneath the palms to await the sun's debut. We lovingly placed orange slices into each others' mouths as we awaited the sunrise. There were clouds in the sky, but the rising sun did not paint them they same way the setting sun so often does. Sunrise was bland: the fiery red ball seemed to instantly appear in the pale sky like bread popping out of a toaster.

Although St. Vincent is only 30 miles long by about 15 miles at its widest point, distances were longer than expected because roads were narrow and winding in the hilly terrain. We toured abandoned sugar mills, with tall, stone smokestacks. We stopped in a little town to ask directions. A tall, slender young man offered his services as a guide to the volcano and petroglyphs. He said the round trip hike took about four hours.

I had hiked on two volcanoes – Diamond Head above Waikiki and Crater Lake in Oregon – but both of those are extinct. Just a year before, Mt. St. Helens had erupted near Seattle, killing dozens of people, filling local rivers with mud and debris and spewing ash around the world. But I had never climbed an active volcano.

The petroglyphs were animal shapes and strange symbols, perhaps depicting some sort of deity, carved into the stone. Along the way, our guide killed an iguana and slung its tail over his shoulder; he also climbed a palm tree to fetch us a coconut, which he cleaved with one clean blow of his machete.

We did not encounter another soul during our hike to the top of *La Soufrière*, which had erupted only two years earlier. A huge black-domed cinder cone had formed in the middle of the crater, with dozens of small smoke plumes puffing out from the edges, astride a turquoise lake. That afternoon, we were enchanted by the sun descending into the Caribbean, with more color than in the morning.

The following year I was in Trinidad during the raucous Carnival, and I couldn't get enough of the bouncy, melodious calypso and dancing frenetic "jump up." Singers had amusing names like Mighty Sparrow and Lord Pretender, but the music bore little resemblance to the romantic calypso ballads I associated with my grandma's Harry Belafonte records. Trinidadians talk in a sing-song mode. Listening to the lyrics belted out in lilting Trinidadian patois, I noticed a recurring calypso theme: a lovelorn black boy whose yearnings are rejected by the desired Indian girl. People of Indian descent make up nearly half of the island nation's populace, and I was intrigued by their culture. It was also my first taste of Indian food. What they called *hot roti* in Trinidad was similar to what many people know as *samosas* in Indian restaurants. When some locals invited me to a Hindu ceremony in a local temple, I couldn't resist. I didn't understand the Sanskrit prayers, but the saffron robes and flowers every color of the rainbow enchanted me. I also looked up a friend of a friend, who allowed me to join a cricket match. As I walked across a plaza in Port-of-Spain, the capital, my feet crunched the thumb-sized cockroaches I squashed with every step. Back in Venezuela, I would later have a girlfriend of Indian heritage who had lived in Trinidad. Nandani had a dark complexion and a mystical look; my friends called her the Nepalese princess. She explained that inter-racial dating and marriage between Indians and blacks was frowned upon in Trinidad.

On another trip I went to Jamaica, where I bounced around the rough roads on colorful wobbly buses and stayed at a remote beach in a crude wooden hut with a straw roof. The tiny community had few walls, just open-air buildings. Faux Rasta wannabees aggressively pushed *ganja* (marijuana) or money exchange. I couldn't even ask for directions because it seemed that everyone had a game. In the interior town of Moneague, two hawkers grabbed my arms and tried to drag me in opposite directions; I had to screech at full volume to shoo them away. The train at dawn from Montego Bay to Kingston was sublime. As it rose steeply out of the fogged-in coastal town, I was reminded of a favorite Bob Marley song, "Misty Morning." In Kingston, I visited Perry Henzel, director of the cult film *The Harder They Come*. He said the protagonist, played by reggae legend Jimmy Cliff, a country boy who seeks success in the city, represents rural peasants with dreams throughout the Third World. Freddy Hibbert, known as Toots and leader the Maytals, ambled in. Toots, whose hair was short cropped rather than typical dreadlocks, sang for me, in between long puffs on his *ganja*-filled pipe, but was too stoned to converse.

I also used my plentiful time off to explore beautiful and varied Texas-sized Venezuela. My roommate and I drove across the green, fertile *llanos*, vast plains filled with swamps, bright flamingoes that looked eerily neon, caimans, long-snouted capybaras, flesh-devouring piranhas, and roving bands of wild horses charging proudly through rivers as if they owned the place. Young boys along the highway sold foot-long catfish dangling from poles. Deep, red sunsets reflected spectacularly off the rivers and swamps.

Before my plane landed in the Andean town of Merida, I saw narrow switchback footpaths carved into the steep mountainsides. I rode the tram to the summit of 16,342-foot Pico Bolivar, where I taught Venezuelan youngsters, visiting the only place in their country that gets regular snowfall, how to make and throw snowballs (I became their first victim). The view from the top was foggy but breathtaking. Near the peak, my friend and I rode donkeys along narrow trails. Down below, walking through a small town, I heard Michael Jackson blaring from a small shop with a Coca-Cola sign in front. I wondered: are these American imports any improvement over drinking tropical fruit juices and listening to *Alma Llanera?*

Work assignments took me to Maracaibo, Venezuela's second-largest city. *Maracuchos* are known for being independent-minded, irreverent, funny and profane. The always-bustling city is spread out, while Lake Maracaibo, where Venezuela's oil industry began a century ago, is populated by houses on stilts called *palafitos* and drilling rigs in every direction. Explorer Amerigo Vespucci, for whom the continent was named, called this area Venezuela, "little Venice" in Italian, because the dwellings along Lake Maracaibo reminded him of Venice. The lake is coated by a fine film of oily residue at the surface, the result not of crude oil seepage but rather diesel leaks from the hundreds of boats that ferry personnel and supplies between the shore and the drilling platforms. Crude oil pipelines run alongshore, on docks, and underwater. At certain angles, the intense sunlight glistens off the oil-slicked water, casting sparkling rainbows. The withering heat might make it tempting to jump in, and I saw boys diving in the lake and spearing crabs. But the dingy water looked forbidding.

We spent a lot of weekends frolicking at beaches with exotic names like Chichiriviche (chee-chee-ruh-vee-chee), my favorite, a secluded cove scattered with a few fishing shacks and weekend cabins that was reachable only by a rugged dirt road. That beach and others had thick bamboo forests on shore. The name of one town, Moron, made us laugh, and we took pictures of each other next to the signs. There we rode a motorboat out to the islands in Morrocoy National Park, where we camped on a beach. I only went to one beach near Caracas but never returned because it was shamefully knee-deep in litter.

The best beaches were at Los Roques, a string of minuscule islands off the Caribbean coast, where we went with friends in their small plane. We landed on a rugged dirt strip on an island with a small fishing village and took a motorboat to an uninhabited island where we snorkeled all day, peering through our masks at the shimmering clear water, a coral reef and fish of every shape, size and color.

The town at Los Roques and even Indian villages in the Amazon, like every other settlement in Venezuela, had a Plaza Bolivar, with a statue or bust of *El Libertador.*

When I could, I got away with friends to small rustic cabins tucked away in the jungly coastal range, a spot so quiet that the only disturbances were the thunderous crashing of mangoes on the tin roof and the squawks of birds.

Still on my list: Angel Falls, the world's highest, in remote southern Venezuela.

Chapter 7

On the Road ... Alone

Leaving Venezuela in late 1982, two years after my arrival, I set out on the road alone but unexpectedly spent little time by myself. I had planned to go around the world not in eighty days, but in two years: one year in Latin America, a short visit back home in the United States, then another year traversing Africa, Asia, Australia, New Zealand and the South Pacific. I had saved more than ten thousand dollars, which would finance this adventure provided I was willing to endure budget accommodations: dank and pungent hotels, quasi-toxic eateries, sinew-battering transportation, the risk of disease, crime and other unseen dangers. Ah, adventure!

All the necessary ingredients were in perfect order: money in the bank, a rough itinerary, heavy dollops of energy and enthusiasm. In fact, I had everything I needed ... except a traveling companion. Many people would be queasy about traveling such a long distance alone in a strange, often risky, environment. Me too. I invited Jean-François, my trusted roommate, with whom I had taken shorter trips around Venezuela, but he had just started a high-paying job and was unwilling to leave as he saved money for grad school. An off-again, on-again girlfriend might fit the bill: she was free-spirited and adventurous, considered it briefly, then abruptly announced her engagement to someone I'd been told was an ex-beau. I decided to go it alone.

There was never any question whether I would take this trip. Amazon riverboats beckoned. Majestic Machu Picchu, Chile's fjords, Rio de Janeiro's beaches all lay in my path, dependent only on my willingness to take the proverbial first step. I was fluent in Spanish, so there would be no major communication problem. I was thirty, single and had financial means. In the future I would likely have a spouse, family to support, a career I was unable to vacate and responsibilities. It all came true. But now, while the call of the wild was relentless, there was only a slight hesitation, perhaps the fear of loneliness, no one with whom to share these extraordinary experiences.

Planning a trip for at least a year without returning home requires immense logistics. Nowadays when I travel, I use a credit card, carry minimal cash, and pay the bills when I get home. But that doesn't work for a two-year, penny-pinching trip when you dine in working class restaurants and stay in bargain hotels that don't take plastic because few, if any, of their clientele own credit cards. Add to that the complication of converting to the local currency in each nation and frightening crime rates. Obviously, it would be foolish to carry ten thousand dollars in cash for such a long trip.

I opened a joint bank account at home with my mother so she could withdraw money to send as I needed it, usually five hundred or a thousand at a time. Because I carried American Express travelers checks, I could receive mail at their offices around the world. My mother sent cashier's checks, which I was able to exchange in most American Express offices.

I usually got as much of the check in U.S. dollars as allowed and then exchanged those dollars on the black market at a much higher rate. The black market in Bolivia paid as much as fives times the official rate, and other countries had similar markups. This led to distortions: the equivalent of seventeen dollars, paid in local currency, for a night in the Sheraton and five or ten dollars for a domestic airplane ticket. After staying in so many smelly hotel rooms for as little as twenty-five cents a night, occasionally I splurged on a fancy hotel. After bumping atop potato bags on the back of a truck, swallowing dust for forty-eight-hour trips through the Andes, a cheap airplane ticket for the same trip in an hour was hard to pass up. Still, by comfortably gliding from one place to the next, I knew I was missing the flavor of everything in-between for the sake of immediate comfort.

I toted long- and short-sleeved shirts, a down jacket, hammock, swimsuit, long pants, shorts, socks, underwear, rain poncho, cap, sunglasses, sleeping bag, tent, tarp, water bottle, iodine pills to purify water (safe to drink but putrid taste), extra film (I shot more than 160 rolls), travel notebooks, guidebooks, reading materials, a mini radio/cassette player, and managed to somehow squeeze everything into a single heavy backpack. In a separate bag, I carried my camera and lenses. My provisions enabled me to sling my hammock to snooze aboard riverboats and at tropical beaches, as well as camp cozily in frozen, remote places without hotels.

My odyssey was more strenuous than relaxing, nothing like a leisurely week lounging at a beach resort. If you want to see a lot of territory, the pace can sometimes be manic. By the time I learned my way around a place, it was time to leave. A long trip in foreign lands can be exhausting, lonely, depressing, and frightening, but all the while enriching.

Even though this extended journey was one of the high points of my life, I rarely wished to stop because I was always moving forward. This was not a journey to savor the moment, but rather one long string of varied experiences and adventures to be relished in their totality, sort of a distinct life within an entire lifetime.

I wonder what makes some people homebodies while others itch with unbridled wanderlust. I got an early start. By age four, I was already roaming around my small town and exploring the Michigan countryside among the cows, horses, sheep, and chickens. I once ran away from a charging bull, but my memory probably exaggerates the danger. Before entering kindergarten, I was reading and writing about faraway places.

On my long trip, I learned tricks to make things easier. One was to occasionally stash my backpack in a hotel's storage room or the back room at a restaurant after eating so I could walk around unencumbered. When I needed a quiet respite in a hectic city, I sometimes ducked into a Sheraton or Hilton and parked myself in a comfy stuffed chair. If an employee asked what I was doing, I simply shot back in rapid-fire English that I was awaiting a friend who was a guest in the hotel. Furthermore, their rest rooms were uncommonly sanitary in a region with filthy, or no, public accommodations.

Maps and guidebooks did not always get me where I needed to go. Curiously, people often provided wrong directions, sometimes using intricate details, not to be malicious, but in a misguided attempt to be helpful.

I sometimes felt that I was the protagonist in a movie about my own life, a sensory explosion, bombarding all the senses simultaneously, dancing a bouncy *merengue* tune with a beautiful girl, sea breeze blowing in warm salt air with the fragrance of hibiscus, the taste of passion fruit in my mouth. Yet my recollections of parts of this lengthy escapade are faded memories, old tattered pictures peeling on the wallpaper of my mind.

The initial step was easy. Jean-François and I traveled together for about ten days in neighboring Colombia before I set out alone. We wanted to spend Christmas vacation in some of the enchanting villages that served as the backdrop for Gabriel Garcia Marquez's "magical realism" tales, as well as toasty Caribbean beaches.

Just a few years earlier, I had ventured on a six-month cross-country jaunt alone in the United States. But many things were different then. It was my own country, so I knew more or less what to expect. I was in my own car, protected and sheltered from unknown elements. And, I visited friends and relatives along the way – California, Minnesota, Michigan, New York, New Jersey, Alabama, Arizona – on familiar ground surrounded by friendly faces. And I wasn't truly alone all the time. A girlfriend accompanied me during the California-to-Chicago leg. A buddy flew to Atlanta, and we journeyed through the South back to the West Coast. And if I got lonely, it was easy to call Mom and Dad or Grandma – collect.

This trek however, covered totally unfamiliar territory. Fortunately, friends in Venezuela had told me to look up their relatives in Colombia, Peru, Argentina, and Brazil. Visiting those contacts briefly helped make the strange surroundings more familiar and less threatening, but comprised only a small part of my time. The adventure and danger lay during those months and miles in-between.

In the end, I'm grateful that nobody joined me because I had to fend for myself, make sense of baffling situations, and along the way forged friendships with people I otherwise would never have met. I accompanied fellow vagabonds from England, New Zealand, France, Germany, Sweden and Argentina and found my language skills handy because some of them spoke little or no Spanish. Several times I hooked up with Israelis, who were fonts of wisdom with generous advice for fellow budget travelers. While most vacationers carry a guidebook, the Israelis are a virtual human tour book on the fly. They exchange tips with fellow Israelis they encounter on the road as well as updating travelers' notebooks at Israeli Consulates in their path. They record the good, the bad and the ugly about places they have been and glean information written by others about cheap hotels, restaurants and transportation, along with where to find the best exchange rates.

Most important, had I not been traveling alone, I would not have stumbled upon the serendipitous coincidences that led to meeting my wife in Brazil. I barely spoke Portuguese and was not looking for marriage. The singles life suited my needs quite well once I had adapted to a solitary existence on the road: a chain of intense – but usually temporary – friendships and romances.

The singular event of meeting Maria changed the trajectory of my long trip around Latin America, and indeed, transformed the entire course of my life. When people ask me how I met her, even thirty years later, it's always complicated to answer. Where do I begin? The moment I walked into a bank in São Paulo and fell in love at first sight with the sensuous teller? The day she arrived in New York, was declared an undesirable alien by immigration officers and ordered back to Brazil? Or earlier in Arequipa, Peru when I met a Brazilian medical student named Flavio, who scribbled down his name, address and telephone and said to call him if I came to São Paulo? The day I flew out of Seattle for Caracas? The morning I departed Venezuela to travel around the world? All of them are good starting points because, absent any single element in this strange series of happenstance, we would not have met. But since I have now told the story numerous times, the narrative thread usually unfolds in the Lima bus station.

Most Peruvians can't afford cars or airplane tickets, so they travel by bus or train. The Lima bus station was modern and efficient, in a Third World sort of way, so I was lulled into thinking that things would work right. Passengers don't carry their bags to the bus. Like at an airport, you check your bag, get a receipt, your luggage is thrown on a conveyor belt, then loaded onto your bus. You don't have to worry about it until you reach your destination, so I was relieved to not lug my heavy backpack.

The bus thrust itself southward through the parched countryside past mile after mile of villages where the walls of *pueblos jovenes* were erected from flimsy woven straw mats. The highway was paved for the entire six-hour journey, surprising after the Pan-American north of Lima was an impassable mess in so many spots. My destination was Nazca, where outlines of giant surrealistic animals were sketched into the sand by ancient peoples. The lines attracted a lot of visitors after the pseudo-science best-seller, *Chariots of the Gods?*, postulated that the drawings were landing instructions for spaceships piloted by prehistoric astronauts. I had read this book, and while I didn't fall for the premise, thought the designs would be worth seeing.

Arriving in Nazca, I went to fetch my backpack. But it was gone. Immediately, I feared I had been robbed of my belongings such as my irreplaceable rolls of film with hundreds of pictures already shot, my clothing, camping gear, everything I needed for two years on the road, much of it irreplaceable in this part of the world. All I carried by hand were a camera bag and a book. The dispatcher called Lima and found out that my luggage had been placed on another bus that passed through Nazca only minutes earlier and was headed for Tacna, 525 miles southward, near the border with Chile. One day in Nazca seemed like enough time to see what I came for, but I was stranded an extra two days – with no change of clothing or toothbrush – waiting for my backpack to return from distant Tacna.

I rode in a small airplane to see the lines from the air, but they were much less distinct than expected, having been trampled and driven over, combined with centuries of wind erosion. After seeing the lines, there was nothing else to do. That allowed me to observe the rhythms of Nazca from the lovely, shaded town square. People awoke early. All the stores were open by eight, and everybody scurried around to shop, to work and school. By noon, temperatures exceeded a hundred, and the entire town came to a standstill during the most sweltering hours when everybody hibernated for a siesta until dusk. Then, like wilted flowers which suddenly spring back to life after watering, the town showed life again. Shops reopened, the town bustled once more, and everybody worked until about eight. By my third day, I was getting acquainted with some locals. A toothless, wrinkled woman asked me to marry her daughter. I was particularly impressed by the affable photographer, who used an old-style box camera, poking his head under a black cloth draped over the back. People posed serious and erect for his shots, which he displayed to customers with a proud smile, making them feel as if he had just taken the portrait of the royal family.

Once I reclaimed my belongings, the next destination was Arequipa, Peru's second-biggest city, an impressive array of colonial churches and elegant homes, many of them white or ochre, with vibrant flower gardens. Due to the higher elevation, the city's climate was much more agreeable. I sat in the town square and read a magazine, shooing away shoeshine boys who insisted on shining my sneakers. Another traveler in the plaza, Flavio, was amused because I did not hesitate to bat away the boys as pesky as flies and thought I might be fun to talk to. About six feet tall with blondish-brown hair, blue eyes and a complexion fairer than my own, he did not fit my concept of a Brazilian. He would fit in at Ballard, Seattle's neighborhood for Scandinavian fishermen. I was surprised that he spoke good English. His father had attended Michigan State University about the same time my own Dad studied there, and he made Flavio and his sister learn English starting from childhood. Flavio and I spent the day touring the colonial churches and museums, then parted ways in the evening. I was traveling up to the high Andes, while he was heading back home to Brazil. Before we split, he generously insisted that I visit him in São Paulo. At that time, I doubted if I would even go there. When I thought of Brazil, I had visions of spectacular Rio de Janeiro, wide sandy beaches and the Amazon jungle. An even bigger version of Caracas had no appeal.

Two months later – after journeying through Bolivia, southward in Chile to Tierra del Fuego, then back up through Argentina, Uruguay and Paraguay – I reached Brazil. The Brazilian Consulate in Paraguay gave me the option of a six-week or a three-month tourist visa. Believing that I would see all I wanted in a month, I opted for the shorter visa. It would be several visas and a year and a half later before I finally would head home from Brazil, all because of meeting the woman who made me change my plans. When I walked into the bank across the street from Flavio's apartment, she grabbed my attention, and shortly thereafter, I knew destiny had brought us together.

In Brazil, I found that fluent Spanish did me little good with Portuguese, which sounded like a confused German trying to speak French. Many words bore little relationship to Spanish or French, and I was dazed.

Ironically, I did not find a traveling companion in Maria. I wheedled her to sail the Amazon and climb Inca ruins, to no avail. For middle-class Americans and Europeans – born into comfort – the notion of journeying all over the Third World has wide-eyed mystical appeal. To someone in the Third World who has clawed out of poverty to reach the middle class, crumbling bus stations, dingy hotels and malodorous restrooms are an everyday fact of life, not something exotic to be romanticized. Thus, my continuous journey morphed into short jaunts, always returning to São Paulo until I wore out my welcome at Flavio's place, my final visa was expiring and money started running out.

I ventured the Amazon and went through the Guianas, homeward bound and alone. My wife-to-be would not leave for the United States until I had a responsible job again. What could I do? I had spent a decade as a tireless flirt, but Maria pinched my soul and love spilled out from every pore.

I still long to journey the Eastern Hemisphere but ironically, my wife and daughter got there first. When we were newlyweds living in New York, Maria accompanied a wealthy Brazilian family to Japan for a couple of weeks as a substitute nanny (their regular nanny did not have a green card and Maria was a U.S. resident by then). Our daughter,

Juliana, who had traveled to Japan in utero, worked in her twenties as a fashion model in Thailand and China, where she adapted easily.

Thirty years later, I still have not started that second half of my original journey.

Chapter 8

The First Step on a
Long, Long Journey

I left Caracas on December 23 at 6 a.m. before anyone else awoke and traffic built up to a beastly mess. I felt as if I had to sneak out of town before something happened to make me stay. I did not know if this was the last time I would see my home of two years, but I was too tired for memories or nostalgia. In my stupor of not having slept enough in weeks – finishing final details for the trip, working at a breakneck pace, short and long goodbyes to casual and close friends – my brain was barely functioning. I only had a brief five-minute goodbye with my Peruvian girlfriend, Ana Maria, after sipping champagne and drifting off into the abysm of sleep just two hours earlier.

I was leaving Venezuela with everything right. No hard feelings with anyone who mattered to me, no debts, no second thoughts. I was fully adapted to life in Venezuela. There was no reason to leave except the thirst for adventure, to explore the vast continent where I had lived on the edge for two years.

My road companion Jean-François and I did not talk much. Both of us were exhausted, so we looked at the scenery and dozed intermittently.

The taxi skirted *ranchos* on the way to the airport as I thought about how I had enough money to spend a couple months in fancy resorts and jet around the continent if I wanted rather than two years of what would be grueling much of the time. I had the money, the time and the thirst to do it my way. A boss once told me that a person needed "screw you money," though he phrased it a bit more crudely, to achieve what he wished. I had done that. I had enough cash that I did not need to depend on the graces of anyone to play my own hand. I was exiting in my own style. We flew to Maracaibo, where the taxi driver taking us to the bus terminal had a vocabulary of non-stop colorful obscenities. He cursed his squealing car, the bumpy roads, other drivers, the traffic, the heat, the government...

The bus ride along the Guajira Peninsula to Colombia bordered an emerald green coastal swamp. When starting out on the road with no end in sight, everything looks charming. Fellow passengers were mostly Colombian Indians; I could barely understand their chatter, mixing rapid-fire Spanish with native words and colloquialisms that had no context for me. The ladies wore dark, loose-fitting dresses. Brass-dominated *salsa* and Colombian *cumbia* burst out at top volume. The ride to the border took just a couple of hours, but the wait to cross – choked with cars and people – was even longer. It took two hours to get the necessary exit stamps, a fitting farewell to Venezuelan bureaucratic incompetence, and another hour and a half to get my passport approved to exit. Next, entry procedures for Colombia took five minutes. The Colombian roadside to Maicao, the closest town, was incredibly littered: discarded boxes, wrappers, food leftovers, just plain junk.

In Venezuela, *ranchos* were made of red brick material about half the size of a cement block. In Colombia, humble dwellings were mud or plywood. In Maicao, most of the buildings were modern and well maintained. The streets were dirt and full of open-air market stalls selling Venezuelan, American and European products. We were bound for Santa Marta, on the Caribbean where Simón Bolívar, the father of independence in the Andean nations, died in 1830. The bus was scheduled to arrive at 9 p.m., but did not reach Santa Marta until 2 a.m. The driver augmented his income by concealing smuggled liquor. Every half hour or so was another police checkpoint. Everyone told us the region was full of thieves and *contrabandistas*, or smugglers.

The most popular contraband in these parts is gasoline. One unmistakable sign that you have crossed into Colombia from Venezuela:

open-air, makeshift gas stations. Vendors wait on the side of the road with the tools of their trade: funnels, siphon hoses and plastic gasoline tanks, usually five or ten gallons each. Gasoline in Venezuela cost a nickel a gallon, the same as it had for decades. Colombians fill the tanks in their cars and trucks in Venezuela, build auxiliary hidden tanks, along with as many plastic cans as they can get away with, to resell at a remarkable profit. Gasoline in Colombia sells at world market prices, similar to levels in the United States, so it's easy to imagine the markup potential from a nickel to three or four dollars. The Venezuelan government is unable to crack down on the smugglers once they cross the border; the Colombian government has its hands full with guerrillas and drug gangs, so gasoline smugglers are not a priority. By late 2013, small-time smugglers had been eclipsed by well-connected gangs carrying huge amounts. Venezuela's Energy Ministry said one hundred thousand barrels per day of gasoline, nearly one third of total domestic demand, was being bootlegged into Colombia.

I learned new vocabulary quickly. Instead of calling you *amigo*, Colombians animatedly call out *sócio*, or partner, the way a Mexican says *cuate*, or an Ecuadoran would call you *pana*.

Santa Marta was mostly middle class, with little extreme wealth or poverty in evidence. Bolivar died in a simple white house, certainly not a remarkable place for the man whose memory is still revered by millions.

After touring Bolivar's home, we were ready to depart for Barranquilla and Cartagena. I had longed to see Barranquilla, a major city along the Caribbean, because of a catchy song: "*Se va caiman, se va caiman, se va para Barranquilla* (the alligator is leaving, the alligator is leaving, leaving for Barranquilla)." *Caiman* is also slang for a disreputable person.

The road passed sparkling Santa Maria lagoon with houses on stilts perched above the mud and roaming pigs. Barranquilla was similar to Maracaibo, a hot, noisy coastal city with a frenetic commercial center.

Cartagena, which draws visitors to its beaches and fort, has resorts for pampered Latins. Our reserved modern beachfront hotel cost a hundred dollars a night, and two nights were enough at that price.

After that, we downscaled to a smaller, simpler place across the street from the sea.

The thick stone walls of the sixteenth-century Spanish fortress envelop bright pastel colonial buildings in the old town, attracting tourists from Colombia and around the world. Also thieves. This was where I encountered my first, and only, money-changing scam. He shorted me a couple dollars' worth of pesos. When I told him, he took the money back and counted it again to my satisfaction by adding several small bills. What I didn't realize was that in adding the smaller bills he removed a large one, handed me back the fistful and vanished before I realized I had been swindled. I lost about forty dollars, but it was a good lesson so early because I would be changing money frequently for two years. Perhaps it was a Christmas Eve gift from fate.

The local girls were beautiful, playful and flirtatious. In one store, a dark beauty told me she liked my eyes. We bantered a bit more and then I asked her out, but she turned me down. The flirtation was nonstop, but I didn't always know how to carry it to the next step. The social rules were different in each country, so I had to learn on the fly.

Most of the tourists were fair skinned, light haired, wealthy people from Bogotá and Medellín, while the locals along the Caribbean were predominantly Indians, blacks and mixed-race.

Fruit vendors, called *paliqueñas,* wore loose-fitting brightly colored dresses and balanced on their heads baskets of pineapples, bananas, watermelon, papaya and other tropical treats. They stashed fierce-looking long knives in their belts. Boys sold cigarettes, sunglasses, hats, or shirts, and other vendors toted coolers to sell beer and soft drinks. One guy peddled ice cream from a bicycle-powered cart.

Yet, just a few miles inland was another world far from the money represented by swanky hotels. Dirt roads took us to towns with lyrical names such as Turbaco, Mahates, San Jacinto and Soplaviento, which translates to "blowing wind." Children rode donkeys; tiny houses had straw roofs. We were immediately whisked into the magical world of Gabriel Garcia Marquez novels set in villages of yesteryear.

On New Year's Day, I reflected on what 1982 had been and 1983 would be. I had worked at several jobs and disciplined myself into strict routines to save enough money to travel. I surmised that the coming year would be freedom from routine and only constant change. But I soon learned that life on the road requires routines, with frequent packing and unpacking, to always keep track of all my possessions, whether in a hotel room or my backpack, to avoid losing things or falling victim to crime.

On my last day in Cartagena, I toured the city on the back of a motorcycle piloted by Carmen, a beautiful architect I met at the beach.

Cartagena was still dressed up for Christmas, with lights festooning noble houses or in poor neighborhoods, scraggly trees. I bade farewell to Jean-François at the airport and took a bus back to Santa Marta. The bus pulled away half empty but filled as we passed through small towns. I went through the same police barricades again, lighted by torches. At night, some towns were lit up, others were dim.

A procession with what looked like a whole village followed a simple wooden coffin hoisted on the shoulders of four men.

The train ride from Santa Marta to Bogotá lasted thirty hours, mostly through hot, sweaty lowlands and climbing the high Andes only at the end. The train passed through Barrancabermeja, an oil-producing area where flares shot high into the air from burning residual natural gas in the oil fields. I hardly slept on the train. Much of the way, I sat on the step between railroad cars alongside new acquaintances.

Bogotá temperatures were generally in the fifties or sixties due to the high elevation. Most buildings were brick with red tile roofs, the boulevards were wide, and pine trees were abundant. The budget hotels, where I communed with roaches and rats, all boasted hot water on their signs, but my shower was icy. Still, I enjoyed chatting with the hotelkeeper's teenage daughter, who talked and sang simultaneously.

In Bucaramanga, I toured the Bolivar Museum, which displayed frightening grotesque skulls which were considered esthetic by Indians who tightly wrapped their children's heads to transform them into coneheads.

My next stop was Neiva in the tropical lowlands. I left the window in my room open with a fan blowing and watched the cockroaches scatter like wild horses stampeding when I turned on the light.

Pitalito had an open-air market where Indian vendors wore sweaters and felt hats, their hair pulled straight back in a tight single braid. Girls wearing red and green dresses walked in perfect unison. I enjoyed interactions with people in small towns and the gorgeous scenery, but I soon found out that they often made too much noise, with loud bells on churches at the town square, and music blasting over loudspeakers. There was no big city white noise to drown it out.

Every town had a church, where beggars, often deformed, installed themselves, pleading, *una limosna para Dios* (an offering to God).

Next was San Agustín, near fabulous pre-Columbian stone carvings. Enthusiastic vendors always assured me they were selling *auténtico* relics. A fellow traveler and I hired a boy to guide us on horseback through the hills to see ruins.

My simple room looked out on a garden blooming with flowers. Walking around town, I came across a bamboo house, the cracks filled with mud and a marvelous balcony overlooking banana plants and the hills. This was my first chance to study banana plants, which have purple pods that eventually burst open to expose numerous tiny green baby-size fingers that grow into bananas. Most people in North America have eaten only one or two kinds of bananas, deprived of many delicious varieties. Some available in the tropics are shorter and fatter, even nearly round, others with orange or pink or purple skin. Bananas bound for export to the United States are picked when still green and shipped in refrigerated containers. Sadly, they are tasteless compared with fresh varieties.

Leaving San Agustín was marked by rapid elevation changes. Some of the lowland houses were bamboo. Then, we rose to higher ground through the Magdalena River Valley. Clouds hung on ridges and filled valleys as the river roared at the bottom of the deep chasm.

The high Andes are incredibly awe-inspiring, dominated by dramatic snow-clad volcanic peaks and deep valleys in quick succession. Houses and terraced farms cling to cliffsides, growing sugar cane, corn, bananas and other crops where it seemed nobody could reach, let alone, farm. Tin roofs atop simple houses climbing mountainsides reflected like mirrors. In a single day I passed above the treeline, cloaked by cold, heavy fog, then back down to the warm tropics again.

Chilly Puracé National Park, at three thousand meters, was nearly deserted, so we ambled through this wondrous collection of odiferous volcanic-fed sulfur springs – green, yellow or red – by ourselves. These were set amid waterfalls and a backdrop of towering Andes peaks. The spiked, hairy-leaf *espeletia* plants resemble a cross between cactus and a bush. Far away, the crack of thunder belched.

At higher elevations, most Colombians wore *ruanas*, brightly colored wool blankets, poking their heads out an opening in the middle. Every color of the rainbow was represented, most notably striking reds and deep, rich blues.

On the road leading to Popayán, waterfalls burst out the side of cliffs. Popayán itself is a wonderful colonial town in which every building seems to be pure, blinding white.

Colombia is packed full of fairy-tale scenery like the blue mountains in the far distance behind emerald green valleys while coming into Pasto near the border with Ecuador. I passed deep ravines and string-bean towns along ridges astride foggy precipices on both sides.

Venezuela and Colombia are fraternal twins, with the same genetic material but noticeable distinctions. Like estranged family members, both sides harbor deep resentments. Many Colombians worked illegally at low-wage jobs in Venezuela, where they were mistreated. Venezuelans blamed illegal Colombians for crime and poverty (sound familiar?). Graffiti in Caracas blared COLOMBIANOS FUERA (Colombians Get Out).

After a few weeks in Colombia, I had already danced in open-air cafes along the coast, felt warm breezes off the ocean, encountered freezing winds in the high mountains, and beheld parrots in jungle trees. Colombians I met were gentle and helpful, and that certainly couldn't be said about Venezuelans in general. Venezuela had the oil money, paved highways, and a higher standard of living, though unevenly distributed. Still, I couldn't help but notice that Colombians, despite their crummy roads, drug gangs and anti-government guerril-las, seemed much happier.

Furthermore, it is pleasant to converse with Colombians, who have precise, sharp diction except for those along the Caribbean coast, who irritatingly speak at a rapid pace and don't enunciate, the same as Venezuelans, Cubans, Puerto Ricans, and Dominicans.

Chapter 9

El Condor Pasa

El Condor Pasa is beloved around the world, but few people realize it is a traditional folk song influenced by haunting flute music that has echoed off the peaks and valleys of the towering Andes for centuries. The effortless flight of the graceful condor has symbolized freedom to the Andean people since the time of the Incas. The mesmerizing song was popularized by Simon and Garfunkel when they recorded it for their best-selling 1970 album *Bridge Over Troubled Waters* (when I saw them in concert in 2003, they sang it beautifully, but to my great disappointment, without a flute).

People worldwide experience the sublime purity of Andean folk music at festivals, street fairs and performed by sidewalk buskers. Hundreds of these groups fan out around the world. They are readily identifiable: the musicians are descended from Incas, often with short stature and clear copper-hued skin, black felt hats cover braided black hair flowing down their backs, and brightly colored vests woven from traditional cloth. They play several types of flutes, a stringed instrument made from an armadillo shell called a *charango,* and drums. One tune they always play is *El Condor Pasa* because it is recognized universally. These musicians are almost always from Otavalo, Ecuador, an enchanting town recognized for its traditional artisans.

Until Spaniards overran the natives, everyone in South America had Indian ancestry. The Europeans then imported slaves, further stirring the racial pot. Some nations, like Argentina, have majority whites, while at least half the people in Bolivia and Peru are indigenous.

Venezuela and Colombia have substantial black populations, especially along the Caribbean.

Simón Bolivar liberated Venezuela, Colombia, Peru, Ecuador and Bolivia from Spain. Argentina and Chile, in the "Southern Cone," have their own national heroes. So, their histories diverged significantly two centuries ago at independence.

Any semblance of cohesion is elusive. Trade groups in Latin American seek to mimic the European Union, but these alliances are only half-hearted. Talk of "Latin unity" is a good applause line, but an empty one: relationships within the region are simmering with resentments. Poor countries in Latin American don't want to sell to their impoverished neighbors. They all seek the world's best markets for their goods – North America and Europe – and they covet shiny, fancy gadgets from places like China, not Guatemala.

As recently as 1995, Peruvians and Ecuadorans killed each other over empty land in the Amazon. Colombia has accused the Venezuelan government of giving safe haven to Colombian rebels who attack targets inside Colombia and then flee to Venezuela, where Colombian soldiers can't pursue them. Landlocked Bolivia believes that Chile robbed its Pacific coastline.

Colombia was my first step away from Caracas. Getting out of Colombia and into Ecuador, however, proved to be more complicated than expected. My last night in Colombia was in Pasto, which seemed drab after the glorious places I had recently visited: Cartagena, San Agustín and Popayán. To protect myself from theft in Pasto, I hid a wad of money behind a picture frame on the wall in my hotel room. Trouble is, I forgot to retrieve the stash come morning and did not realize my error until I was at the border after a ninety-minute bus ride. That meant that I had to return to my hotel to retrieve my cash and take the long trip back to the border a second time. The stunning scenery, however, merited another view. The serpentine highway passed tiny villages perched atop steep hillsides where residents hiked single file up and down steep, narrow paths. Motorcycle riders were adorned in *ruanas*: modern technology and Andean tradition speeding the death-defying curves together. Even some bicyclists somehow braved the rock-studded roadway. One village, Imbabura, named for a volcano and surrounded by parched brown hills and cactus, seemed to have all black residents, while the rest of the towns were populated principally by people of Indian lineage.

The Colombian side of the border, near a town called Ipiales, had a huge military fort and was occupied by hundreds of bazooka-toting soldiers. Across a deep ravine lay relaxed Ecuador. Another immediate improvement in Ecuador was a paved Pan-American Highway with a white line painted in the middle. Three hours down the highway is Otavalo, a charming cultural center with cobblestone streets, a looming volcanic peak, and a colorful market. Besides the great scenery, Otavalo conveys an air of calm; the people have a gentle, innocent nature.

Five hours away is Quito, where the first amazing view is from high on a hill outside the city, spread out neatly below in a bowl. The capital is well preserved, with Spanish architecture and steep winding cobblestone streets, amazingly, without ruts. It had far fewer slums than Caracas or Bogotá. I enjoyed Quito, in fact, until I got some kind of food poisoning that weakened me for several days. Another hassle was that there was no centralized bus station; rather, numerous bus stations were scattered here and there. Although Quito looks colonial at first glance, it also has a modern section, in which embassies are located, where imperial red double-decker buses that look right out of London scoot by on wide boulevards.

Outside Quito was the tranquil, picturesque town of Baños, blessed with mineral hot springs and nearby waterfalls. It made me wonder why I wasted so much time suffering in rundown hotels in boring, dirty cities and riding uncomfortable buses with endless streams of vendors instead of kicking back in a gem like Baños. Another pleasing town was Calderon, where the villagers make marzipan figures used as Christmas ornaments, a tradition which began for godparents to give religious figures to their godchildren on holidays. I still have marzipan llamas for my Christmas tree three decades later.

A couple hours outside of Quito is an extinct volcano, Quilotoa, where I hiked ten kilometers above thirteen thousand feet past brilliant green farmland where farmers inhabit straw huts, to the rim of an extinct volcano filled with a blue lake. In some ways it resembled Crater Lake in Oregon, but the special bonus was seeing terraced farms holding onto steep slopes inside the volcano, humble peasants blessed with a million dollar view.

A different hike in the mountains outside Quito afforded a sunset which painted a snow-draped volcano dark pink above a fog-rimmed valley.

Ecuador, of course, isn't only the Andes. I detoured to Ecuador's amazing Galapagos Islands. My flight from Quito connected through Guayaquil, Ecuador's most-populous city, on the Pacific coast. On the first leg of the flight, I chatted briefly with a fellow passenger, presidential candidate León Febres Cordero, whose rapid-fire oration I had witnessed the previous evening at an outdoor rally in Quito. What I remember most about Febres Cordero, who won the election, was the sound trucks in every town in Ecuador blasting out campaign slogans, *León es la verdad,* interspersed with bouncy music. Sound trucks are commonplace throughout Latin America to peddle political propaganda as well as fresh produce.

From the air, the Galapagos are a motley collection of barren rocks set amid emerald lagoons. The airport is on relatively flat Baltra Island, nothing but volcanic rock – red, black, brown and grey – tossed about haphazardly. A bus takes travelers from the airport to the dock for a ferry to Santa Cruz Island, where they stay in noisy Puerto Ayora if not boarding a boat immediately. This route shows mangrove poking through rocks on shore while pelicans plod the shoreline.

I joined an Israeli, some Colombians and a Dutch couple to contract a fishing boat to take us around the islands for a week. We each paid twenty dollars a day, food included. We slept aboard the boat and ate freshly caught fish, mostly tuna (far more flavorful than canned). Some days we feasted on plump, juicy lobsters, and one day they butchered a stray goat wandering on an island to make stew. Besides the captain, the boat had a licensed guide and a deckhand who doubled as cook.

Iguanas were everywhere, long, fat and scaly, with green lumps on their backs and yellow bellies; they tore the fruit off cactus and let humans approach. One dashed across a rock, its head crowned by a spiny trail leading to the tip of its tail. It stopped to let the sun soak into its scaly skin. After warming up, it gracelessly plopped into the cool water and paddled away.

The aquamarine water was perfectly clear, allowing a view of bright red and blue angelfish, others striped, spotted, small and large, and long slender trumpet fish which play follow the leader, even behind people. Sea lions, which often seemed to be sneezing, playfully nudged up against us in the water and on the beach. Midget penguins seemed to behave like humans as they embraced one other. Pink flamingoes flocked in a salt water lagoon. Sand and coral beaches crunched underfoot, but movement is restricted by law in places where the weight of people could break lava tubes and thin layers of lava. We played Superman, hoisting above our heads lightweight lava rocks as big as basketballs. Sugar Loaf Peak was four hundred meters high, accessible only by trudging up a forty-five degree incline in the baking sun. The return trip felt like skiing in the hot sand. Blue-Footed Boobies had huge, bright blue feet and emitted a whistle-type noise as a warning. They lay nests on the ground in the thick overgrowth, and their offspring are fluffy cottonballs. Male red-breasted Magnificent Frigatebirds inflate their chests into a bright, translucent red globe to attract females. How can any lady frigate refuse an offer from such a magnificent specimen? Binocular-toting ornithologists were living in a crude camp to study mockingbirds, which, they assured me, don't mock. Inside the crater on Daphne Island were hundreds of Blue-Footed Boobies flapping their wings and screeching sounds identical to a *zampoña*, a traditional Andean panpipe. Each one lets out a unique pitch, recognized by their chicks for feeding.

I had snorkeled at many beaches in numerous seas, but diving into the water over an extinct underwater volcano was uniquely eerie. The water is transparent hundreds of feet deep; and it was a bit overwhelming – when snorkeling at coral reefs I couldn't usually see more than twenty or thirty feet down.

Back in port, I spent the next day hiking to remote, empty beaches and to a reserve for giant tortoises. The lumbering creatures, some of them five feet long and weighing a ton, retreated into their shells when I got close or tried to snap photos. The trail was not marked, and I got lost on treacherous paths where I suffered the tortures of the damned, my legs torn apart by wicked thorns.

After leaving the Galapagos, every time I saw someone with a pointed nose and beady eyes, it reminded me of a masked booby; the inflated vermillion chest of the frigate is a dead ringer, figuratively, for preening machos strutting in streets the world over.

After flying back to the high elevation of Quito and other towns in the Andes, the weather was cool, but it got much hotter when the road dropped down to the sizzling Pacific coastline. Along the border with Peru, the houses were perched on stilts along the rivers. We were trapped at the border crossing on the Pan-American Highway until it opened at eight in the morning.

In Peru, the buses stopped wherever the highway washed out. Several times, the passengers all got out, tromped through mud carrying their bags, then clambered onto a different bus on the other side.

It was so hot that sweat seeped out all my pores and nostrils. I constantly wiped my face with my only hanky until it became grey, sticky and smelly. This desert no man's land was infested with flies more numerous than sand dunes and oil pump jacks. In some places, mud was piled ten feet high on the side of the road, evidence of recent landslides. A boulder the size of a semi truck rested atop a wall of mud.

Peru was extremely dangerous then. Police maintained frequent checkpoints in the desert, jungle and mountains. Maoist Shining Path guerillas, or *Sendero Luminoso*, were on a mad killing spree, while police and soldiers also brutalized civilians with impunity. My friend, Peruvian journalist Carmen Valdivieso Hulbert, is probing the massacre of eight journalists in a remote Andean hamlet in 1983. Her documentary, *Uchuraccay*, is scheduled for release in 2014.

I was beset by various minor ills which sapped the thrill out of traveling: the dramatic scenery, colorful costumes, and funky little towns all seemed drab as I struggled with muscle aches, runny nose and sneezing. Bumps in the road seemed rougher, lumpy beds felt like torture racks, and the crummy food was inedible.

Extreme sleep deprivation can lead to a break with reality, even insanity. I had strange delusions on two occasions; my journey was becoming a scary acid trip without drugs. I endured hardship to see the scenery, which I often ended up missing because many of the buses or trains I needed only traveled all night or required starting at an ungodly hour. I would often get up at four to catch a bus or train scheduled to depart at five, only to wait in line for hours and lose sleep for nothing. Even routes that were scheduled to arrive in the late afternoon or early evening were often delayed by breakdown or road closures, and I would reach my destination long after midnight. On trains, I got jostled by all the baggage carried by passengers; some even brought live chickens on board, which is amusing but noisy and messy. I got virtually no sleep for consecutive nights several times on my long journey. The cumulative sleep deprivation as well as lack of effective medicine for my illnesses made me briefly hallucinate bright red spots, flaring lights, and cartoon characters in my midst, all too incredible to believe. I nicknamed the dreadful buses wheeled cockroach traps.

The initial overriding impression of Lima is brown: the color of sand dunes, flaking cliffs, and passing countryside. Houses of mud, adobe or thatched cane leaves are all brown. Fires infested the air and nostrils, intermingled with the stench of garbage and decaying flesh. I stayed with a friend's family, so I was able to recuperate from my illnesses and fatigue.

I'd been told it never rains in Lima, so I was surprised to see windshield wipers clicking and unprepared people shielding themselves with hunks of cardboard. One woman walked her pig on a leash. But the most bizarre sight in Lima was the collection of mummies, many of them in jars in a fetal position, at the Larco Museum.

In Peru and the other Andean nations, poverty, ignorance, and malnutrition cause tragic deformities from birth defects and disease. Far too many children had to sell things instead of study or play. Some had the oddest clothing: a boy hustling drinks wore a T-shirt depicting an obese rich man chomping a cigar, bearing the telling slogan YA DON'T WORK, YA DON'T EAT. Another shirt said "I'm related to the

South American monkey and have a teenie weenie to prove it!" while many T-shirts misspelled the names of American universities.

I ventured into the high mountains to the Pampa Galeras reserve, where soldiers on horseback protect vicuñas from poachers. The beasts romp free, squeal at outsiders, protecting their territory and a dozen or so wives. They look you straight in the eye, make high-pitched screeches and bellows, sounding almost like a bird, then turn around and gallop away. The reserve is in a bowl-like valley with gently sloping hills, wind-blown smooth, and bare except for sparse grass. At four thousand meters, the sharp, dark blue air is thin. The harsh conditions dry the skin quickly. The few local residents were mostly farmers and herders living in piled stone houses with straw roofs, along with national guardsmen, one of whom begged me to help him stage a coup. With no hotels, I slept cozily in my one-man tent and down sleeping bag.

Remote Machu Picchu can be inconvenient to reach. Most travelers ride the railway through breathtaking canyons from historic Cuzco up to Aguas Calientes, where they might stay the night before the short bus ride to the ruins. When I visited, Peru's train workers were on strike so I hiked the distance with some Argentines. The day we saw Machu Picchu, no more than a few dozen people roamed the ancient stone structures and terraced apartments on steep hillsides. When cool raindrop fell mid-afternoon, most of the others left. I followed the swirling tunes of a sweet flute to its source: some *antioqueñas*, young women from Medellín, Colombia wearing ruanas had taken refuge in a windowsill overlooking the majestic site as fog crawled in and out of the valley. One moment we had a clear, commanding view, and seconds later it was misty and obscured. The improvised, hypnotic flute music, spellbinding ancient city and thin air made me float effortlessly, transcending time and space.

Archaeologists tell us the Incas were advanced in many ways; why then did they have human sacrifice and torture chambers? I spent several days going to other ruins, all with perfectly fitted stone walls and buildings: Ollataytambo, Saqsayaman, Tambomachay, Pukapukara, and Pisac, where I spied a little hunched-over man lugging on his back a pile of sticks nearly his own size, presumably to use as firewood.

At deep blue Lake Titicaca, I took a boat to visit islands seemingly untouched by the outside world except for tin roofs that replaced straw on many stone houses. Veiled women tending flocks of sheep seemed to exist in their own distinct, charming world. What could go wrong on such a pleasant outing? On the return trip, rain pounded fiercely, and wind whipped up oceanic-scale waves. The little boat rocked, rolled and reeled on the waves. I held on for dear life for an hour as the boat tipped and swayed and crashed into each threatening breaker. Once the storm broke, the water calmed and the sun's golden rays shone magnificently, displaying a vivid double rainbow and turning the lake's green grass into a golden shimmering floating garden. Fishermen paddled by in reed boats the shape of dugout canoes, as if they had emerged from a canvas painting.

One of the most common foods is *pez de rey*, a small bony fish that is fried in the public markets along the lake. In Puno, I was treated to out-of-tune brass bands and dancers swinging colorful hoop skirts in the Virgen de Candelaria parade.

Lake Titicaca straddles the border of Peru and Bolivia. Each country's residents claim that their side of the lake is the *titi* and the other nation gets the *caca*.

On the Bolivian side, I climbed a steep hill from Copacabana, a village for which the famed beach in Rio de Janeiro was named. The view from the top resembled an endless sea, along with Island of the Sun and Island of the Moon. A magnificent sunset over the lake was announced by lighthearted Andean flutes.

The mountains in Peru and Bolivia were far different from the northern Andes in Colombia where I started my trip. In Colombia, it seemed that I crossed more than one cordillera every day, constantly up and down vertiginous hillsides. In Peru and Bolivia, however, I stayed in the treeless high *altiplano* – a long, wide high plateau – for weeks. Roads were rarely paved but were much easier to traverse. Glacial runoff spawned milky rivers, the largest of which we crossed on bridges, while the bus charged and splashed straight through the smaller ones. Hailstorms occasionally dotted the brown earth all white. At higher elevations, the only creatures were gaunt llamas and alpacas with stick legs chomping on sparse, pale yellowish-green plants.

The elevation, besides making it difficult to suck in enough sparse oxygen molecules, inflicted odd, unexpected pains: my knees ached as if I had arthritis, my tongue became sore and particularly sensitive to salt, and infections plagued my nostrils. Unsanitary conditions, lack of sleep, and a heavy backpack exacted a cruel toll on my body. I came down with colds, runny nose, blisters, cracked lips, stomach ailments and diarrhea, skin rashes, lice, neck and backaches, throbbing headaches, and exhaustion. It could have been worse. A gaunt twenty-something gringo stranded in Copacabana was stricken with hepatitis, which made him urinate brown and black. Fortunately, I avoided hepatitis, along with other serious illnesses such as yellow fever, dengue, malaria and Chagas. Still, when I got home I slept twelve hours a night for a month to recover from the accumulated fatigue.

Sucre is the constitutional capital of Bolivia, but the de-facto administrative capital is La Paz, which means "peace." The history of La Paz, however, is anything but peaceful, with violent coups overthrowing presidents more times than anyone can count. The city lies in a deep ravine more than two miles high in the Andes, with views of distant mountain peaks seemingly topped by whipped cream. There, Bolivian television broadcast the most horrifying interview I had ever seen. Nazi Klaus Barbie, called "the Butcher of Lyon" for his role as regional head of the Gestapo which exterminated thousands of human beings, fled to Bolivia after World War II and became an army officer. Interviewed during his extradition flight back to France, where he was convicted for his ghastly war crimes, Barbie was asked whether he regretted anything in his life. Just one: no regrets about joining Hitler or slaughtering innocent people, only "getting caught." I will never forget hearing those candid words spoken with no emotion, sending an icy *frisson* up my back. Barbie was not alone. Thousands of Nazi war criminals took refuge in nearby Argentina, Brazil, Chile, Paraguay and Uruguay. Argentina's most-accomplished actress, Norma Aleandro, visibly recoiled when she told me about a kindly old neighbor she knew as a child and later discovered he was a Nazi whose lampshades were made of human skin ripped from Holocaust victims; she was still revolted by the haunting memory decades later.

Likewise, many countries throughout the region still grapple uncomfortably with fallout from their anti-communist "dirty wars" that killed thousands of civilians. A Panamanian whose cousin apprehended dictator Manuel Noriega's opponents said the now elderly man is unapologetic. "I told him that he doesn't have a cross to bear, rather, the cross will carry him," she said.

In La Paz, I entered a so-called Mexican restaurant, but it had no tacos, burritos, or enchiladas, in fact, nothing but Bolivian food with Mexican names. It reminded me of an alleged Italian eatery in Quito that had no spaghetti, pizza or any Italian dish. La Paz is a bustling, crowded city overwhelmed by poverty. In Potosi, the bowels of the earth have been torn and pried apart for silver and tin. I toured a mine six hundred meters underground, in over one hundred-degree Fahrenheit heat, slopped in mud and bumped my head on the low ceiling.

The highest elevation I ever reached was Bolivia's border crossing with Chile, at four-thousand six-hundred meters, or more that fifteen-thousand feet. That is higher than the glacial summit of lofty Mt. Rainier, the silent sentinel that looms over Seattle. The border crossing was so high, in fact, that the mountain peaks which towered over La Paz and the surrounding area, such as 6,542-meter Sajama, were reduced to small lumps of vanilla ice cream as I approached. That night, I wore a T-shirt, long-sleeved shirt, sweater, and down jacket and still shivered in morgue-like temperatures while waiting in line to cross the border. By four-thirty in the morning, I arrived in coastal Arica, Chile and headed to a palm-fringed park where I stretched out on the grass in a T-shirt to snooze a couple of hours. Sleeping out in the open risked theft, so my backpack doubled as a pillow. It was a hot, heavy, steamy night after the shivering cold only hours earlier. I gulped moist, sweet, salty, oxygen-rich air and slept immediately and profoundly to the sound of waves slapping the rocky coast. I was startled in the morning by something spooky crawling up my arm – one of those lethal scorpions that proliferate in the Atacama Desert? But I was fearful for nothing: annoying, but ultimately harmless, ants. Arica was the first of a series of enchanting Chilean cities which, after the depressing poverty of Bolivia, exuded a magical, fairy-tale feeling. The next city down the coast was Iquique (ee-KEE-kay), where sea lions playfully begged for food along with squawking pelicans, which scooped up entrails of the fish gutted by fishermen. Everywhere I went, Chileans gleefully stuffed popcorn – coated with sugar – into their mouths.

The Atacama Desert in northern Chile forever altered my perception of dryness as I passed through places where it had never rained in recorded history. The brown hills were so smooth that they had not even formed rivulets for water to trickle down and looked as though they had been raked smooth. Traveling south, the scenery changes ever-so gradually as minute cracks appear in the hills where small amounts of water have flowed and tiny plants grew. Even farther south, those cracks slowly grow to where dry streambeds appear before a glimpse of real year-round creeks.

I traveled the length of shoelace-shaped Chile, from the searing northern desert to Tierra del Fuego, buffeted by frigid winds blowing unabated from Antarctica. Chile's topography is a mirror image of North America's West Coast. Northern Chile is the equivalent of Baja California's deserts. The Atacama gradually yields to golden grassy, oak-filled valleys that resemble Central California. The road ends in southern Chile at green, rainy Puerto Montt, with pine forests, clear rushing rivers and topography much like the Pacific Northwest. South of Puerto Montt is Chiloé Island, reminiscent of Vancouver Island in British Columbia. The ferry to Punta Arenas glides past evergreen rain forests, snow-crowned volcanic peaks, jaw-dropping fjords, and glaciers spilling into the sea, almost a dead ringer for the Inside Passage between Seattle and southeastern Alaska's Panhandle region. Mostly barren Tierra del Fuego shares common features with northern Alaska's tundra.

After Chile's desolate north, it was nice to see trees and greenery again. In Santiago, a Victorian mansion was converted into the Hotel Londres (London) where the furniture in the sitting rooms had red velvet cushions, elaborate crystal chandeliers dangled from high ceilings, and the wood floors were polished. As my traveling companion and I looked out the window, surveying the working ladies prowling Calle Londres, she asked me the meaning of the lyrics to the song by Jose Luis Perales that was playing, *"parecen mariposas de la noche,"* I translated "they look like butterflies of the night" and we agreed that was a fitting description of the scene spread out before us. Who needs TV when real life is so entertaining?

Santiago was marvelous, having a European air and nothing in common with the other capitals I had seen: Caracas, Bogotá, Quito, Lima, La Paz. The buildings were graceful, the boulevards wide, and the people were well dressed. Just one catch: Chile at that time was ruled by the military junta led by General Augusto Pinochet which overthrew the elected government of socialist President Salvador Allende a decade earlier with U.S. government assistance and imposed unspeakable cruelty on its fellow citizens. I visited Chile Stadium, where thousands of people who opposed the coup were deemed enemies and murdered by soldiers. The walls were still pockmarked by countless bullet holes, with no attempt to plaster over the savagery.

Military juntas tend to rule in the most backward nations with the poorest educational and income conditions in Africa and South Asia. Nonetheless, the most ferocious military dictatorships in Latin America ruled for years in Argentina and Chile, two of the most advanced nations in the region, as well as laggard brethren such as Bolivia and Paraguay.

I longed to see Viña del Mar, Chile's premier seaside resort, which every year holds the most celebrated music festival in Latin America. Some houses were built into the rocks along the coast, one with a swimming pool overlooking the pounding surf. I chatted with fishermen who carried their humble wooden boat from shore to the water. For the most part, however, Viña resembled other beachside refuges for the wealthy – mansions, chic boutiques and crowds – in other words, boring. I'd seen it all before in Miami, Waikiki, Malibu, and the Italian-French Riviera.

On the other hand, Santiago's nearby seaport, Valparaiso (vahl-par-uh-EE-so), is fascinating, with fifteen short funicular railroads, called elevators, which lift people atop a steep hill. The houses are old, wooden, crumbling, colorful. I was captivated by a bewitching dark-haired student I met and was so enthralled that I forgot to get her phone number. I also stumbled upon graffiti on a wall boldly proclaiming PINOCHET = HAMBRE (Pinochet = hunger), for which the spray painter could have been shot on sight.

The train ride was comfortable from Santiago to Puerto Montt, the farthest southern city reachable by rail in Chile. I passed through oak-filled golden valleys and swam in the cool waters of deep azure lakes such as Villarica and Llanquihue in the shadows of magnificent glacial-draped volcanoes.

I reached far southern Chile aboard a three-day ferry ride, from Puerto Montt to Punta Arenas, which stopped in small fishing villages populated by indigenous people who wore wool caps and thick sweaters. Some of them touted strangely shaped crustaceans which looked like mutant versions of familiar shellfish.

I tramped around Torres de Paine National Park, scattered with jagged sawtooth mountains, mirror-image lakes, and deep-blue Grey Glacier, but the best views of the fabulous twin peaks were mostly obscured by overcast weather every day I camped out there. Similarly, I never got an unobstructed view of Mt. McKinley while hiking in Denali National Park in Alaska. Extreme locations are accompanied by extreme weather. I returned to Punta Arenas and rode a short ferry to Porvenir on Tierra del Fuego where Yugoslav immigrants hung portraits of their homeland's long-time leader Josip Broz Tito on the walls of their homes and shops.

There were no buses, so the only way across the island's lone, sparsely traveled dirt roadway was to hitchhike to Ushuaia, the Argentine city which boasts being the southernmost burg in the world, flanked by the Darwin Mountains on one side and Cape Horn on the other. In Tierra del Fuego National Park, I hiked among the brilliant fall colors and woke up to a dusting of snowfall in early April, the equivalent of October in the Northern Hemisphere.

Crossing into Argentina, the border guards gave me a booklet to be stamped every day at the local police precinct. Sometimes the police station was several miles outside the town where I was staying. This was Argentina's way of punishing Americans for their government's support of Britain in recently fought the Falklands War. Weeks later, upon leaving Argentina for Uruguay aboard a ferry, I presented this booklet which had been stamped by police all over Argentina. The Argentine immigration officer, instead of verifying the information, simply discarded it without looking.

Chapter 10

Hitching From Patagonia

The last time I saw Thomas, he thrust his head out the window of a departing bus and shouted, "You'll never get out of here" as I stood stupidly, thumb outstretched, at a lonely truck stop in Patagonia, nearly a thousand miles south of Buenos Aires, without enough money for a bus ticket. I had a million pesos in my wallet, but they were only worth ten dollars. I wasn't really broke. A five-hundred-dollar check awaited me at the American Express office in Buenos Aires and another one for an equal amount in Montevideo, Uruguay.

The only hitch was getting to Buenos Aires to pick up my loot. I had already waited two days at this truck stop outside the dreary, unwelcoming town of Comodoro Rivadavia and worried that before long I would run out of money for food. What charity in a Third World country with real poverty of its own would help a wayward middle-class *estúpido* gringo?

On other occasions, I'd waited all day for a bus or a truck, which sometimes come and sometimes don't. But I had never been marooned this long. When I had needed a ride recently, it came so fast that I missed a chance to set my camera on the tripod for a self-portrait in front of the Tierra del Fuego sign in Chile. That trucker left me several hours later at *Bahia Inutil*, or Useless Bay, where I camped out as I waited seventeen hours overnight for the next ride. The wind sliced like a razor blade, and I reckoned that frigid land should be called *Tierra del Hielo* ("Land of Ice") rather than *Tierra del Fuego* ("Land of Fire"), so named because early European explorers noticed lots of fires, which warmed the natives.

Thomas, a German I had met a week earlier, gave up waiting. Together, we had hiked to frigid Lago Argentino high in the Andes, where we camped in the shadow of Perito Moreno Glacier, which from the distant plains of Patagonia glimmered like a bejeweled Land of Oz. We crawled into our sleeping bags weary after the glowing sunset briefly illuminated swabs of red cotton clouds, momentarily tinting the glacier an eerie crimson. Under the moonlight, the sharp cracks of calving, house-size ice blocks wriggling loose from their moorings and heaving into the water with a titanic splash, startled us with explosive snaps louder than thunder.

I yearned to climb into a little boat and go exploring even closer. To reach a lagoon, we hiked along a narrow ledge with a solid wall of ice on one side and the lake far below on the other. A falling chunk of ice would have swept us into the lake with no chance for escape. It was spooky, mysterious, yet thrilling. In the sunshine, the glacier glared a blinding blue, contrasting with the dull, milky greenish-white lake which resembled liquid antacid.

Doubting Thomas had sufficient cash on hand to buy a bus ticket to Buenos Aires but not enough to lend me bus fare too. His cruel parting words were ominous and certainly unwelcome to a poor fool in my miserable predicament.

I would have used my credit card to pay for a ticket, but Visa canceled my card without explanation and no way to find out why from so far away. I often bashed Third World stupidity and inefficiencies, but this was modern Bank of America that messed me up.

It was the second time I had run out of money on this long trip and it wouldn't be the last. A year later, I would arrive in Lima with the equivalent of two dollars in local *soles*. I had the choice of getting a cheap room or eating dinner. It took me more than an hour walking through dodgy areas to find a hotel I could afford until I could retrieve my check the next morning. But I'll never forget the first time. It was three months earlier when I arrived in Quito without much money, in anticipation of picking up my check. The American Express office, however, only had a notice telling me to get a small package at the Customs Office. I was notified on the cusp of a four-day weekend that the Customs Office at the Quito airport would be closing in minutes. I ran out to find a taxi but realized that traffic was hopelessly snarled and the only way I would make it on time would be with my own two sore feet.

I had less than fifteen minutes to jog two miles, zigzagging past cars trapped in the city's constricted, two-lane cobblestone streets. I had run cross-country and track in high school, more than a decade earlier, but that was at sea level. Quito lies 9,350 feet up in an Andean valley. Thin air is troublesome at first, giving most people headaches while gasping for sparse oxygen particles. The Quechua language spoken by the Incas had a word for it, *soroche*. I had no alternative but to keep going and prove that I had not lost my speed, stamina or determination. I was the kind of runner who usually took second place in competitions, but this time second-best would not do. I had to win the race against my only opponent: the clock.

I smoked cigarettes off and on and had been trying to quit, but Ecuador was too tempting. Everybody smoked, even ladies in colorful hoop skirts and bowler felt hats. Worse, for someone trying to kick the habit, was the fact that vendors sold individual cigarettes for a nickel. It's easier for an intermittent addict to resist the inducement to buy a whole pack than it is to take "just one more" puff. Even though I only smoked a few cigarettes a day, it wasn't long before thin oxygen and smoky lungs proved that I was no longer a teenage gazelle.

The coughing consumed me as I zoomed unhindered through the streets. I regretted every cigarette I had ever stuck in my mouth, starting with the first one with giggling friends after school when I was fifteen. My body was now paying me back for the mistreatment to which I had subjected my lungs, my heart, and my nervous system. My chest pounded, heart thumped fast, head throbbed, sides ached. Wheezing, I reached the airport and Customs Office at the exact moment they were closing the door. I begged the agent to not turn me away, that I was broke before the holiday weekend and needed the check inside my package. The small care package also included necessities of life I could not find on the road: snapshots of family members, newspaper clippings from home, Chap-Stick, brownies, Oreos. After paying a small tax with my remaining money, I offered the friendly customs agent a brownie, which he had never eaten before and enjoyed immensely. Seeing his dark eyes light up was more joyful than the taste of Mom's brownies.

I rode a bus back to the city center and found the bank where American Express had directed me to cash my check. Ecuador, which had tight currency exchange restrictions, did not allow me to make the transaction at American Express. Feeling dizzy and twisting in self-inflicted pain, I recalled one of my favorite films, Stanley Kubrick's *A Clockwork Orange*, in which the beastly protagonist was subjected to nonstop graphic depictions of sex and "ultra-violence," unable to close his eyelids to block it out. At first he enjoyed it, but after several days of this aversion therapy, he was overwhelmed and became docile, as if lobotomized. I was experiencing a similar effect with cigarettes, my wheezing and suffering caused by smoking. I was hacking for days afterward. Thirty years later, I have never smoked again or felt any temptation to pick up a cigarette. Even a faint whiff of smoke acutely brings back the same nauseating sensation.

Three months later in the wastelands of Patagonia, this aversion therapy was just a faint memory. All I needed was a driver willing to take me on the three-day ride to Buenos Aires and, so far, nobody would do that. I was even willing to ride with a smoker. After all, I could not walk the distance. Strangely, other hitchers were getting rides after only short waits while I was ignored. Passing cars and trucks spit noxious fumes while flinging unwelcome gravel and dust toward me. Autumn temperatures plunged to near-freezing at night, so my down jacket was always within reach.

There were few consolations during the long, lonely hours I waited. I enjoyed brilliant leaves swirling in whirlpools around me, yet I would rather have watched the colors whisk by through the window of a vehicle, any vehicle.

I didn't miss Thomas. Although I had no companionship, I did not need his negativity. The night he left, I felt an intense glow from the first genuine act of kindness since getting stuck. I had been silently mocking an obese man in the restaurant for gorging himself on two of everything: juicy, thick pork chops and hefty mounds of fries. Then, as he left the restaurant, he told the waiter to bring over the rest of his bottle of red wine to me, tipped his beret, and flashed a warm, friendly smile my way. I had been drinking tap water to conserve my rapidly depleting cash. After savoring the *Vasco Viejo* wine, I peeled the label and preserved it in my travel diary along with leaves, flowers and a miniature wheat stalk.

Luckily, food in the truck stop was cheap, only a dollar for a basic meal of pasta and bread. A TV in the corner seemed to play the same soap opera, *Todos los Dias la Misma Historia* (every day the same story) whenever I ate. For four nights I slept outside this lonely pit stop of humanity and washed in a grimy sink.

Getting desperate, I began to beg rides from truckers as they filled their tanks. One after the next, they turned me down. I felt like cursing those who rejected me, but something inside fought back the temptation, telling me there was no reason to bear them ill will.

Thomas had become hostile and bitter about being stuck, but I had resisted letting him dampen my own spirits. I felt it was necessary to keep a sense of humor and balance. When I told him in one conversation that I was enchanted by Andean culture dating back to the Incas, the vibrant blankets, the felt hats, the bewitching flute music, Thomas bellowed: "That's not culture. That's just primitive people. Culture is Wagner and Goethe, not Indians with llamas and flutes." To this day, I eschew effete snobs and continue to derive pleasure from many cultures such as Andean tunes and Brazilian samba, as well as highbrow classics.

When one trucker responded that he did not pick up riders, I shot back politely that I was skinny and didn't take up much space (well, I *was* slender in those days). He opened the door and motioned me on in. Juan was a cross between Merle Haggard and Jack Nicholson, with dark hair slicked back and a roughly carved nose and chin. He was friendly and wanted to chat, which we achieved by shouting over the loud drone of the engine. Hobbled by a sore throat, my voice had descended into a rasp the duration of our time together.

I wanted to buy him food with my remaining money, but instead, he insisted on treating me to meals, which always included wine. I could not insult my kind host by refusing. He taught me that in Argentina, you never utter "wine" to a waiter. Doing so would give you away as an outsider. Instead, you simply order *tinto* for red or *blanco* for white.

By watching Juan, I deciphered signals given by truckers drumming on their dashboards to alert fellow truckers to a police car or weigh station ahead like Africans pounding rhythmic messages to neighboring villages.

In a country divided by sharp political polarities between the barbaric right-wing military regime in power at the time and violent leftist opponents – many of them Eva Perón fans – Juan was surprisingly moderate and flatly rejected both extremes. After encountering many illiterate peasants in recent months, he was educated and well-informed. He stopped every so often to fire up a camping stove over which he boiled water for *maté* tea, sipped from a tall, slender cup through a metal straw. I sampled the bitter potion but never understood its appeal. Instead, I filled my own cup with hot water and a tea bag. We both urinated freely beside the highway, which was a dirty ribbon winding and stretching over numbingly nameless territory.

After being in Argentina for a couple of weeks, I'd begun to reach some conclusions about the people. Most are descended from Europeans, unlike the mostly Indian populations in other countries. Argentines were more like Americans or Europeans than other South Americans: better educated, reserved and seemingly cold and methodical at first, but kindhearted when you pry beneath their skin a bit. Most outsiders, especially Latin American neighbors, can't see beyond Argentine arrogance, which is viewed as the local version of French haughtiness. It appears to come from the Argentine view that they are cultured Europeans stuck on a continent full of backwards illiterate monkeys (as they describe neighboring Brazilians). It was a matter of breaking through the external barriers to see what lay beneath the Argentines.

As we drove northward, the barren landscape became gradually more verdant and lush. The closer we got to Buenos Aires, the more it looked like American Midwest farmland: tall grassy fields of green and gold, corn, wheat, grazing cows and sheep, more trees. Yellow flowers were abundant, and so was a strange plant that resembled a dried sunflower without the petals. I glimpsed this world through a dirty windshield riven with spider-web cracks and miniature gravel-propelled holes.

On the third day of our truck ride, in sprawling, but still rural, Buenos Aires province, the highway was now smoothly paved unlike the cratered roads back on the pampa. It was still Indian summer here. Everything was green, and fall had not yet descended as it had in now-distant Patagonia.

I craved the amenities of civilized life again. I had not showered in a week or slept in a bed for two weeks. Buenos Aires was a spectacular city that radiated a feeling of being the center of the world, a sensation I had experienced in New York, London, Paris and Rome. The feeling was even more intense after the slow trek through Patagonia. From the freeway, the utilitarian skyscrapers on both sides gave airs of an American metropolis. Rather than just a massive collection of people and buildings, Buenos Aires had everything, a teeming fishing hole to extract whatever you wanted. It was the first place on this trip that beckoned me to stay rather than continue my weary travels through more uncivilized territory.

I dropped by the English-language *Buenos Aires Herald* and was offered a job. It was tempting, but I wanted to keep moving on. I had only been on the road four months at that time, and the wanderlust still had a grip on me. That job seemed like returning to what I had left in Venezuela, only in a new city and country. I needed to move onward, not backward or tread water.

In the city center, I found a hotel with a balcony and shuttered windows that reminded me of the French Quarter in New Orleans. For the first time in two weeks, I had a room to myself. I was intrigued, turned-on, charged-up, and excited by my bustling, noisy, hectic surroundings. I was enchanted and understood why *porteños*, Buenos Aires residents, felt superior to the peasants in countries surrounding them. Seriously, don't we grant New Yorkers and Parisians a bit of leeway for rightful pride in their cities?

A favorite joke in Argentina, recounted by numerous Argentine friends as well as foreigners, goes like this: What's the easiest way to get rich? Buy an Argentine for what he's worth and then sell him for what he thinks he's worth.

Buenos Aires was stunningly beautiful, with wide boulevards and expressive fountains everywhere. Brightly painted buildings of every shade made the bohemian section, La Boca, hypnotic. Yet, the alluring city appeared to be a living museum trapped in a bizarre time warp. Tango seemingly had not evolved since its greatest singer, Carlos Gardel, died a half century earlier when my parents were toddlers. Tango seeped out of every café. Almost every car was a vintage Ford Falcon identical to those back home in the sixties. People wept at the tomb of Eva Perón, who died in 1952 and was idolized to the point of obsession.

The most iconic Argentine besides Evita is Che Guevara, the scruffy bearded Marxist guerrilla who battled alongside Fidel Castro in the Cuban revolution and was executed while trying to lead an uprising in Bolivia. The word *che* has no political significance; in Argentina, it simply means "hey" or "buddy," or even "hey buddy."

I rode a ferry across the Rio de la Plata to lilliputian Uruguay, which felt more like a province of Argentina than a distinct country. Uruguayans have the same Italian-inflected accent as Argentines, eat the same food and feel like ugly, neglected stepchildren.

My ordeal in Patagonia far behind me, I was relieved. As Juan and I bade farewell, I asked him why he had given me a ride. He had found my response to his initial rejection quick-witted and thought I would make an amusing travel partner and conversationalist for the endless, lonely hours. Surely, he would not have offered a ride to someone with Thomas' sour disposition, so I credit my positive attitude for getting me out of there.

Chapter 11

The Illegal Alien

My first visual impression of South America came from the movie *Black Orpheus*, the Greek tragedy *Orpheus and Eurydice* transposed to Rio de Janeiro's colorful Carnival. I saw the 1959 film when I was junior high school age with my father, who was right in assuming that I would enjoy it. As a child I was interested in all things foreign, despite not visiting a foreign country other than Canada or Mexico until I finished college. Before I entered kindergarten, Dad taught me scraps of Japanese he had picked up as a sailor during the occupation, words I still remember (*arigato, sayonara, ichi, ni, san, shi, go, roku ...*). I delighted in French cinema and Italian opera and read about faraway places. I peppered family friends and neighbors from places like Lebanon, Italy and Panama with questions about their homelands.

I had befriended Brazilians while living in Venezuela and along the road. I was convinced that Portuguese would roll smoothly off my tongue by virtue of my fluency in Spanish and basic knowledge of French from school days.

I arrived at the Brazilian border from Paraguay. The bus ride from Asunción, in western Paraguay, lasted six hours to its eastern border. In Asunción, a Taiwanese immigrant had ushered me all over town on his motorcycle, took me to cheap meals in Chinese restaurants, and introduced me to Paraguayan girls. Lou sold costume jewelry, which the locals call *fantasias*, in small towns. I had entered Paraguay at Encarnación, across the Paraná River from Posadas, Argentina after touring the ruins of Jesuit missions, the history of which was recounted in the tragic 1986 film *The Mission* starring Robert De Niro. Barefoot peasants sold items in the dirt streets, and Indians spoke to each other in their native Guarani language.

Ciudad Stroessner, named for the dictator who ruled that nation for thirty-four years and still held power the first time I went there, was a jumble of outdoor bazaars, muddy streets and touts. The bus marooned me in the middle of a crowded market rather than a bus station. There was nothing in the ramshackle city that interested me, and I was anxious to explore a new world on the other side of the border. Money changers juggled dollars, Brazilian, Paraguayan and Argentine currencies, so I changed enough to get me through the weekend at Iguaçu Falls and bus fare to São Paulo. Many Paraguayans in Ciudad Stroessner spoke *Portuñol*, a mishmash of Spanish and Portuguese words that is used by those who speak one of those languages but only bits and pieces of the other, much the way some talk *Spanglish* elsewhere.

I asked how to find a bus to Brazil, but nobody seemed to know. I walked around in a daze before spotting a city bus with a sign saying *Frontera* on the windshield. I hopped aboard, paid my fare and assumed it would drop me off at the border.

The bus chugged slowly across the bridge, about a quarter mile over a deep ravine, but never stopped at the border. There was no gate or fence. I saw a kiosk manned by border guards, but they never looked at the bus, which did not stop. This was the first time I had crossed a border illegally and was baffled as the bus kept moving. By the time it stopped, I seemed to be a mile away from the border. I could either trudge back to the border carrying my backpack or leave it in a hotel to walk back unencumbered.

The hotels all posted prices on the wall, so I did not have to inquire in Portuguese. For only three dollars a night I found a room that was much cleaner than most of the places where I had stayed. I noticed the odor of bleach and rubbing alcohol, my first glimpse of the Brazilian compulsion to keep clean and sanitary. The city streets were asphalted and the sidewalks were inlaid black-and-white patterned tiles. This was modern civilization again, a whole different world from the bedlam right across the bridge in Paraguay.

Unburdened of my backpack, I walked back to the border. I had been accustomed to uniformed guards, often stern-looking soldiers, at most other border crossings, but the Brazilian federal police agents wore casual clothing.

I handed my passport to one of them. He told me, *"Você precisa de um visto. Tem que voltar na segunda-feira."* (You need a visa. You have to come back Monday). I looked at him dumbfounded. Not one word sounded anything like Spanish.

I asked him in Spanish, *"¿Que está diciendo?* No hablo portugués. *"*

He repeated the same thing, again in Portuguese, this time adding, *"Vai no consulado brasileiro no Paraguay. Você pode tirar seu visto lá."*

I recognized enough words to realize that I needed to obtain a visa at the Brazilian consulate in Ciudad Stroessner. I had not even checked in advance whether I needed a visa.

"Monday," the officer emphasized in English.

It was Friday afternoon. I certainly did not want to spend the weekend in Paraguay, especially after already renting a room on the Brazilian side.

I asked him in Spanish if I could stay the weekend in Foz de Iguaçu and then get my visa Monday. I'm not sure he had any idea what I was saying. He just shrugged his shoulders and nodded. So I returned to my room wondering if I was headed for trouble. I remembered in Venezuela how joggers in parks without ID were jailed, sometimes for days until someone could get them out. Brazil at this time was still officially a military dictatorship, so I feared trouble. And, if I had *problemas* with authorities, I could not even explain my situation clearly.

I was awestruck by the thunderous falls and spent a leisurely weekend, one full day on the Brazilian side and the other on the Argentine side viewing them and snapping pictures from every possible angle. They looked like dozens of Niagaras, gushing out of the jungle at all angles. Numerous catwalks go right to the edge, affording frighteningly close views; one goes straight to the edge of falls appropriately named Devil's Throat.

The weather was warm and a bit clammy, a welcome change from the frigid temperatures just two weeks before in Patagonia. Butterflies were everywhere, particularly the blue morphos common throughout Brazil. They landed on railings, flowers, and even my arm.

During that first weekend, I met a fellow American traveler who recommended two great features of Brazilian life that I enjoy regularly many years later. One was *guaraná*, the national drink. It is a zingy carbonated beverage with a kick, made from a red fruit native to the Amazon rain forest, and some believe it holds medicinal value. The other was *pão de queijo*, golf ball-size cheese puffs made from tapioca flour, with a thin crunchy shell and chewy innards. Little could I guess that years later, my Brazilian wife would introduce her own iteration of this tasty product to groceries and specialty markets in Seattle.

Another thing I noticed shortly after arriving in Brazil was a sweet odor, vaguely reminiscent of cotton candy, in every town. It took me a long time to realize that it was the scent of locally produced ethanol, which became a popular fuel years ago, to lessen expensive oil imports.

On Monday, I came down with a cold and stayed in bed instead of getting my visa. I was not feeling up to an irritating bureaucratic ordeal, so I put it off until Tuesday.

After spending three days and four nights in Brazil, I was not ready for Paraguay again. It was jumbled, confusing, hectic and filthy compared with the relative order and cleanliness of Brazil. People at the Brazilian Consulate in Ciudad Stroessner were friendly and spoke fluent Spanish; I only had to fill out a form and give them two pictures. I walked back across the bridge this time because I did not want to get stuck on a bus far from the border crossing. But they still would not admit me into Brazil, legally, until I went back across the bridge once more to get stamped out of Paraguay.

During my multiple trips across the border, I occasioned upon a group of Africans from Zambia and Senegal who were in limbo, unable to get stamped legally into either country and did not speak Spanish or Portuguese. I interpreted for them by explaining their situation to the Paraguayan border police, who relented and finally admitted them.

I'll never know if I did a favor for some helpless wayward souls or aided a band of criminals. Years later, I learned that this border region was overrun by smugglers from around the globe, including some really evil characters with Mid-Eastern terrorist connections.

Once I was legalized, I went to find a bus to São Paulo. It was at the bus terminal that I realized why they did not have controls at the border. You can't get out of Foz de Iguaçu unless your documents are in order.

A sixteen-hour bus ride lay ahead, away from the comforts of proximity to a Spanish-speaking country and rolling through a strange new world where few people spoke either Spanish or English.

Chapter 12

Riding on Bolivia's "Death Train"

The train which connects Santa Cruz, Bolivia's most-populous city, to Brazil, is called the "Death Train." The origin of the nickname depends on who you talk to. Because it once carried yellow fever victims? Because murders have occurred on board? Because passengers have died in horrific crashes? Nowadays, it breaks down so often that travelers start to wish they were dead instead of being helplessly trapped in this over-packed, uncomfortable tin can. A seemingly endless ride turned into my own vision of Dante's *Inferno*: eternity on this train in a state of exhaustion, unable to sleep or rest with the noise, light, vibration and filth.

I made this trip for a curious reason. Only a week after arriving in São Paulo, I met an enchantress named Mariesa. As we strolled along Avenida Paulista, the throbbing heart of South America's wealthiest financial district, she was mesmerized by the Bolivian sweaters hawked on street corners. Some were brightly colored alpaca wool; others were grey-and-white llama wool with outlines of those intriguing dromedaries. Both were scratchy, but I wore one I bought in La Paz. Winter in São Paulo called for long sleeves, and the sweaters were simply delightful. They were unusual and splashy, definitely not something off the shelf from a mall.

I did not speak enough Portuguese to understand the vendors' patter, but Mariesa, who spoke passable English after living in England, learned that the sweaters were fetching about twenty-five dollars apiece. I was astounded. In Bolivia, they were three to five dollars each. I told her that I had seen them all over the place in La Paz a few months earlier and had bought one for myself and mailed others to my family back home. A born schemer, on the spot she concocted an idea to travel to Bolivia and buy armloads of sweaters to sell in Brazil. That would give her money for school and adventure at the same time. And, why was I on the road for the past five months if not for a series of new adventures?

We had met only a few days earlier, with no effort on my part. Mariesa had boldly introduced herself to me, and I was open to new friendships. I was instantly bewitched by her cute turned-up nose, uncanny resemblance to Kate Hepburn, and sultry Lauren Bacall voice, an irresistible combination. She was about as unconventional as possible: she lived on a farm with Argentine artists and sold honey for a living. From the start, we held heart-to-heart discussions until late at night. Instead of goodbye or goodnight, she always said *"Dorme com os anjos"* (sleep with the angels), a Brazilian expression deeply embedded within me still.

A few days later we were rolling on the "Death Train" after an auspicious start. We rendezvoused early one crisp morning at *Estação da Luz*, the aptly named Station of Light where trains departed for Brazil's interior, a vast swamp called the Pantanal, and eventually the border with Bolivia. Sunlight danced in the station through stained glass windows, shafts of light illuminating elegant curved iron arches and graceful rounded angles. The train was clean, passengers were energetic; this was the perfect genesis for the ideal trip.

Indeed, it was perfect all morning. The city gradually yielded to lush green countryside and copper-colored earth where some of the world's most fertile farmland grew soy and coffee. Big humped Brahma cattle grazed lazily. One small town after the other rolled by. The sense of perfection, however, didn't last. When we arrived in Bauru that afternoon, we had missed the train for the next leg of our journey by about fifteen minutes. Why it failed to wait for the train from São Paulo made no sense. We were faced with waiting twenty-four hours for the next train, but Mariesa was too resourceful to waste so much time. She quickly marshaled us into a taxi; we raced to the next stop and beat the train by ten minutes.

That train chugged all night; the next morning we awoke passing through the soggy Pantanal all the way to Corumbá, on the Bolivian border. There, a taxi took us to Puerto Quijarro, Bolivia. That short distance crossed from a world of paved streets, sidewalks and clean aluminum counters in restaurants with numerous food options to a mud-and-insect-infested hell where the only eateries cooked foul-smelling fare in open-air pots over a wood fire. The train station was pandemonium. All the tickets for that day's train to Santa Cruz had been sold the day before, and it left without us. But they did not sell the next day's tickets until right before the train left, so we had to wait in line twenty-four hours to buy tickets. To keep our place in line, we needed to sleep on the cement train platform in the open air.

This required using the poorly ventilated, stinking unisex restroom: about a dozen stalls, some with doors, and swarming with flies and other bugs. There I encountered the person with surely the worst job in the world. Because there was not enough water pressure to flush the toilets, a boy used a water bucket to flush after people were finished. The one lad was so busy that he only flushed after two or three people had used a toilet. For his work, he collected tips, the equivalent of pennies, for each flush. Since then, when people complain to me about having a lousy job, I recount this experience to let them know there are worse.

But, at least there was a bathroom! Bolivia has few public facilities. In La Paz and other big cities, many people have no alternative but to relieve themselves in the street gutter or empty lots. Ladies in their layered hooped skirts squat in the street to do their business, whether liquid or solid, requiring that pedestrians watch their step. In fact, Bolivia and Peru placed signs warning people not to "perform necessities" in public, which begs the question whether the offenders had any other options. Similarly, Brazil is the only place I ever saw a sign, on a weed-strewn empty lot, which cautions: "Don't throw trash or dead animals." Are there so many surplus animal carcasses in Brazil that people come from near and far to dispose on this guy's property?

After waiting at the Puerto Quijarro train station all night, we finally bought our tickets. When the train was ready to leave, the organized line instantly morphed into the mall on Black Friday, with the frenzied throng pushing to get on. A local explained: "It's simple. They just love to push. That's all." Are they any different from Americans who wait in line all night on Thanksgiving to jam into crowded stores before sunrise?

The train ride was as numbing as the ocean washing sand over rocks and slowly polishing them. We passed through flyspeck towns, with ramshackle outdoor eateries called *comedores*. The train was so crowded that some people slept in the aisles. Others jammed into walkways between cars. Many passengers who called themselves *piloteros* brought goods, such as rice, macaroni, and sugar, to resell in Bolivian cities. It was the reverse of what Mariesa was doing with sweaters. The bathroom on our train car had no door. I couldn't sleep when twits chattering like woodpeckers tapped out nonsense into the air while others blared radios or tape players.

The train station in Santa Cruz was total disorganization and madness as if run by inmates on a work study program for the criminally insane. When the train pulled into the station, the *piloteros* unloaded their boxes so quickly that their clutter tripped departing passengers. Our hotel room was decorated with magazine pictures taped to the walls. I heard crickets outside my room, making me think they had more class than to stay in that rathole.

Mariesa and I visited small villages outside Cochabamba and bought sweaters from people who made them on simple hand looms in their own homes. Most of the houses were crumbling adobe with peeling paint on dusty roads. But inside, some had beautiful open-air courtyards with fragrant flowers. We bought enough sweaters to fill two enormous flour sacks. They cost us four to five dollars apiece, and Mariesa planned sell them for about twenty-five dollars, giving her a profit of hundreds of dollars.

The return trip by rail was just as crowded and miserable, the bumpy train as jumpy as popcorn.

Crossing back to Corumbá was a thrill. The unshaven driver who took us across the border reminded me of Charles Bronson. He seemed to know everybody on both sides. He stuffed our big bags on either side of the engine and slammed the hood shut. He was driving a shiny new truck with brand new tires, the only good tires I ever saw on any of my four trips to Bolivia. We got stuck at a flag-raising ceremony at the border as soldiers stood rapt at attention. After that, the driver chatted briefly with the guards, and they let us pass.

The Brazilian guards waved us right through. The driver only charged us a few bucks for the trip. Once across the border, we ran to get a taxi and sped to the train station. The train had already blown the whistle and slowly started to chug out of the station as the immigration official at the station diddled with our passports. Mariesa had already thrown the sacks of sweaters on the train and came back to retrieve her passport. By the time our passports were stamped, we had to run and jump on the slowly moving train, as Frank Sinatra's character tried to do in *Von Ryan's Express.*

Cash was tight, and after buying our tickets we barely had money for food on the twenty-four-hour journey. When the train pulled into the station of a small town near the Pantanal, I spotted an unclaimed five-thousand-cruzeiro note on the ground, worth about eight dollars at the time. That prompted me to dive out the window headfirst, giving me the money to buy a frosty beer and real meals, not just the loaf of bread we had bought for the trip.

This exhausting journey doomed my short-lived romance with Mariesa. I saw her only a few more times back in São Paulo. Her parents desperately wanted this relationship to work out, but Mariesa's erratic behavior and unpredictability wore me down. The last time I saw her was nearly a year later in coastal Porto Seguro, seven hundred miles northeast of São Paulo, near the spot that Pedro Cabral discovered Brazil in 1500. She described selling sandwiches during Carnival and earning enough to live cheaply for a long time; this made me remember what a survivor she was. Running into her struck me as some sort of cosmic prank. We chatted briefly in the street while a radio in a nearby store blared out a popular song, *Menina Veneno* ("Poison Girl"), with the lyrics, "the world is too small for the both of us."

Chapter 13

Blame it on the Bossa Nova

Midway through 2013, just a year before the World Cup was scheduled to get underway in Brazil, the unthinkable happened. Masses of Brazilians called on the government to cancel the games. What started as protests against higher transit fares erupted into huge events akin to the earlier "Occupy Wall Street" movement in the United States.

The demand to move the 2014 soccer championship outside Brazil defied belief. Would Romans kick the Vatican out of the eternal city? Would Indianapolis halt the 500? Would Parisians urge that the Eiffel Tower be dismantled and carted away?

Yet, here they were, people in the land of soccer clamoring to not be the host. It's not that they dislike soccer. Far from it. Instead, they were protesting the expenditure of billions of dollars on stadiums and cost overruns they believed were pocketed by dishonest officials, as well as corruption scandals in Brazilian soccer. Over the past year, several high-level officials had been convicted of corruption, but, up to that point, none of the top culprits had ever seen the inside of a prison cell (later, these scoundrels went to prison – where they shamelessly lived in luxury). At the same time, basic services like schools and hospitals were chronically underfunded and people were being evicted from their homes to make way for World Cup construction. It looked like the extravaganza would bestow additional profits on the already wealthy and once again exclude the poor.

I had seen other mass movements in Brazil. I was in São Paulo in 1984 when citizens clamored for an end to two decades under the yoke of the military, which had deposed an elected civilian government.

The protest movement and World Cup are both Brazilian to the core. The Brazilian way of doing things is like putting off your term paper until the last minute, cramming all night to finish it, and in the end getting a B minus. The intent is there, but execution is scrambled, and every time they get started on the assignment, friends drop by or something else intrudes. In the end, they get it done, just not as well as it should or could have been. That's what makes Brazil the biggest success story in the region. Using the same analogy, Brazil's neighbors end up never handing in their term paper, flunk the class, and blame others for it.

Many Brazilians from all walks of life worried that the country was unprepared to stage the World Cup because infrastructure projects – highways, electrical plants, and stadium construction – fell behind schedule and went way over budget. Inefficiency, haphazard planning, labor unrest, and corruption skewed timetables. Nonetheless, things in Brazil usually turn out better than the sky-is-falling crowd fears but not quite as good as the rosy-eyed promoters promise.

Still, it would be unfair to point fingers at Brazil as backwards. For all its shortfalls, Brazil has many innovations others could learn from. For instance, when a member of the U.S. Senate dies or resigns mid-term, the rules vary widely by state on how a successor is chosen. Brazil's system makes it easy. When someone is elected, the *suplente* (replacement) is already elected along with the candidate and ready to step in. Brazil's overseas Consular officials travel to other cities to help Brazilians who need their services. For instance, officials at the Brazilian Consulate in San Francisco travel several times a year to Portland, Oregon and Seattle to help local Brazilians with passports, birth registrations, taxes and other necessary functions. Brazilian law forbids one parent from taking minor children out of the country without notarized permission by the other parent, thus preventing one estranged parent from running away from the other. One huge defect in Brazilian law, however, is mandatory voting, which leads to a lot of blank and soiled ballots, as well as votes for fictional characters or deceased people. If people don't care enough to vote, even those who were denied that sacred right for an entire generation, forcing them to vote is pointless.

When I first arrived in Brazil in 1983, I could never have imagined that my own future would be so intertwined with this bewildering land where I could not even understand the language. My earliest impression was an accurate and lasting one, that Brazilians are warm and welcoming. The first thing Brazilians say when greeting someone is *tudo bem?* (everything fine?). They make the assumption in advance that things are great, and that infectious positive attitude permeates society. Despite all the country's ills, there is a certain pride in being Brazilian, which led to the saying "God is Brazilian," without the snobbery of Paris or Buenos Aires. For years, Brazilian travelers have applauded when their airplane coming from a foreign destination lands back home.

Brazil was still a nearly blank slate to me as I journeyed from the Paraguayan border toward São Paulo, marveling at the rich, red soil. Every few hours there was a rest top, where the restaurants and bathrooms were surprisingly clean. It was the first time I had ridden a bus in South America that was better than a Greyhound. Despite language barriers, those early days in Brazil went smoothly. Numbers were close enough to Spanish pronunciation that I could order food or get a hotel room. I began to do the same thing I had done in Venezuela: learn by immersion. I bought newspapers and spent a lot of time thumbing through a dictionary to learn words.

I had not intended to stay with Flavio, whom I had met in Peru. He had given me his phone number, so I thought of inviting him out to dinner and then leaving for Rio the next day. I checked into a hotel and called him, but he was not home. I left a message with his sister, Virginia, and told her where I was saying. Then I headed out to walk around São Paulo and eat. When I returned to my hotel, Flavio was waiting for me at the entrance and insisted that I come home with him. He and Virginia lived in a modern apartment in a neighborhood that could easily be mistaken for Los Angeles, with new high-rises sprouting up everywhere and no slum next door. Their mother had died, and their father lived with a new wife they disliked.

Flavio talked me into staying the weekend so I could attend a party and meet his friends, some of whom invited me to go places with them. One friend took me to a BBC film series about Charles Darwin at MASP, the modern art museum. He and I went together several times, until one day he was unable to attend and I went alone. That day I met Mariesa, who became my girlfriend and traveling companion to Bolivia (see Chapter 12). After I returned from Bolivia, Flavio and I went into a video shop to rent a movie. At the time, VCR tapes were new in Brazil, and few movies were subtitled. When the owner of the video shop heard us conversing in English, he offered us a job putting Portuguese subtitles on the movies. Flavio would get a month vacation from medical school, so if I was willing to stay longer, we could work together and earn about forty dollars apiece per day. Because of high inflation, we went to the bank every day to cash our checks, and there I met Maria (see Chapter 7), who today is my wife.

Translating films pushed me from barely conversant in Portuguese to fluent in only a month. We listened to short passages, then stopped the movie and discussed how to translate it. Because Flavio could not type and I typed quickly, I dutifully punched away the words that he told me in Portuguese. Talk about immersion, in no time at all I not only acquired a full and varied vocabulary in Portuguese but I could also spell.

Even as I learned Portuguese, I had the occasion to continue using Spanish. Strangely, three different times in this city crowded with millions of people, I ran into fellow travelers I had met earlier in other countries: a couple from Spain, a Chilean, and a pair of Peruvians.

Unlike machine gun staccato Spanish, Portuguese has a mellifluous, lyrical flow. With a smooth, lush sound, the melodic language gives joy to the ears even if you don't understand all the words. Millions of people who don't speak a word listen to *bossa nova* and other Brazilian music, or watch Brazilian movies.

Learning languages enlivens appreciation for the process of toying with words, employing distinctive expressions, bending meanings to suit tastes and moods, devising double entendres. Words – as delicate as early morning mist or coarse as sandpaper, as circumstances dictate – can provide exquisite pleasure. Isn't that one reason why reading can be so satisfying? And, isn't it a joy to listen to polished elocution, such as the crisp diction enunciated by the finest British actors?

Portuguese is fluid, ever-changing to accommodate the whims of its speakers in mother Portugal, Brazil and former Portuguese colonies spread across Africa and Asia. The flexibility, elasticity and resilience of Brazilian Portuguese allow many piquant variations, rich and ornate without being overly flowery. Brazilians took a garden variety Romance language and remade it in their own image: colorful, expressive and boisterous. They added ingredients from indigenous and slave tongues and invented a vibrant, unique concoction. Without the French resistance to pollution from other languages, Brazilians joyfully embrace or adapt any word or expression that fits their impish nature.

Although Portuguese is the world's seventh most-spoken tongue, with more than two hundred million native speakers, more than French, German, Russian or Italian, many people think it's the same as Spanish (the world's second most-common language, after Mandarin). The two are sister languages but certainly far from identical twins.

Learning a new language always has pitfalls as well as *faux amis*, words that appear to be one thing but are something entirely different. Upon my arrival in Brazil, I saw signs for *moveis*, which I took to be a bastardized spelling of movies. Nothing doing. *Moveis* are furniture. Signs for *magazine* were perplexing because they don't point you toward a newsstand to buy *Time* or *National Geographic* (those are *revistas*), but to a department store. A *funilaria* is not an undertaker (that's *funerária*) but instead is an auto body repair shop. Another tricky word is *motel*, which is not where weary travelers get shuteye. Rather, a motel perched along a highway on the outskirts of town is rented by the hour and designed for quickies by people who are not using a bed for sleep. A purely Brazilian oddity is the *drive-in*, which is not a place for showing movies but somewhere lovers can park their car in a garage-like setting to get frisky without the risk of someone shining a flashlight through the window. It's easy to get confused between the similar sounding *verbo*, meaning verb, and *verba*, which is a government expenditure. In Spanish, one of the most deceptive words is *tuna*, which does not mean canned fish, but prickly pear. Most people recognize *niño* as signifying baby in Spanish, but they would be mistaken if they hear that exact word spoken by a Brazilian because *ninho* means bird's nest. *Chico* in

Spanish means small but in Portuguese is a nickname for *Francisco*. *Oficina* means office in Spanish, but is a workshop in Portuguese. In Spanish, a *propina* is a gratuity, such as given to your waiter in a restaurant, but the same word in Portuguese is a bribe.

A waiter who offers indigestible food won't get many *propinas* (in Portuguese, *gorjeta*). The most unappetizing menu I've ever seen, also the world's worst translation, offered Venezuelan diners fungus (I can't imagine they got many takers). What this establishment really served was mushrooms, but the menu proved how a translating dictionary can be a dangerous weapon in the hands of someone with no knowledge of a language because the Spanish word *hongo* means both fungus and mushroom. Similarly, if tourists in Brazil who see *lagarto* on the menu start thumbing through their dictionaries, they will see "lizard," while instead the menu item is a more edible "eye of round roast." Of course, I mangled translations just as clumsily. In Venezuela, I pointed out the number of *piernas* (legs) in a bumpy road when I mean to say *piedras* (stones). Worse, I once offered someone *pecado* (a sin) when I meant *pescado* (fish).

Brazil's revered, eloquent songwriters were the leading innovators in language before TV began to homogenize the language. Since *The Girl From Ipanema* first sashayed around the world in the 1960s, the most common exposure people outside Brazil had to Portuguese was through its expressive music, most notably *bossa nova* and *samba*. *Bossa* means "talent" or "thing" and *nova* is "new." Survivors among the *bossa nova* movement are now in their 70s, with many still at peak popularity and productivity.

While the themes of *samba* are often parochial, parodying economic woes, incoherent politics, devastating corruption or sexual mores, they sometimes achieve universality. A word that rhymes with *samba* is *bamba*, which means a master of samba, an old pro.

Even the word for slang, *giria*, has the magic touch. Some words sound exactly like what they mean. For instance, *bagunça* means mess, *babaca* is a fool, *bunda* means rear end, *nojento* is nauseating, and *besteira*, which I use frequently, is nonsense. Some of my favorite words flow from the mouth like honey (*mel*), including *preguiça* (laziness), *pipoca* (popcorn), *doido* (crazy), *cala* (shut up), and *vapt vupt* (right away). *Gato* or *gata* (cat) signifies an attractive person, while someone unappealing is called *canhão* (cannon). *Sapatão*, literally "big shoe" describes lesbians. A knife or scissors so dull that it won't cut is called *cega* (blind). English speakers say "it's raining cats and dogs" (does that make any sense?); Brazilians use the much more descriptive *chovendo canivetes* ("raining jackknives"). *Bacana* is a way of saying "fantastic," while *legal* means both "legal" and "great." One incredibly diverse word is *bico*, which means a bird's beak or breast nipple, as well as a moonlighting job.

Intermarriage among all the races in Brazil has created what is proudly called the *raça brasileira*, or Brazilian race. *Mulato* doesn't carry negative baggage as in English. In fact, *mulatas* are the most sought-after girls on Rio beaches and as Carnival dance partners. *Caboclos* are a mixture of white and Indians, while the pairing of blacks and Indians are *cafuzo*.

More than a million people of Japanese ancestry live in São Paulo, which has the largest Japanese population outside Japan. The Japanese have integrated themselves into Brazilian society and frequently inter-married with Brazilians of all races.

Japanese immigration began in the 1930s, when most of the new arrivals settled in rural areas outside the growing city. They bought farms, and today Japanese faces are common at farmer's markets, with their distinctive names stamped on produce boxes.

The Japanese government has encouraged young Brazilians of Japanese descent to work in Japan for a year or two to perform low-skill labor. That leads to clashes of culture because the young Brazilians of Japanese heritage don't act like Japanese; they behave like Brazilians. News reports in Brazil frequently carry stories about these youthful Nisei who get into trouble in Japan because they are loud, boisterous party animals who don't fit into the staid, starchy mannerisms of their ancestors.

São Paulo, Brazil's biggest melting pot, has people from all over the world, similar to New York. Millions trace their roots to Spain, Italy and Germany. Nazi horrormaster "Angel of Death" Josef Mengele lived unnoticed near São Paulo for years before he drowned at a beach in 1979, following stays in Argentina and Paraguay. São Paulo also has significant immigration from the Middle East, including Mayor Fernando Haddad and two of his predecessors, Gilberto Kassab and Paulo Maluf. Middle Eastern foods such as *esfiha* and *kibe* are found everywhere in São Paulo.

The overwhelming majority of Brazil's presidents carry Portuguese surnames, with a handful of Italian and German names. But the family tree of the current office holder, Dilma Rousseff, was planted in Bulgaria. And one of her most popular predecessors, Juscelino Kubitschek, who moved the capital to Brasília to spur development in the interior, traced his family history to a Czech grandfather. João Goulart had French heritage. Even the names of presidents with Iberian surnames are colorful: Floriano Peixoto, Hermes da Fonseca, Venceslau Brás, Epitácio Pessoa, Isiais de Noronha, and Getulio Vargas. By comparison, the United States has been led by guys with plain vanilla names like John Adams, John Tyler, Andrew Johnson, Herbert Hoover and Gerald Ford.

One curiosity is the profusion of Greek names, although I never met a Brazilian of Greek heritage and only a handful who had ever read *The Iliad and the Odyssey* or Plato's *The Republic*. *Socrates* starred twice in the World Cup, *Diogenes* was a family friend in my wife's home town, and *Laertes* was a messenger at a friend's office. I also heard names like *Euripedes, Erasmo, Homero,* and *Virgilio.* One of the most popular soccer clubs is *Corinthians.* These Greek names with a sonorous lilt have the sole intent of an appealing sound, without any literary symbolism. While you meet plenty of people with traditional names such as Pedro or Maria, you also encounter people with first names like Jackson, Kennedy, Wilson or Jefferson, not to mention Washington, with no political overtones.

Brazilians of European descent populate the South and the largest cities. Along the Northeast coast, Afro-Brazilians are the biggest group, while the Amazon and interior have many Indians.

Brazilian public life has more than its share of kleptocrats and uninspiring starched-shirt yes-men, but Brasília also had one of the most colorful politicians prowling the halls of the ultra-modern Congress for years. That was Mário Juruna, a Xavante Indian and son of a *cacique* (chief) who drew plenty of attention by battling for rights of indigenous people while wearing a full-feathered headdress and native outfits in Congress. He prominently carried a tape recorder everywhere he went to tape his conversations and hold public officials to their promises.

Spoken words are only one part of intricate interpersonal communication with Brazilians, who are far more evocative and demonstrative than most North Americans or Europeans. They frequently touch your hand or tap your shoulder to make a point and use your name frequently when speaking with you. A greeting is frequently accompanied by a hug or a kiss on both cheeks, while a farewell – in person, by telephone or email – often is accompanied by the expressions *beijos* (kisses) or *abraços* (hugs), though you might be less inclined to offer a beijo to someone who is *banguela*, missing front teeth. Brazilians also have a unique farewell – *Disculpe qualquer coisa* – which loosely means "I apologize for anything I might have done to offend you." Even more expressive than words are bodily gestures. A universal demonstration of approval is the thumb's up sign, while a wag of the index finger and tongue clucking denotes a resounding "no."

Brazilian deference for their elders or social betters employs using the third person to address someone: *o senhor* or *a senhora* rather than the common *você*.

Even begging is an art form in Brazil, where an outstretched hand is not accompanied by a curt "brother can you spare a dime?" when instead they can tell you their whole life story until you relent with some change: "My *patrão* (boss) told me to go out and pull all the weeds on his property, then to plant a lot of flowers, and then to water the flowers, and after that to hose down the driveway and wash his car, but he hasn't paid me yet ..." These long, involved stories by beggars are so varied and ornate and embellished that comedians mimic such lines and work them into their stand-up routines.

Just like Eskimos have various words for ubiquitous snow, the tropics necessitate distinctions for ever-present insects we know by one name: *mosquito, pernilongo, muriçoca*, or *borrachudo*. I've been explained the distinctions, but once you are stung it doesn't seem to matter which one it was. The omnipresence of insects makes me wonder why nobody in Latin America puts screens on windows – especially when a display at the Panama Canal tells how Dr. William Gorgas used window screens as one of his weapons to control the malaria and yellow fever epidemics that were killing canal workers.

When a situation gets so diluted as to become ineffective, such as watered-down legislation, it becomes a *pizza* or *salada*. A major problem is an *abacaxi* (pineapple). The Spanish word for pineapple, by the way, is the totally unrelated *piña*.

This home to so many brilliant butterflies describes them with a lyrical word: *borboleta*, which has fluttered into the Brazilian consciousness. *Borboleta* is slang for turnstile or a fickle person. To butterfly means to put on a costume during that most enchanting of all magical times: Carnival. When people dress up during that four-day blowout, they wear an aptly-called *fantasia*.

Puxa saco (sack puller) is an obsequious flatterer, while *encher o saco* (fill the sack) is to annoy someone that he gets a *saco cheio*, (full sack), or fed up. That's the effect of an *amigo da onça* (friend of the jaguar), or false friend, whom you might get rid of by telling to *vai tomar banho* (go take a bath) or *cai fora* (literally "drop outside," but figuratively "go away"). A true friend is an *amigo do peito* ("friend from the heart").

You would call a jerk *chato*, which means flat and also body louse. If you are angry with someone you are *bravo*, which does not mean brave. If you are really upset, you will *fica puta* (become a prostitute) with someone. You can imagine all the jokes that leads to, especially the inevitable headline about a prostitute upset with a cheapskate customer: *Puta Fica Puta!* (I really saw that headline). In fact, references to prostitutes permeate the language in this Catholic country, always to show displeasure, with *puta da vida, puta que pariu*, and *puta merda*.

Two of the most delicious words describe my least favorite person: *picareta* and *cafajeste* are colorful ways to describe a swindler. Another great word is so simple and utilitarian: a light switch is called an *interruptor*, which makes sense because it interrupts the power going to a light. One word identical in Spanish and Portuguese is *propaganda*, which appropriately enough means advertisement (it also literally means propaganda). A curious pair of words, similar in both languages is *pessoa física* and *pessoa jurídica*, literally meaning physical person (human) and legal person (corporation). That lends a whole new dimension to the debate in the United States over whether "corporations are people." And one very deceptive word is *decepcionar*, which can mean "deceive," which it sounds like, as well as "disappoint." Equally deceptive is *pretender*, which in both Portuguese and Spanish means to "intend" rather than "pretend." *Parentes* are not "parents," but rather "relatives" while *pais* are "parents," not to be confused with *país* (with an accent), meaning "country." You could cause a big embarrassment if you mix up *plástico*, which is "plastic" with *plástica*, which is slang for "plastic surgery." If you hear someone using the word *receita*, you need to listen carefully. They might be discussing a cooking recipe, pharmacy prescription, or even income revenues.

Brazilian children learn to say *cocô*, equivalent to our "poo-poo." But you don't want to confuse it with *coco*, pronounced with a different inflection on syllables, to describe a coconut. A friend recounts the stunned reaction he got from a vendor when he ordered *agua de coco*, or coconut juice, with the wrong pronunciation.

Brazil is a land of stark, vivid contrasts where the term Belindia describes how the most developed regions might resemble efficient Belgium while the rest of the country is as backwards as India. Few places on Earth offer the juxtaposition of a peasant driving an ox-drawn cart amid the Space Age buildings of Brasília or Amazon Indians in feathered regalia chatting in their native tongue on a cellphone. I didn't always have a camera ready when such a scene appeared before me, but I remember distinctly the bicycle that whisked by me in Campo Grande carrying a woman on the back who was breast-feeding her baby.

Many such paradoxes pop up in everyday life. Carnival is celebrated with reckless abandon, some soap operas show flashes of full nudity, and unwed pregnancies are rampant. At the same time, men in shorts or shirtless are improper in many situations despite the tropical heat.

An indignant doorman once upbraided my wife and me for kissing passionately (fully clothed) while waiting in front of a friend's office, less than a mile from where dancers would disrobe a month later to paint their bodies and dance topless or even nude in the Carnival parade. The Catholic Church's influence guarantees that abortion is officially illegal, yet abortions are easy to obtain from competent medical professionals in not-so-clandestine clinics. Small town people frown on homosexuality, yet gays and transvestites cavort with San Francisco-like abandon in Rio and São Paulo. Two-thirds of Brazilians identify themselves as Catholics, yet the incumbent president and her predecessor are both evangelical Protestants. And these aren't just transplanted Baptists and Methodists. Brazil has its own home-grown Universal Church of the Kingdom of God, its biggest Protestant sect, with eight million adherents in Brazil and another four million overseas.

Despite the overwhelming affiliation with Christianity, many Brazilians also believe in African spirits which Americans and Europeans label voodoo. It's not just the unschooled, impoverished people, but some highly educated white people also believe in African cults which go by exotic names like *candomblé, macumba,* or *umbandu.* The African slaves brought their beliefs with them, and when Catholicism was forced on them they prayed to a certain patron saint which was synchronized with an equivalent African deity. In Rio, millions of people of all races flock to the beach on New Year's Eve for the celebration in which white-robed, white-turbaned women throw flowers into the sea as an offering to the African goddess *Iemanjá.* Gilberto Gil, who together with Caetano Veloso invented the *tropicalia* music movement in the 1960s, pays homage to this purely Brazilian syncretic phenomenon in his song *Banda Um.* Intelligent, educated people really believe that someone can cast the evil eye on them and that setbacks in life can result from chants and spells. I attended an all-night *jaré* ceremony in the backwoods of northern Brazil in which a cigar puffing, white robed *pai de santo* (holy father) sacrificed chickens while others danced in a whirling dervish type of frenzy that reminded me of "talking in tongues" hysteria at charismatic churches in the United States. When I grabbed a bunch of fresh flowers I found on the way home in

São Paulo, my wife was furious, believing they had been used in some *macumba* ceremony and would portend dire consequences for us.

Brazil's green, yellow and blue flag has the words ORDEM E PROGRESSO emblazoned over a globe. For years, everybody joked that the country was neither orderly nor progressive, but that parody faded as Brazil has made major strides. During the 1980s, Brazilians frequently joked that Brazil was the country of the future – and always would be. In other words, its potential was always slightly beyond grasp. Since then, the standard of living for most Brazilians has risen substantially. Case in point: my wife's home town had only a handful of telephones and cars when I first went there in the 1980s. Now, almost everybody has a phone or cellphone, and cars are quite common. Electricity and running water were a rarity on the farms outside town; now the hinterlands have been electrified.

The city of Governador Valladares is prosperous from all the Brazilians who worked in the United States, mostly in New York and Boston, and brought money back to buy property and start businesses. The pleasant city has gardens everywhere and even bicycle lanes painted in the streets.

Despite the horrendous traffic, frightening poverty and crime, terrible air and water pollution, and crowds, São Paulo was surprisingly livable. I enjoyed the frenetic activity on Avenida Paulista, the Portuguese coffee barons' stately mansions, art deco buildings scattered around town, open-air farmers markets, numerous small parks tucked in hidden places, and the proximity to beautiful beaches a couple hours away. My favorite sights in city parks were sloths, who hung from tree branches and stared at people with a goofy grin that spookily resembled an intoxicated human. Multi-colored parrots and toucans in parks were a joyful sight. At the same time, the expressway which circles the city is built alongside the stinky, polluted Tietê River that floods every year and turns the key route into an impassible swamp. The glaring contradictions of São Paulo kept reappearing in different forms everywhere I went in Brazil.

Chapter 14

A Continent in a Country:
The Length and Breadth of Brazil

I've been to more places in Brazil than most Brazilians and crossed the border in about a dozen places. I've seen every kind of topography the country offers, every region and major city and have a firm grasp for the country as a whole.

By the time I began to travel extensively around Brazil, I already had capable Portuguese skills, so I was able to fully appreciate this enchanting land and all its nuances. By then, the wayfarers I kept running into in Colombia, Ecuador and Bolivia had long since returned to Europe, or North America or Israel. As I traveled around Brazil, I instead met almost exclusively Brazilians.

One trip took me to the Pantanal, a great wetland which I had passed through all day to and from Bolivia. Insects were so plentiful that they smacked my eyes and burrowed into my nostrils and ears while I traveled by train or truck. I landed an assignment to write about this fertile uterus for *Geo Mundo,* a Spanish-language *National Geographic* wannabee. My report was about the impact of poaching on the fragile ecosystem. Hunters killed alligators for their valuable skins and dumped the carcasses into the swamp. Piranha populations skyrocketed, then swarmed nearly every body of water and began to devour everything in sight, including range animals like cattle and horses, as well as capybaras, emus, monkeys and other wildlife. I traveled and stayed for a week with wildlife biologists, ranchers and cowboys (a Brazilian cowboy is called a *peão*). Floods provide the best opportunities to see wildlife, forced to crowd together on smaller patches of dry land. I awoke every morning before dawn to a melodious symphony of chicks calling – loud squawks, chirps, squeaks and peeps – for food. My surroundings looked and felt like the primordial beginning of time, before any people existed. A big-eyed brown monkey the size of a grown cat nimbly climbed a tree with a screaming infant on her back. Alligators performed giant bellyflops in the water, and wild pigs bolted across meadows. A rancher recounted his long, lyrical poems expressing his love for the Pantanal. Sunsets showed off a red-tinged sky gulped quickly by inky blackness.

The Pantanal was just as compelling after dark: fiery red eyes became intense burning coals resembling miniature highway reflectors shining through the blackness, without giving a clue about what kind of critters they were.

In southern Brazil, mountain towns such as Garibaldi and Bento Gonçalves held wine and champagne festivals during winter, when they get frost and sometimes a light dusting of snow at higher elevations. Southern Brazil, populated by immigrants from Italy, Germany and Yugoslavia, is a prosperous region with heavy industry and fertile agricultural land. Buildings in Blumenau look more like Bavaria than Brazil. Odd pine trees are shaped like a candelabra. Men wear baggy pants and leather hats secured by a thin strap while they sip maté tea like their *gaucho* counterparts in Argentina and Uruguay. People from this region are called *gauchos*, but pronounced differently (gow-OOO-sho, not the Spanish GOW-cho).

While in the South I visited towns named Mostardas, Novo Hamburgo, and Tubarão (shark). Other enchanting city and state names include Cascavel (rattlesnake), Pirapora (in the lyrics of a touching song by Elis Regina), Jacarei (alligator), Puxa Faca (pull the knife), Aracaju, and Pernambuco. There is even Americana, a town founded by disgruntled members of the U.S. Confederacy after they lost the Civil War so they could continue slaveholding (Brazil refused to abolish the practice until 1888).

When I left São Paulo for my first long journey all through Brazil, I took several days to reach Rio de Janeiro along the coastal roadway, akin to winding slowly through Big Sur instead of taking Interstate 5 between Los Angeles and San Francisco. I was amazed how undeveloped and pristine some coastal areas remained despite their proximity to the most populated metropolis on the continent. A decade later, when I lived in São Paulo with my family, we spent weekends and sometimes a week in this coastal area. We drove five minutes to the beach in the morning and stayed until it started raining at about two in the afternoon. Then we went back to our rented house, lunched, and napped in hammocks on the patio, lulled to sleep by heavy raindrops ferociously pounding the red tile roof. When the sky cleared in the afternoon, we swam in a small man-made lake created by damming a cold river that plunged down from the precipitous coastal range, about a thousand meters high, immediately behind us. At night, we delighted in the entertainment provided by *vagalumes* (fireflies) and chatter of *cigarras* (cicadas).

As a traveled away from São Paulo, I needed much of the first day to reach Ubatuba, where I stayed the weekend with a friend at his beach house and went wind surfing. Leaving there, it took nearly all day aboard buses on serpentine coastal roads to Paraty, a colorful colonial town blessed with historic churches and pastel buildings, where I spent a couple of days. From that point, I needed most of yet another day to reach Rio. By contrast, the inland divided highway between São Paulo and Rio only takes about six hours by comfortable bus.

I had been to Rio a couple of times with Flavio for brief trips, but this would be the first time I could spend as long as I wanted, which was a week. I rode the funicular railroad to *Cristo Redentor* (Christ the Redeemer) statue atop *Corcovado* (hunchback) peak seven hundred meters high, towering over the gorgeous city, coastal range and ocean. I hiked around the hills taking pictures and marveling at every angle of the view in all directions. Later I discovered that bandits hide in the brush to rob tourists, then disappear into the surroundings. The tram to the top of *Pão de Açuçar* (Sugar Loaf) provides an expansive feel for the city's topsy-turvy layout, from the top as well as during the ride, both night and day. I swam little at the crowded beaches, deciding to devote more time to beaches later in the empty stretches of sand in the Northeast. Copacabana is a cross between Waikiki beach and old Times Square: crowded with upscale residents, tourists, thieves, *travestis* (transvestites) and *putas*. Ipanema is more laid back and residential.

My favorite place in Rio is *Floresta da Tijuca*, the world's largest urban forest and a sanctuary of purity and sanity above the scenic but chaotic city which is constantly bursting in rapid forward motion. The park is but a small remnant of the vast rainforest that once hugged the southeastern coastline; now only five percent of the original forest is intact. The resplendent greenness of trees a hundred feet high intermingled with patches of bright red, yellow and orange flowers. Profuse butterflies of every imaginable shade, some even appearing neon, landed on flowers and innocently alighted on my arms. I strolled through the park with Brazil's most renowned butterfly expert, Dr. Luiz Otero, who told me their apparent abundance was deceptive and that more than two dozen species were on the endangered list. Cooling mist from waterfalls splashed my face as I wandered; spring water gurgling up was more refreshing and sweeter than any soft drink.

I also hiked the steep paths through the massive *favelas* clinging to hillsides abutting Copababana and Ipanema. Amid the squalor, some squatters had views that would command millions of dollars if they were seen instead from opulent homes. Sewage ran through troughs like babbling brooks as barefoot children raced through the stinking effluence.

After Rio I visited Ouro Preto, one of Latin America's finest historic cities (on a par with Taxco, Mexico and Cuzco, Peru). Once the capital of Brazil, its many colonial churches are ornately gilded inside; lights resembling antique gas lanterns adorn the streets. Cobblestone streets race up and down vertiginous hills, leaving no flat spot in town. I have been to Ouro Preto at least a half dozen times, and every time I lose at least five pounds and get sore legs from all the huffing and puffing. It was here that a scruffy bearded *Mineiro* (resident of Minas Gerais state) wearing a weathered, round leather cap taught me the local custom of how to balance a plate on my legs and eat with one hand while sitting on the leather seat of a low three-legged stool. Ouro Preto had few tourists or accommodations the first time I went there. Now dozens of hotels are available for all incomes as Brazilians and foreigners have discovered this priceless gem. This attention, fortunately, resulted in many decrepit buildings being restored to their original splendor. On one trip, I also visited other well-preserved historic towns nearby: Mariana, São João del Rei, Tiradentes, Congonhas and Diamantina.

From Ouro Preto, it was a full day's ride, bouncing on a dirt road that thrashed my body to bits to reach Maria's home town, Virgem da Lapa, for the first time. Since then, I've been back at least a dozen times. My first view coming into town was of a fairy tale village, the bus winding down steep switchbacks for ten minutes above the red tile rooftops, cobblestone streets and bright pastel adobe houses. I stayed for several days, met her siblings who would later become my brothers- and sisters-in-law and went to some parties. I also met an American and an Irishman, both engineers, who worked with *garimpeiros* (miners) who used crude sluice boxes, shovels and buckets in local mining operations seeking gold. In fact, Maria bought a gold nugget from a prospector in her home town, from which a jeweler made our wedding bands. Nobody in Virgem da Lapa was wealthy, nor were there any slums; no one was starving. With no *Toys "R" Us*, the local kids enjoyed simple pleasures, like lassoing cicadas with string and running around while flying them on a tiny leash. Girls fashioned dolls from rags. People told me that they did not bother to lock their doors at night because crime was negligible. I met the mayor, a family friend, who was constantly interrupted in his office. It seemed that the whole town came to him with whatever problem they had, day or night. He had to be a doctor, dentist, priest or banker, depending on who needed him and when. Later, he was elected to the state legislature.

Heading northward, massive granite boulders emerged out of rolling green hills, some shaped like giant anthills. I had to change buses in Feira de Santana, where the guard at the bus station used a sharp poker to awaken people who snoozed while awaiting buses. From there, I went straight to the widely praised capital of Bahia state, coastal Salvador. The bus, however, was late, and the city looked frightening rather than scenic after midnight; too many people slept in the streets, and too many scary-looking characters prowled around.

Salvador was enjoyable during the day, showing off colorful old buildings with peeling paint. So scenic, in fact, that many movies are filmed
there. Black ladies, many of them heavy set wearing white robes and
turbans, sold spicy fishcakes and seafood recipes of African origin.
Even today, some of my favorite foods are *comida bahiana*. The best is
moqueca, a seafood dish indigenous to coastal Brazil with a delicious
blend of spices which is always my first choice when I stumble across
a Brazilian restaurant outside Brazil. Despite this great food, I got a
strange hankering for pizza and had the worst one ever. The cook
grabbed a frozen pizza shell from the fridge, poured ketchup on it,
threw on some thin slices of cheese and tossed it on a grill. I was
stuck with it because I had to pay in advance, but it was inedible and I
handed it to a beggar outside.

On another occasion, I attended Carnival in Salvador because it
spills out into the streets. By contrast, viewers in Rio and São Paulo
watch from huge grandstands. A perennial favorite in Salvador is *Filhos
de Gandhy* whose participants dress in white Indian robes to honor the
Mahatma's devotion to peace.

Along the coast near Salvador is Morro de São Paulo, a settlement
on a tiny island with no automobiles or paved roads. People ride donkeys, which also pull wagons with heavy loads. A lighthouse arises on a
peak, and I climbed all 109 steps to the top to view the sunset, a brief
brilliant orange globe before disappearing into the clouds.

Farther up the coast, I rode a flatbed truck to a tiny remote fishing
village called Gaibu, where a fisherman rented me his one-room palm
thatched hut for the night. With no hotels, my alternative would have
been to string my hammock between palm trees. As I stretched out on
a woven reed mat atop the sand, I watched stars winking at me through
the thatching. The village then was just a collection of simple huts on a
wide and empty beach. I have not been back but recently looked it up
online and saw that it now boasts expensive resorts.

I headed inland to Lençois (len-SOYS), full of historic buildings
with nearby rocks in which cracks yielded moist mini-climates where
epiphytes thrived without roots. A hike took me to Roncador (snorer),
a series of waterfalls linked by a single, iron-permeated river. Some

pools were black and others bright yellow. It seemed that every water-fall had another farther up and that this would continue indefinitely.

Much of the Northeast is barren before you reach the Amazon rain forest farther north. It was so hot and dry in Piauí (pee-ah-WEE) state that even palm trees were sad and drooping. In the state capital of Teresinha, a new concrete stadium rising out of the dirt was incongruous with the worn-out, heat-prostrated city surrounded by drought in all directions.

Crossing into Maranhão state, the occasional palm tree immediately gave way to thick palm forests. Most houses had fan-palm leaf roofs, which seemed to be constantly replaced by new green leaves atop the older brown ones.

Near the mouth of the Amazon River is Belém (Bethlehem), with one of the most vibrant waterfronts I've ever seen: fishmongers jostle for space amid fruit and vegetable hawkers, as well as local herbs and spices. *Guaraná* and *açaí* were sold in both powder and berry form long before both became worldwide health tonic rages in recent years. Vendors in the *Ver-O-Peso* ("see the weight") market sell herbs and spices in colors ranging from bright red, to orange, to yellow and black, spread out on towels and in glass jars. Some jars, looking like they belong in a high school biology lab, contained disgusting animal parts that made me cringe.

From the depths of the Amazon, I headed back to Venezuela to visit friends and then circled around South America a second time so I could return to São Paulo and see Maria again. Before the border was the city of Boa Vista, the other side of the Rio Branco River via ferry. But we reached the ferry landing right as they were leaving for lunch and had to wait an hour in the withering heat before we could make the five-minute crossing. Boa Vista (Beautiful View) had less of a frontier feeling than other remote cities. Streets were paved, while other out-of-the-way towns had dirt streets with a Wild West, anything-goes atmosphere. North of Boa Vista, the Amazon rain forest gradually yielded to rolling hills and grassy savannah. I rode on the back of a series of flatbed trucks carrying cargo, choking on fine powdery red dust the consistency of sifted flour. The drivers stopped whenever we passed a river, stripped down to birthday suits, and we all swam in the refreshing water.

Long past nightfall we reached Pacaraima, the final town in Brazil at the Venezuelan border. At a thousand meters high, I shivered in a down jacket after enduring triple-digit heat all day and feeling the early stages of heat stroke, with dizziness and nausea.

Chapter 15

Bolivar's Ghosts

Glancing across the border to the rolling red hills in Venezuela, I thought about familiar faces, especially my old roommate Jean-François, and sleeping on clean sheets in a comfortable bed. Life on the road is liberating but also exhausting and sometimes lonely.

The Brazilian border guards in chilly Pacaraima were friendly as I expected. But after being away from Caracas for a year, I was unprepared for the hostility that would greet me on the other side like a *cachetada*, Venezuelan slang for a slap in the face.

The Venezuelan border guard at Santa Elena leafed through my passport, already filled with stamps at many border crossings, and zeroed in on my long-expired Venezuelan resident visa. I planned to enter the country on a tourist card.

"You used to be a Venezuelan resident?" he quizzed.

"Yes, but no longer," I answered

"Why not?" he pressed me.

"Because I left to do some traveling," I responded honestly.

"You lost your residence in Venezuela. You had the right to become a Venezuelan citizen eventually. Not everybody is lucky enough to get that chance," he growled.

"Yes, I know that, but I wanted to travel," I said.

"How could you give up the right to Venezuelan citizenship? That's the stupidest thing I ever heard," he barked back, his face getting redder as the veins bulged out of his thick bulldog neck.

"I decided to move on. I got a Brazilian girlfriend," I said, thinking this would appeal to Latin machismo. Instead, it only agitated him further.

"Don't you know that Venezuelan girls are *más bonitas? Miss Universo* is Venezuelan. *Miss Mundo* is Venezuelan," he challenged. He was becoming increasingly hostile over my decision to leave his homeland, taking it as a personal affront. If this were a game show, I would have gotten a loud buzzer for every wrong answer. "You gave up your right to Venezuelan citizenship. That was so stupid," he yelled.

The worst thing would have been continued honesty, that I would have to be a fool to stay in Venezuela when the world offered far better options. This wannabe warlord was standing between my right to entry, and it seemed that I was running a huge risk of being turned away, so I decided to go along with him.

"Yes, it was unwise to give up my residency. I will check with the Diex when I get back to Caracas to see if they will restore my resident status," I told him.

With that response, the tension disappeared. He smiled and stamped my passport willingly.

The next day I passed through a town called El Dorado, tucked into red rolling hills, though it had no fountain of youth.

After a few days, I was back in Caracas, which was familiar and much more civilized than many places I had visited. But it seemed crowded after having spent months on the road in the wild: mountains, jungles, beaches, and vast, wide-open plains. Caracas was an infection spread into each crack in the valley, oozing its disease into everything where it didn't belong.

Besides the abrupt difference in mannerisms, I also noticed that Venezuelans seemed to lounge around quite a bit, whereas in Brazil I saw people of all ages working and going to classes much of the time. It was painfully obvious how Venezuela and the other Bolivarian nations had fallen so far short of the dreams of their founder, Simón Bolivar, who envisioned hard-working, honest people forging a prosperous, free, unified nation modeled on the United States.

The Daily Journal editors invited me to work briefly during the presidential election. I was jolted back into my previous lifestyle in which every minute was filled even before it arrived. But the interlude was just what I needed – a short bit of regularity, clean sheets, and familiar faces – before I would be ready to tackle another year of vagabonding. After working for a few weeks, this exercise in lunacy made me appreciate my wandering ways once again. Where I'd grown tired of the discomfort, I began to thirst for liberty again.

Life on the road is a separate reality. While sleepwalking through our daily grind, life is mostly numb and predictable, and we long for freedom to do whatever we want, be it retirement in the future or winning the lottery right now. But the road also means loneliness, fear, and the requirement to adapt to the unexpected all the time.

I visited parts of Venezuela I had not seen when I lived there, such as the Guacharo Caves, perhaps Venezuela's most intriguing natural site. Inside, some rocks were smooth and shiny. Others were rough, as if with wart-covered skin, while some rippled rocks resembled the rib cage of a decomposing corpse. Far from the entrance, the light from the cave opening resembled a thin flashlight beam, making the darkness even more mysterious and overpowering. The blackness was spooky, even more so when listening to the weird guacharo birds cackle and flap, seeming an evil mutant cross between bats and roosters. I wondered what would happen if our single lantern failed, conjuring up images of Tom Sawyer and Becky wandering lost in the cavern. An hour's visit left my pants and shoes layered with mud.

The caves are near the town of Caripe, set amid one of those rare garden paradises scattered about the Earth. The overriding feature is fertility: rich, productive soil; hills stacked with thick green foliage; bright violet, red and yellow flowers. It exudes health and vitality; everybody was smiling, unlike in stressful Caracas. I walked back to town from the caves to see orange trees, coffee bushes, banana groves, and seemingly sculpted mountains, all close up.

Historic Cumaná is blessed with a charm rare in Venezuela: proud, bleached-white colonial buildings, an imposing Spanish fort, and surprisingly few visitors. Many historic towns in the region were sadly ignored. The poor people in Latin American who can afford to travel usually visit family and don't appreciate historic sites. Middle-class people head to beaches or resorts in warm places with swimming pools. And the wealthy jet off to North America, the Caribbean or Europe. The percentage of people interested in their own history and culture was minuscule; most tended to favor Parisian or Roman culture over their own.

After my work and travels around Venezuela, Jean-François and I went to Colombia for a second time. This year, instead of riding a bus to Cartagena, we took his car to remote villages in the Andean foothills. After he headed back to Venezuela, I was still weary from so much traveling in substandard conditions and working in Caracas, that I needed a vacation from my trip. I had been guided by the wind, carried by the currents, tumbled by the waves. So I rested for a couple of weeks at a meditation retreat in the mountains above Medellín. There, I spent an afternoon with coffee pickers at a *finca*. I watched their fingers skillfully pluck the plump red coffee berries, carefully strip the branch, and empty each handful into a slowly filling wicker basket. A cool wind dried the trail of sweat on their backbones as they cleanly sliced nettlesome weeds with machetes. The leather straps holding their increasingly heavy baskets dug grooves into their backs. When they got a break, we took seats on a soft pile of freshly shorn weeds and chatted. A condor swooped overhead, not twitching a muscle as its wings caught the winds beneath the brilliant sun in the rich, azure sky. Butterflies flit about the plants in all directions.

After this much-needed interlude, I returned to Medellín and boarded a bus for Ecuador, bursting from the cradle of peace and comfort into the unknown, chaotic world once again.

Twenty years later, I returned to Venezuela on a short work assignment and found the country in rapid meltdown, ruled by fear. Fear of crime. Fear of oppression. Fear of doing something that would displease President Hugo Chavez or his strutting *chaveto* martinets. Political strife was rending the country into scraps. Chavez, who served time in prison for leading a military rebellion against the government before being elected a few years afterward, employed increasingly strong-arm tactics. Formerly bold broadcast and print media were intimidated. Venezuela had devolved from a fast-developing regional leader into just another flailing banana republic. Social order is disintegrating as the nation now spirals out of control into a nightmarish dystopia of wanton crime and murder.

Chapter 16

Homeward Bound

The meandering, muddy Oiapoque (OY-ah-POH-kay) River slices through endless overgrown rain forest, separating gigantic Brazil from diminutive French Guiana. Like the Rio Grande splitting the United States from Mexico, the Oiapoque River is a crossroads between a major world power, France, and a developing nation, Brazil.

The Brazilian side of the river had all the sights and smells to which I had become accustomed: muddy roads, ramshackle slums, familiar foods, and the facility of speaking Portuguese. The French side was familiar in some ways and strange in others: the streets in St. Georges were paved, and the houses were all solid. I followed a pleasant, familiar scent that wafted from the bakery, leading me to my first warm, authentic croissant in years. Something else struck me. These two towns are in plain view of each other, yet no adults in St. Georges spoke Portuguese, and I could not find anybody in Oiapoque who spoke French. But the French children all seemed to know Portuguese, perhaps because of Brazilian TV and radio available locally over the airwaves.

These twin towns were isolated, cut off at the time from the rest of their nations, and the world. The road from Oiapoque to Macapá, the capital of Amapá state, took three days to travel, and was either dusty or muddy, and barely passable in many spots. The French side had no road. A daily flight went to the provincial capital, Cayenne, in a little puddle-jumper that carried about a dozen passengers, which was booked far in advance.

Brazilians I met planned to ride a boat illegally to Cayenne under the cloak of darkness, leaving them at an empty beach near town. I didn't like this option – I had heard stories about passengers drowning on overcrowded boats that capsized. I also saw Brazilians sleeping along the waterfront and at the airport. Some were sneaking to Cayenne to work illegally, while others were planning to sell things. I got stuck several days waiting for a flight, and no hotels had rooms available. I ended up sleeping on a covered, open-air platform at the airport; I did not want to risk missing a flight by staying in a hotel across the river in Brazil.

Thirty years after I first traveled this route, there is now a paved road all the way from Macapá to Oiapoque, a bridge over the river, and a paved highway from St. Georges to Cayenne. Progress has at last arrived.

Oiapoque was the last place I set foot in Brazil for years. It was a strenuous ride from São Paulo, requiring weeks of bouncing aboard miserable buses over jaw-grinding roads. I had two options: I could fly relatively cheaply from São Paulo on Paraguayan Airlines by connecting through Asunción and onto Miami, or I could travel a slow, torturous overland route through territory I had not yet seen. It would take much longer and cost more money. But, once more, the magnetic lure of the unknown was irresistible. Flying out would deny me the experience, albeit coated in drudgery, of knowing the length of the country, from glittering São Paulo, to the nearly impassable Amazon.

On the road for nearly two years, it was time to head home. I was getting tired of living like a peasant and hoped Maria would accompany me, but she was nervous about giving up the middle-class life she had achieved in São Paulo. Since meeting her, I had circled back through the Spanish-speaking countries and taken numerous trips around Brazil, always returning to São Paulo to see her. I was in a holding pattern, and my money was running low. Once I made up my mind to leave, I was homeward bound.

Flavio saw me off at the bus station. At that time, I didn't know whether I would return to Brazil or if I would ever see him or Maria again.

From São Paulo, I headed straight northward through the nation's center. At first glance, futuristic Brasília looked very un-Brazilian to me. While most Brazilian cities are a haphazard, chaotic jumble, Brasília is spread out, with huge empty spaces between buildings, wide boulevards and parks. Government buildings lie in the center, and commercial and residential areas radiate out on grids which from the air resemble wings. Furthermore, there were no *favelas* jerry-built on vacant spaces as in every other Brazilian metropolis, and things seemed organized. I missed the spontaneity. Was I in the same country? Upon closer inspection, however, I noticed many shattered windows in buildings, peeled window tinting, and broken sidewalks, making it more Brazilian.

Slums are distant from the city center, requiring a bus or train ride. As well, affordable middle-class housing is located in commuter "satellite cities" surrounding Brasília. Those towns resembled their counterparts all over Brazil – crowded, noisy and barely manageable.

From the capital, I rode a train westward through the vast *cerrado* plains, Brazil's breadbasket. All around were curious emus, a cute relative of the ostrich, and what resembled three-foot-tall anthills, which were termite nests.

The plains continued all the way to Cuiabá, and from there I went northward where the rain forest started. Entering and leaving Cuiabá was the very Brazilian phenomenon of motels. I had grown accustomed to motels lining the highways in major cities, but this was a Wild West frontier town with almost no paved roads. The only other place I saw such motels was in Panama, some with names like "Love Camp" and "Beautiful Dream."

Traveling into the heart of the forbidding Amazon, an uneven dirt roadway alternated with washed-out pavement. Craters, a foot or more deep but seemingly the size of those on the moon, sent passengers flying toward the roof like a jack-in-the-box on a tightly coiled spring.

Before venturing into the Amazon, I had imagined pristine virgin forest, which still exists but is rapidly disappearing. In some places, the jungle was reclaiming, even devouring, what they call a highway, and the buses and trucks swished through new growth. Many trees had wide-spreading branches laden with dried brown pods; the shape of every seed was visible, like an embossed print or sea fossil with fish bones, while brilliant red, orange, purple and yellow flowers seemed even brighter contrasted with the dominant green and brown.

Still, the impact of deforestation was painfully evident. In many places, not much jungle was left. Along the main rivers and roads, it is slashed away or coated with dust. Some foliage was so brown and dusty that it looked as if it had been napalmed. Once forest is razed, it devolves into a wasteland of worthless scrub and weeds. Many towns need water trucks to moisten the dry, dusty streets where jungle had dominated for millennia until recently.

The forest often was entirely burned out, with only isolated sticks poking up over bushes and felled trees, a ghastly pall of death.

The ever-present dust made everyone on the buses cough, with many breathing through handkerchiefs. My nostrils were so infested with dust that when I blew my nose, out came mud.

Pedestrians left trails of dust puffs in their wake.

Settlers used hand-cranked wells to draw water at humble homesteads. At some hotels, the stench of nearby sewers was overwhelming. Yet other jungle cities were brand spankin' new, looking like suburbs of big modern cities.

At a state border crossing late at night, health workers pulled everyone off the bus, lined them up and injected mandatory yellow fever vaccine. I didn't need one because before leaving the United States, I had surrendered my arms as pin cushions, not knowing what disease I might encounter. I also took anti-malaria pills in jungle regions, which rendered me unable to donate blood for several years afterward.

The Amazon is so hot that pedestrians, and even bicyclists, clutch umbrellas to protect themselves from the intense, hostile sun. Before European settlers intruded, the Indians lived in dense jungle, so they spent much of their lifetimes in the shade.

Nightfall is sudden along the equator. The sun blazes, withers and punishes all day. Then, in just minutes, the fat orange globe sinks into the land, and night's cloak descends.

Human encroachment offers neither cleanliness nor privacy. Many towns experience a sudden influx of newcomers to exploit the natural resources such as mining or logging, which overcrowds the hotels and boarding houses. Newcomers and visitors who can't find a room sling their hammocks in parks or anywhere they find space. Even if you manage to get a hotel room, the mildew-choked walls don't reach all the way to the ceiling so the sizzling air doesn't get trapped. That means you can hear your neighbors snore, burp, and fart, or have sex, and, likewise, they hear you. Ants, mosquitoes and other bugs invade every space.

Amazon Indians live in round or oblong straw huts, with numerous families or even whole villages under the same roof. (With such a glaring lack of privacy, I wondered how baby Indians are conceived). Local houses borrow the wide-open design from Indian huts, with many homes lacking doors between rooms to guarantee badly needed ventilation.

Between Belém and Manaus, I paid eighteen dollars to ride a riverboat for five days. Passengers scurried to find two pegs from which to suspend hammocks, their bed and stateroom for the duration of the trip. Hundreds of hammocks ran multi-level at all possible angles and directions. I stretched mine above the crowds and clambered up and down like a monkey. Fellow voyagers showed me how to tie a *boca de lobo* (wolf's mouth) knot to shorten my span and not intrude on my neighbor below. Despite torrential humidity and the constant equatorial heat of at least a hundred degrees, passengers were required to wear shirts at all times. I took several showers a day but was always sweaty. It was tolerable only when the boat was in motion because of the breeze, but it was hard to sleep with all the commotion among hundreds of other people. Some passengers listened to soccer games on their scratchy radios late at night, followed by loud music in the morning and garrulous, energetic shouting at all hours.

The powerful Amazon is so wide that sometimes you can't see the other side of the river, feeling more like a vast inland sea. Villagers paddle up in small dugouts, waiting for passengers to throw them a bunched-up T-shirt or other gift. After the ferry passed, their little boats bobbed in the wake like tiny corks. Massive clumps of water plants were floating islands of vegetation. Islands had houses on stilts along the waterfront connected by plank walkways. Lumber mills belched out black smoke as they processed the valuable hardwoods felled in the jungle. We stopped in ports large and small, including Santarém, which I had once seen in a movie, but passengers were not allowed to disembark to explore.

The most amazing sight was the dramatic convergence of the Amazon and Tapajós River, forming what seemed from a distance to be a demarcation, where the Tapajós reluctantly surrendered its translucent blue waters to the Amazon's muddy, milky *café com leite* tone.

We approached Manaus, a metropolis of more than a million people which looks out of place along the Amazon after chugging through wilderness. Even more alien is the massive pink Renaissance-style opera house in the city center, a relic of the short-lived rubber boom of the late nineteenth and early twentieth century which seemed more appropriate for France or Italy. With few roads, the river is the lifeblood for remote communities. Manaus, which receives ocean-going freighters and containerized cargo, is the principal distribution point for the whole Amazon region, including towns upriver in Colombia and Peru. The waterfront stinks of sweat, rotting fish, urine and untreated sewage, but it is never boring. It is a beehive that hums with excitement: dozens of riverboats of all sizes, many of them double-deckers, traveling to every imaginable destination. Most are white, with blue or green trim. Porters, barefooted or wearing rubber flip-flops, scurried through mud and water up and down narrow loading ramps. They heaved heavy bags on their backs, carried even heavier oil barrels, and toted food and beverage containers off and on. Some boys unloaded clumps of bananas as big as themselves from a boat near the trash-strewn shore. Freight loaded onto these riverboats was a hodgepodge: furniture, appliances, bicycles, even cars. The upper decks were festooned with brightly colored hammocks swaying in the gentle breeze.

When I slung my hammock among hundreds of others on the riverboat, I had no expectation of privacy. But when I rented hotel rooms, I did anticipate at least a modicum of personal space. I rented a room one night in Porto Velho, the capital of Rondônia state ready to descend into some deep REMs. But when I awoke in the middle of the night to urinate, I was shocked to see a stranger sleeping in the other bed in my room. I awoke the owner to complain. His excuse: sharing rooms, sometimes even beds, was customary in a region with an acute shortage of hotel availability. At this hour, I had no choice but to return to my bed.

Few bridges exist in the Amazon. The rivers are far too wide, and expensive bridges could not justify their cost in the remote region. Ferries, mostly simple barges, were the best way to get over these rivers, some of them muddy and others clear. I swam in the Amazon and other rivers every chance I got to cool off, and so did other people. They explained that swift-moving rivers have no piranha problem; I still have all my limbs, toes and fingers.

Slowly I inched my way northward. My last hurdle in Brazil was Amapá state's dusty roads with jungle encroaching on both sides. Aluminum doors in the capital, Macapá, loudly echoed every fierce raindrop. A cabdriver, explaining how he avoided hold-ups, told me he spotted robbers right away because they avoided looking at him. The criminals instead looked out the window because the driver is a mark, not a person. If a passenger seemed suspicious, the driver stopped at a police kiosk, saying he must pick up documents. There, he would tell the officer what he suspected. One time, he said three passengers looked scary, and when checking, the cops found two guns and a knife "this long" motioning with his index fingers a foot apart. The dirt ribbon wound through the jungle to Calçoene, where I slid on slippery rocks through the river's gentle rapids with the local children. That cleaned the dust off me, luckily, because the hotel did not have running water, curiously, in Brazil's rainiest city. From there, it took one more day to reach the border at Oiapoque.

After my extended wait in St. Georges, I flew into Cayenne, which looks like a small, storm-battered, down-on-the-heels version of New Orleans. I only stayed one night and headed out the next day for Suriname. I looked forward to the efficiency of the industrialized world after so much confusion throughout South America. Guiana, after all, is part of France, one of the most advanced nations on earth.

But it seemed that no matter how hard I tried, I could not escape the Third World. I got stuck halfway between Cayenne and the Suriname border in a comedy of errors befitting *Monsieur Hulot's Holiday*. The driver forgot to gas up the bus. We stopped in Sinnamary, but there was no gasoline in a town where the roofs were all overhanging tin and all the windows were shuttered to keep out the violent storms which erupt without warning and quickly disappear. A truck delivering gasoline arrived, but the pump was broken, so we had to wait further for a repairman to fix the pump. After five hours, they started to siphon gas from another vehicle for the bus. Then the bus had a tire problem, followed by further mechanical woes. We were doomed to comic misadventures.

My first sight of Albina, Suriname across the Maroni River, was much more elegant than my final view of shacks in France along the water. Once the ferry crossed, I saw rows of Chinese-owned shops on the main street.

I had taken thousands of pictures during my long journey, but I was warned not to photograph police or police vehicles or vessels in Suriname. I heard that a Frenchman had the daylights thrashed out of him for unknowingly taking a picture of a police boat, which resembled a fishing boat.

In Suriname, vehicles drive on the left like in Britain and former British colonies, which seemed odd for an erstwhile Dutch colony. Signs warned TENEZ VOTRE GAUCHE (stay to the left) for French-speaking drivers. Ivy engulfed the trees. I also saw the first nudity since visiting remote Indian villages in the Amazon; some women wore a skirt but no top.

Bus passengers in Suriname were subdued, not noisy like counterparts in Latin America. There were surprisingly few hotels in the capital, Paramaribo, and the entrances were on the side of buildings or an alley rather than facing the street. Some hotel lobbies were several flights upstairs. I found what seemed to be a clean, acceptable place. Then at 9:30 at night, the owner started playing loud music and the bar in the lobby suddenly filled with hookers and their customers. The next day, I found a nice quiet family hotel, which the owner promised me did not offer such intrusive entertainment.

There wasn't much to do in Suriname. Consider the national obsession: birds. All the young men carried bird cages through the streets and taught them to whistle. At a contest every Sunday on the lawn in front of the presidential palace, the loudest bird tweet was the winner. Seriously.

Fear was rampant. Dictator Desi Bouterse ruled with an iron fist; less than two years before my visit, fifteen prominent critics of the regime were slaughtered by the military. Locals whispered to me that the United States should come in and straighten it up like the Caribbean island of Grenada, which U.S. forces had invaded a year earlier after a Marxist coup overthrew the government. Luckily, I was able to get out of Suriname the next day.

I wanted to continue overland to Guyana and fly from there, but Guyanese consular officials informed me that it would take weeks to get permission to visit. It was never clear why it took so long. I had come all this way and endured all this discomfort but was denied bragging rights that I had set foot in every country in South America. Instead, I flew out of Suriname through Curaçao, which I had visited when I lived in Caracas.

Ironically, airfare from Suriname, just a short hop over the Caribbean, was more expensive than it would have cost to fly back to the United States from São Paulo. But I would have flown over everything, and my view of Brazil would have been woefully incomplete. And, for what it's worth, I would have missed out on French Guiana and Suriname altogether.

Still, getting out of Suriname was not that easy. Strict currency controls meant I was unable to exchange my pocket full of local guilders, which are worthless elsewhere. Luckily, I met Orlando, an official with the national soccer federation who was traveling to Curaçao. He paid for a hotel room we shared in Curaçao. I gave him the rest of my guilders, which he could spend upon his return to Suriname. In Curaçao, life was once again orderly. People waited in line without pushing or cutting as in Latin America. What a relief. That same morning I was Miami-bound. After clearing customs I found a flight to Detroit, and before dark I was riding a bicycle on scenic, tranquil Belle Isle with my beloved Uncle Bill and Aunt Helene.

I would not set foot again in South America for nearly four years. By then, I was working for The Associated Press in New York, and Maria was pregnant with our first child when we visited her parents together for the first time in rural Minas Gerais. It was nine years before I lived in Brazil again, when I returned to São Paulo as the bureau chief for Dow Jones newswires.

Chapter 17

Fear of Crime Lurks
Just Below the Surface

In the pre-dawn hours of July 23, 1993, off-duty police officers in plainclothes opened fire on homeless children sleeping in front of the Candelaria Cathedral in downtown Rio de Janeiro, killing eight of them. The bloodbath grabbed the attention of the nation, and indeed, the world, casting a harsh, searing spotlight on the largely ignored crisis of homeless children in Brazil and impunity of law-enforcement and vigilantes. President Itamar Franco expressed his horror and went to Rio with members of his Cabinet to make sure the perpetrators were caught and punished. Sadly, such massacres were commonplace, though usually unpublicized. Street children were routinely taken to out-of-the-way places and summarily executed, according to Amnesty International and other independent organizations. Typically, such grisly executions were performed on a smaller scale at a landfill site, where the bodies would soon be buried by garbage and then smothered with dirt. No witnesses. No evidence. No one to care.

Three of the eight police officers prosecuted for the murders were convicted. One of them testified that the children were shot because they had thrown rocks at police cars the previous day.

The elegant cathedral, with a baroque façade, dates back to the eighteenth century. The children, having nowhere to go, slept out front because people at the church provided food, blankets, and other assistance.

More than sixty homeless children sleeping in the plaza survived the shooting, but reporters trying to track them down a decade later were unable to find most of the survivors. The ghosts of Candelaria still haunt Brazil.

Fear puts people on edge in Brazil's biggest cities, and in much of Latin America, all the time.

Less than a year before the Candelaria carnage, prison guards and police stormed the Carandiru prison in São Paulo to quell an uprising which claimed 111 inmates. Many were gunned down after surrendering, and the government still conceals information about that and other prison incidents. Public opinion polls show a large bloc of the crime-weary Brazilian populace supports "anything goes" by police.

Authorities apparently learned little in the two intervening decades. In late 2012, police killed suspected car thief Paulo Nascimento, pleading for his life after he was captured and subdued near São Paulo. It would have been just another in the long succession of police killings except that an anonymous neighbor recorded the shooting, which was broadcast on television the next day. Four police officers went on trial for murder.

The Candelaria rampage revolted a society complacent with everyday summary executions because so many children were killed at once on sacred ground next to a church in downtown Rio. A body or two scattered willy-nilly in the junkyard every day doesn't grab attention. I wish I could say that bringing these facts to light was one of my finest hours as a journalist. Instead, I must confess that I stumbled.

When that news broke, I was working on the international news editing desk at The Associated Press in New York. The story arrived the same day as Mideast strife, Sikh violence in India and multiple wars in Africa. I dutifully edited the story quickly, making sure it had the requisite background and context, and sent it out to readers. After that, I moved onto the next story, or so I thought, until the international editor arrived. He called me over, scowling, to ask why I treated this as a routine dispatch with six or seven paragraphs. My boss saw this story through a different prism. He immediately recognized what had escaped my jaded mind initially, the potential for this tragedy as front-page news worldwide. My error in judgment became apparent quickly.

None of the facts in the story was wrong; it was well written and reported. The correspondent in Rio did a skillful job, and I had edited it adequately. But both of us, sadly, were inured to the wider meaning. Quality journalism demands perspective and insight as well as clarity and precision. We both knew that street kids were slaughtered every day in Brazil and simply saw it as one more tragedy, like another traffic fatality. But this was no routine car crash; it was a major pileup with eight victims. As well, the wanton homicide of children made it even more shocking.

A government commission was convened to investigate the butchery, but its progress was set back when two of its members were killed by unidentified gunmen. That is emblematic for most problems in Brazil: Every step forward to resolve a problem, however earnest, is matched by another one backwards that hinders resolution.

Considering my experience, I should have recognized the importance. I headed a team of AP reporters who produced an excellent series of stories about street children. For our efforts, we won the 1991 Tom Wallace award from the Inter American Press Association. Armies of these kids proliferate through the region – Colombia even has its own word for them, *gamines* – but nowhere were they so numerous as in Brazil.

Bands of glue-sniffing pre-teens survive by begging, robbery or both. They might be runaways from abusive families or abandoned by parents who can't afford to support them. Public and private resources devoted to caring for these children or preventing overpopulation fell far short. I have met foreign missionaries who run shelters and orphanages, but they are woefully limited to helping only handfuls.

Tragically, people who are too poor to raise children have the highest birthrates. Until recent years, an ineffectual health care system failed to reach those who most needed access to contraception. The Roman Catholic Church's influence for years pushed to prevent contraceptives from reaching those who need it most. International aid to family planning was stymied for years by lobbies in the United

States which block such assistance to other countries under the guise of preventing abortion. Simply put, ignorant, impoverished people in Brazil and other Third World nations have millions of children they cannot feed and shelter.

Depicting these stark realities was a 1981 Brazilian movie, *Pixote*, which means "kid" or "pee-wee," by Argentine-born director Hector Babenco, who also made *Kiss of the Spider Woman*. Both films are start-to-finish tragedy interlaced with brief moments of awkward but poignant beauty, underpinned by outrage and pity. *Pixote* chronicles the brief life of a runaway who ping pongs between a heartless juvenile center and the cruel streets, where he discovers a sense of community with other discarded youth. Surrealistic reality steamrolled art and invention: slum-dwelling child actor Fernando Ramos da Silva – who played the eponymous role – was gunned down in real life at age nineteen in 1988 by police, who blamed him for armed robberies.

Middle-class people fear street kids, and business owners see them as a threat to their livelihoods. Put yourself in the shoes of a small business owner, perhaps a lunch counter, in a big Brazilian city. Street kids and other homeless people forage through the trash can for anything edible or to ask a sympathetic employee for something to eat. They beg for spare change from your customers, or they might start robbing your clientele. Customers avoid your establishment because they fear a mugging, so they patronize a competitor where they feel safer. You ask police to shoo away the kids, but that just scatters them momentarily. The cops can't focus on your puny concerns; they are so overwhelmed by dangerous thugs and heavily armed drug gangs that they can't devote much time or effort to petty crime.

Word gets around quickly. The street kids have figured out that your customers are easy marks, and your business plunges overnight. You told the kids to scram, but a pack of them threatened you with a knife and you were forced to back off. Then you decide to take the next step: you pay a private security guard or cop to do something about your problem. Don't hurt them, you say, just move them somewhere else. In reality, that is no more effective than capturing the coyote terrorizing your pets and dropping it off in another neighborhood.

Brazilian law makes it nearly impossible to prosecute minors for petty crimes.

Police and vigilantes know the most effective way to deal with the street kids. They round up the children at night from the places they sleep in plain view and take them for disposal where everyone else unloads the trash: the dump. When a truck drops a load of garbage over the bodies, they will never be seen except by hungry vultures and rodents.

There certainly is no excuse for the behavior of the shopkeeper who hires someone to eliminate his problems, the way you hire an exterminator to get rid of an insect infestation. The business owner is not doing it to be cruel; he is also in a battle for survival. His priority is to preserve his business from insolvency when it is under attack. The problem of street children has numerous culprits but no easy solution.

My office window in São Paulo looked out over a downtown area where a knot of street kids slept under a bridge. They were loosely knit, around eight or so boys about seven to twelve years old. Statistics show that only a tiny percentage survive to adulthood. I sometimes saw one of these boys running away from someone whose pocket they had picked or purse they had grabbed.

This group often stumbled about, high on cobbler's glue. They sat on steps and sniffed an old filthy sock with glue inside, the cheapest rush available. They could not afford *maconha* (marijuana) or *cocaina*, drugs of choice for people with cash. A bottle of glue sold for less than a dollar and got the whole gang high several times all day.

The kids I watched were pretty tame. A couple of blocks away was a more vicious flock which held up people at a stop light. Unsuspecting motorists stopped for the light, and if their window was open, a boy of about ten thrust his clenched fist to the driver's neck, clutching a jagged chunk of glass. Frightened drivers handed over money and the boy scooted away. This happened to my wife with our toddler son wiggling in his car seat. She was terrified that something could have happened to Joseph and rushed straight over to my office. A driver at the taxi stand in front of our building took her back to look for the ragamuffin who had attacked her, but he was gone. Learning about that incident was even more frightening than any of the half dozen times I was robbed, knowing that my wife and infant son's lives were imperiled.

Since Candelaria, the federal, state and municipal governments have made a major push to get kids off the street to put them in shelters, boarding schools and orphanages or provide basic sustenance so their families can support them. That was one of the major accomplishments of the administration of former President Luiz Inácio da Silva, known as Lula. The problem is not nearly as bad as before, but it certainly has not been solved.

With that background, I'm always apprehensive when in Brazil. I rarely let down my guard in the cities and am sometimes astonished by an experience that defies my preconceptions.

One trip took me to Belo Horizonte, Brazil's fourth most-populous city, with two million residents. The downtown restaurants weren't open the advertised hours, and a pizza joint that looked good on the outside turned out to be full of smoke and jarringly loud music. So, I settled on McDonald's, the cheapskate's choice in the United States but far more expensive than bargain eateries in Brazil. After two tiresome weeks of rice and beans ever day, even a fish fillet sandwich sounded tasty. I had picked up the latest *Newsweek*, so I could catch up on some of the events I missed while I was out in the hinterlands beyond the reach of newspapers and TV.

As I began to eat, an energetic little Shirley Temple of a moptop began to interrupt my meal. She asked me about my family and my name, then ran around and quizzed a couple of teenage girls at a nearby table. She looked to be three or four years old, and volunteered her own name, Sabrina. Then she wanted a sip of my milkshake, which I denied her, fearful of germs. I looked around and asked where her parents were. She just giggled and ran around some more. Well dressed and clean, she was obviously with a family and was not an abandoned urchin turned loose to beg in the streets.

Despite this lighthearted scene, the fear of crime hovered on the other side of the window. In the crowded street outside were abandoned youngsters and a swarm that surely included thieves. When the nearby teenage girls made a move to leave, the tot begged them to stay longer. One of the girls responded: "My mom is expecting me soon. The streets are dark and getting unsafe, so I'd better get home now."

Kidnapping for ransom is quite common in Brazil; anyone seen as having the wherewithal to make a payoff is a potential target. Besides random robberies, there are surely plenty of criminals who would love to nab a kid they thought would get them fast cash. So, this adorable little girl was a prime target, as were my own children.

Back in the United States, where kidnapping for ransom is uncommon, you rarely see children interacting with adults out of their parents' sight. There is such a deathly fear of sexual predators and criminal sociopaths that most kids have the innocence beaten out of them by their parents before preschool. When he was younger, my own son refused to respond to people who made comments in my presence, such as "You're such a very well-behaved boy."

When asked why he remained mute to friendly entreaties, his answer was always, "You know, Dad. I'm not supposed to talk to strangers." It's complicated for a child to distinguish proper from improper contact.

Despite horrendous violent crime and high-profile cases involving pedophiles, most Brazilian youngsters, even those in the crime-infested cities, retain a degree of innocence and childishness that their American counterparts have lost. The little girl's behavior was really quite typical.

Is there a way we can protect our children from harm without beating exuberance, spontaneity and a zest for life out of them?

During another trip to Brazil, I stopped in São Paulo for the day before a twenty-hour bus ride to visit relatives in Maria's remote home town.

A friend and I set out on foot for a restaurant near the city center. After eating, we went to the Praça da Republica, one of my favorite places, where I browsed local crafts and bought a few gifts to take home.

Bill and I are both experienced expatriates with well-honed street smarts. We conversed *sotto voce* in English to avoid attracting attention. Walking near us along the busy avenue was an American talking loudly into his hands-free mobile phone. He was just an arm's length away from us.

This is an attractive area, with European-style and art deco buildings, well-maintained streets and no slums. We saw nobody who fit the profile of ruffians, usually teenagers and pre-teen boys dressed in rags who assault pedestrians and motorists. Although we were only a few blocks away from the corner where Maria was robbed several years earlier, I had no reason to recall that incident as we enjoyed a fine spring afternoon.

Suddenly I felt someone push me from behind. At first I thought that Bill might be slapping me on the back before we heard a loud cry "Help" in English. I knew immediately that it was the American who had been chattering away.

Bill and I turned around as two bandits wrestled the middle-aged man to his knees. The robbers were dressed like any other men in their twenties and blended in with the crowd. Seeing the tourist pulled down reminded me of *National Geographic* nature films when hyenas or wolves tackle a deer or gazelle and devour it moments later. These human predators were just as barbaric.

We slowly approached the scene. Bill, experienced at martial arts, assumed an attack position. When one of the criminals motioned that he was reaching toward a gun under his belt, we slowly backed off.

Seeing a police car across the street, we ran to alert them about the mugging in progress. Three officers were talking to some civilians and one told me, "I can't come now. I'm busy with something else."

I pleaded, "But officer, that man is being robbed. He needs help."

I pointed across the street, but he did not even look up. His priorities were firm. "I'll go there later."

Bill interjected, "By then the criminals will be long gone," to which the officer cut us off with, "Go mind your own business."

As we walked cautiously back to Bill's apartment the streets suddenly looked menacing. We kept looking behind us to be sure we weren't being followed.

The next day I recounted this incident to relatives, and nobody was surprised. "The police were probably involved," my bother-in-law concluded. "Instead of arresting them, they just shake down the thieves for some of the loot."

I have been robbed so many times at gunpoint and knifepoint that I just don't remember them all.

After I was mugged in Belém, I found the closest police officer manning a kiosk on a nearby plaza. He told me that based on my description, he had a notion of who the robber was and would go search for him ... if I paid him for the service. It seemed pointless, so I declined.

One night in São Paulo, I was at a bank ATM, in a small enclosed room intended to prevent robberies. When I arrived, several people were in line in front of me. Suddenly, I realized that I was alone with two criminals. One had his hand in his pocket and appeared to be holding a pistol. They politely told me to withdraw the maximum allowed, about three hundred dollars, grabbed the cash and fled. They never laid a hand on me. They did not take my ATM card, credit cards or anything else. It occurred to me that they were smooth professionals. Any item with my name on it would be incriminating evidence if they were stopped by police. With just my money, there was no proof they had robbed anybody. I felt lucky that was all they took. The news every day was filled with tragic tales about middle-class or wealthy people who were killed or maimed by robbers, who, ironically, often fled without the loot they were seeking.

Through the years, crime has only gotten worse, leading people to question the legitimacy of democratic governments that respect human rights. They remember the days when the military ruled by brute force. Criminal suspects were often shot on sight, no questions asked, no trial, no bleeding hearts allowed to wail over human rights. Totalitarian states – Cuba, the Soviet Union, China, various Mideast nations – have or had little street crime accompanying the absence of freedom. Liberty is a messy system. Dictatorships can effectively minimize street crime. But what is the real cost?

Simply being a gringo made me a target, even if I wore blue jeans, sneakers and Che Guevara T-shirts, even if I traveled by bus or train and slept in cheap hotels. Maybe it was my six-foot stature in nations where Indian populations were a head shorter, or my Anglo-Saxon paleface surrounded by darker-skin folks. Savvy criminals spotted me and deduced I was carrying cash. I may as well have worn a target on my back an engraved invitation for bandits.

Several times I was robbed by taxi drivers. My practice has usually been to pay more than what is posted on the taximeter. But, spotting an accent, some drivers asked for huge amounts, for instance fifty dollars for a brief ride when the meter showed the equivalent of five dollars. When I protested, some drivers threatened me with guns or knives. A taxi driver in Mexico City pulled a knife on me when I offered him four times the rate on the meter. When I got out, he chased me, so I threw some bills at him, hoping he would stop running to grab them. Other times I was robbed by muggers brandishing a gun or a knife on a dark street near a bus or train station. Sometimes it seems that every corner of a big city has its own horde of beggars and bandits. Nearly everybody I knew who lived in Latin America – locals and expatriates alike – had been mugged. Back home in Seattle, none of my acquaintances has ever been threatened physically.

In São Paulo, I was also the victim of fraud in the days when credit card purchases were run through a machine making a carbon copy. But the bank took the loss, not me. Some store clerks in Brazil commonly made two copies of your card. The first one went to the store to collect payment for the purchase. The second one was sold to thieves, who used the imprint to fabricate fake cards with a matching name and account number. My monthly bill once showed a purchase for more than two thousand dollars at a pharmacy in Rio. I had not been to Rio in months, and I wondered who ever spends that much money in a pharmacy. Shouldn't the merchant demand identification for someone making such a huge purchase?

While on the road everything I owned was in my backpack, so I had to be extra judicious about crime. I was in the habit of dividing my assets. That way, if I was robbed, they would only get a portion of my money. I kept small stashes of cash in my wallet, front pants pocket, folded in a money belt, in a sock-type sleeve I wore on my leg and a stash hidden inside my backpack. Thieves were typically in a hurry, so they gladly take the wad you hand over and scram. On most occasions, I only lost about fifty or a hundred dollars at a time. Others I met weren't so lucky.

I had the uncanny experience of seeing people again after several months and thousands of miles on the road. Once I ran into a pair of young Peruvians I had met earlier as they traveled through Bolivia bound for Brazil to work illegally. During that long train ride, their faces lit up as they excitedly described the opportunities they thought awaited them, the ability to earn a hundred dollars a month as unskilled laborers, quadruple what they could earn at home. A couple months later, I saw them on a city bus in São Paulo, their forlorn faces bloodied and bruised. They had worked hard and saved their money, but bandits beat them up and took everything they had. Their fantastic voyage had just barely begun and was already over.

Fear of crime is so visceral that many people avoid traveling to Latin America's major cities, or shun the region altogether. That is understandable, but I was the victim of violent and non-violent crime numerous times when I lived in New York City. Yet ironically, many people who live in or visit the Big Apple wouldn't even consider venturing to Latin America.

Rampant crime led to the death of someone dear to me. Jules Waldman founded *The Daily Journal* in Caracas in 1945, but by the time I got there in 1981 he had retired and was no longer involved in day-to-day operations. In his late sixties, he came to the office a couple of days a week, always dressed in a crisp suit and perfectly knotted tie, to write editorials. He took a liking to me and occasionally called me into his office for lengthy discussions about recent Venezuelan history, from the days of the dictatorship. He knew everything about everybody in Venezuela and reminded me of a kindly emeritus professor. After I left Venezuela, Mr. Waldman was tied up by bandits in his home and robbed. He was hospitalized for shock and soon afterward succumbed to a stroke at age 77.

Chapter 18

Mexico: Distant Neighbors
in the Labyrinth of Solitude

I was about ten the first time I set foot in a country outside the United States or Canada. My grandparents took me to Tijuana, little more than an hour's drive from their home in San Clemente, California, the scenic beach-side community where Richard Nixon would retire in disgrace a decade later. Mexico was my first experience with the seamier and steamier side of life. Having never been exposed to the most impoverished sections of Detroit or Los Angeles, where I had lived, I was stunned by the poverty and filth: tumbledown ramshackle buildings; dirt streets; children in tattered clothing; beggars everywhere; disease-ridden, mangy dogs. Gramps, who could pass for a Hollywood leading man a few years past his prime, was propositioned by a tout offering "companionship" with his "sister"; that became a joke in our family for years. I bought two comic books in Spanish, one *Superman* and one *Batman*. They were the exact same comics produced in the United States, with dialogue translated into Spanish. I was amused by how the Joker's laugher was translated into *ja ja*, not realizing that the "J" in Spanish is pronounced like an "H" (think *José*) in English.

The next time I went to Mexico was a few years later, when my parents took our family to Ensenada for the weekend. That was a couple hours' drive along the rugged, empty coastline beyond Tijuana. My most pungent memories of Ensenada involved the stench of rotting fish at the docks and a swordfish bigger than an adult human dangling from a hook, blood dripping from its snout like a leaky faucet.

151

Appalled by these sights and smells, I picked and pecked at my food, fearful of getting some dreaded food-borne illness.

Little did I realize that a quarter century later I would be living in Mexico City and would zip down to Ensenada on a modern freeway that would bypass most of hectic Tijuana. As an Associated Press correspondent in Mexico, I had an appointment with Ernesto Ruffo, the thirty-eight-year-old folk hero mayor who was running for governor of Baja California state. The cognoscenti dismissed Ruffo's chances because of his membership in the conservative National Action Party, known as PAN. The ruling Institutional Revolutionary Party, or PRI, had dominated the country for sixty years with a combination of bullying, patronage, and outright fraud. Most people simply assumed that PRI would steal the election, as it frequently did when facing a strong challenger.

While I waited outside Ruffo's office for my scheduled interview, I overheard a couple of men in their early twenties seated near me chatting in Portuguese. I found out they had been accused of a traffic offense by an allegedly crooked cop and were appealing the violation to the mayor. It turned out that one of them was the son of the Brazilian Consul in Los Angeles. When Ruffo came out to meet me, I told him the story of these young men and offered to interpret for them. He asked them a couple of questions through me, and, satisfied with their answers, made a phone call to get their car released from impound so they could head home.

Ruffo impressed me right away as a "can-do" sort of guy who was serious about reform. His municipal administration in Ensenada was considered among the most efficient in Mexico, and in a country rife with corruption, his reputation was spotless.

Several months later, I returned to Baja California to cover the voting. No surprise, the PRI's henchmen did try to steal the election, as usual, but this time public scrutiny interfered. I rode in a car full of Mexican reporters chasing a truck with PRI toughs who had stolen ballot boxes in precincts with strong support for the PAN. In the end, President Carlos Salinas de Gortari relented, and the PAN won it fair and square, for the first time in sixty years. Of course, Salinas himself was not so generous earlier when the vote count showed leftist opponent Cuauhtémoc Cardenas winning in 1988. The PRI machine stopped the vote counting, and Salinas squeaked by with – surprise, surprise – just a smidgen over fifty percent of the "official" vote count a few days later. Salinas, curiously, avoided me at every event I attended, exactly the same as Bill Gates did a decade later when I attended Microsoft events in Seattle.

But the cornerstone had been laid. PRI could not persist with its strong-arm tactics, and a few years later, Vicente Fox, a member of Ruffo's PAN, became the first non-PRI president in generations. The Mexico I encountered in the early 1990s was in rapid transition to a more pluralistic, modern and democratic nation.

While in Baja California during the Ruffo election, I had my own encounter with the police that was a direct opposite to the experience of the young Brazilians. Driving a rental car in Mexicali, within spitting distance of Calexico, California, I accidentally ran a red light. A police car pulled me over, whereupon I displayed my American driver's license, explained my confusion, and confessed my guilt. I expected a ticket or sticky fingers extended, but instead he beseeched me to be more careful and sent me on my way. While we were talking, I thought about a Mexican friend who got in trouble by calling a policeman *vato*, the equivalent of saying "hey dude" when he get pulled over, but I did not make that mistake. I was lucky that time, but I know people who have been forced to pay up to three hundred dollars in bribes to Mexican police for traffic offenses they never committed. How many billions of dollars in tourist revenues does Mexico lose every year due to foreigners' fear of corrupt police, drug gangs and street crime? Fittingly, the Mexican slang for bribe is *mordida*, which means "bite."

Of course, fear and distrust run both ways. Why do Mexicans fear the United States? Our ancestors grabbed nearly half of their country. All of the American Southwest, including California, used to be part of what is now Mexico. Consider this: if Canada had stolen Washington, Oregon, Idaho, Utah, Montana, Colorado, Wyoming, and the Dakotas from the United States, do you think Americans might harbor a bit of a grudge? (And where would we put Mt. Rushmore)? That was long ago, but if they haven't yet gotten over the Spanish conquest of the Aztec half a millennium ago, how can they reconcile the U.S. incursion less than two centuries ago? Remember that many Europeans still resent Germans for taking over their homelands in the World Wars, while millions of Asians (and Pearl Harbor survivors) begrudge the Japanese over World War II, even though those horrors occurred decades ago.

Countless times, the U.S. government has meddled in the affairs of its Latin neighbors by backing coups or supporting oppressive dictators. That policy has improved in recent decades, but there is still bitterness by people who were tortured by military regimes or who lost family members in those struggles. In some backward countries, a handful of plutocrats owned and ran everything for centuries, with U.S. support for their neo-feudal societies.

Much of that ill will can be softened if we butt out of their internal affairs and stop spying on their leaders. Do we want Mexicans or Brazilians telling us how to run our own affairs?

Mexico, by accident of geography, has its own cross to bear that the others don't: sharing a border with the United States. Imagine that you lived in a dirt floor shack without running water across the street from Donald Trump. Wouldn't you feel resentment watching him eat caviar and show off his Rolls Royce? The U.S.-Mexico border presents perhaps the starkest contrast in the world, where the most powerful, wealthy nation abuts the Third World. People in Ecuador are just as poor, but their nation borders Colombia and Peru, so they aren't reminded constantly of their own poverty contrasting a next-door neighbor's wealth.

Alan Riding discusses that phenomenon in great detail in *Distant Neighbors*, an insightful, penetrating book. Few books about Latin America are as good. For instance, some writers label the border a "scar" or a "metaphor." Others describe the border as a region unto itself, neither wholly American nor Mexican. Rubbish. Godawful hyperbole. There is no border "region." This is a true delimitation between one world and another, with no more telling reminder than the shacks on dirt streets in Tijuana or Ciudad Juarez in the shadow of gleaming steel-and-glass towers in San Diego or El Paso.

I frequently conversed with Mexicans peering through the fence at California or across the river to Texas, waiting to cross the border at night. Some returned to Mexico voluntarily to visit family but then experienced difficulties crossing back again. Others were sent back by immigration officers, called *migras,* short for *immigración.* They recounted stories of working in a meat-packing plant in Iowa, picking fruit in Montana, or washing dishes in New Jersey. These folks generally liked the United States and few blamed the immigration officers for deporting them. However, I heard countless horror stories about being shaken down by Mexican authorities to extort money upon their return. This became so frequent that the Mexican government devised a program to encourage its citizens to report cases of abuse.

When we think of illegal aliens, we generally consider the United States as their destination. But people illegally cross borders everywhere for a chance at a better life. Many Paraguayans, Bolivians and Peruvians work illegally in Brazil, Argentina or Chile because of better opportunities. Guatemalans, Nicaraguans, Salvadorans and Hondurans seek a comparatively better life in Mexico or Costa Rica. Colombians flock to Panama for higher wages. I visited a refugee camp in southern Mexico which sheltered Central Americans fleeing civil wars. A Mexican official told me the aliens streaming over the country's southern border were "like a trail of ants." Many reported abuse by military or police in their homeland, and some complained about ill treatment by Mexican officials, bus drivers, and alien smugglers, called *coyotes.* The movie *El Norte* starkly depicts the lives of a pair of young Guatemalans headed northbound to the promised land.

It was hard to adapt to Mexico City. The high elevation and choking pollution made my wife and infant daughter constantly sick with bronchial disorders. And the barely disguised Mexican resentment toward the United States, lurking an inch below the surface, gets tiring.

Mexicans, acutely aware of the shortcomings in their own society, take pride in their direct bloodlines to the ancient Mayas and Aztecs, who had some of the most advanced societies in the ancient world.

It would be pretentious to say I managed to penetrate the complicated Mexican psyche. Instead I defer to the nation's great author,

Octavio Paz. *The Labyrinth of Solitude* explores the Mexican identity and their attempts to mask their profound solitude. My own experiences with that tangible solitude were revealing.

I was living alone in Mexico while my wife and daughter had to stay in Brazil for five months to care for my father-in-law as he recovered from botched surgery (see Chapter 19). Midway through this lengthy separation, I took a week off to visit them in São Paulo. I spent as much time as possible at a nearby playground with my daughter, then barely a year old. Juliana played in the sandbox with other toddlers, and their parents invariably initiated conversations. It was so easy and natural, very Brazilian, and always enjoyable. When they got back to Mexico a few months later, we took Juliana to the parks in Mexico City and found the opposite environment, guarded by invisible walls we could not penetrate. The children were discouraged from playing with kids they did not know, and the parents did not interact with strangers. Each family unit seemed to be distinct and isolated from others, belying John Donne's quote about no man being an island. We invited neighbors with kids to accompany us to the park so Juliana would have playmates. Because I did not live outside Mexico City, I don't know if that isolating behavior is the norm nationwide. It would not be accurate to extrapolate the habits of New Yorkers as representative for all Americans, so I can't generalize that all Mexicans take after *Chilangos* in Mexico City. Many Mexicans in the hinterlands dislike residents of the capital, whom they see as snobbish, aggressive, pretentious, and dishonest.

Besides poisonous air and high crime, Mexico City carries another potentially lethal danger: earthquakes. I had lived through big quakes in California, but my first one in Mexico was among the most frightening experiences of my life. The high-rise building in the city center where I worked rocked back and forth, felt as flimsy as cardboard, and seemed on the verge of collapse. Remembering the 1985 quake which killed more than ten thousand people and flattened hundreds of buildings in the city center, everyone, myself included, stampeded down the stairs. In seconds, Paseo de la Reforma, an elegant wide boulevard with monuments in the center divider, was jammed with refugees from all these tall buildings. After the quake stopped, people streamed back inside. Only one person did not panic. Back in the office, Eloy Aguilar, the AP bureau chief, pressed his nose against the floor-to-ceiling window surveying the city, dictating a story to the desk in New York. In an instant, all the legends about Eloy came to life: never flinching in the face of countless natural disasters and Central American wars. Eloy's favorite put-down was that someone "couldn't even find a whorehouse in Juarez."

The center of Mexico City, built atop a dry lake bed, is prone to devastating temblors, while nearby areas resting on more solid ground remain unscathed. When I got home from work that night, Maria, who was miles from the city center, was not aware there had been a quake that day.

By coincidence, Maria and Juliana were flying back to Mexico from Brazil at the exact moment U.S. forces invaded Panama to topple dictator Manuel Noriega, known as *Cara de Piña* (Pineapple Face). The flight path between Brazil and Mexico goes directly over Panama. After working all night at the office to report the invasion, I went to the airport to greet them, only to find the flight information board saying SEE AGENT. My chest froze and I got dizzy, knowing that is the exact message you get when an airplane crashes. The airline had no information, and, I was horrified that they could have been accidentally shot down, as can happen to civilian aircraft during wars. It took several nail-biting hours before I was informed that the flight had been rerouted away from Panama. It had been sent to Miami, refueled, then sent onto Mexico. The diversion made their flight about six hours late, but once I knew they were safe and coming home, I was relieved. Juliana did not recognize me after not seeing me for three months and did not even let me even hold her until she got used to me again.

The most emblematic story I've ever seen from Mexico was written by a fellow AP colleague about the trash pickers' union. Mexico's version of untouchables were strong-armed into paying dues to a *sindicato* so the head of that organization could live in palatial luxury. The shameless union boss, a leader in the PRI, brazenly boasted about exploiting the poorest of Mexico's poor who barely survive by combing through mountains of garbage at landfill sites.

Foreigners often complain about the "siesta culture" in Mexico and other places in Latin America. But in Mexico City, that is a thing of the past. Every event I attended at *Los Pinos*, the presidential palace, or the "perp walks" (when criminals are trotted out by law enforcement) started punctually. In fact, Mexico's domestic airlines frequently left ahead of the scheduled time. I traveled by air quite a bit, and Mexican carriers still had a smoking section. Smokers, however, wanted to stay in the non-smoking section to avoid breathing the noxious fumes of their fellow smokers, and they always seemed to sit next to me. When I politely reminded them about the smoking and non-smoking sections, it always caused an argument in which a flight attendant would enforce the rules and tell the smoker to put out the butt or move to another seat. Similarly, once at a hotel in Brasília which caters to big-spender clientele, a man lit up in the elevator. Without saying a word, I simply pointed to the PROIBIDO FUMAR sign, and the smoker became so agitated that a bellboy had to come between us to prevent violence. The lowly bellboy, however, did not tell the smoker to extinguish his cigarette.

I discovered early on that the life of a foreign correspondent is not devoted to socializing on the *Champs-Élysées*, but rather to working long, tireless hours doing whatever it takes to get the stories out, whether big or mundane. Famous people die, trains crash, pipelines explode, wars break out. Big news events don't just happen nine to five Monday through Friday. The foreign correspondent must be willing to drop everything to pursue the big story, even at personal sacrifice. I once missed a party my wife and I were throwing to celebrate our wedding anniversary because I was covering Central American peace talks. Any foreign correspondent who does not beg to cover the breaking news should go back home and write press releases instead.

Humdrum, however, is also part of the mix. In Mexico, for instance, whenever an American tourist or businessman died – whether drowning in Acapulco, crushed by a bus, or under suspicious circumstances, which was remarkably frequent, given the number of Americans in Mexico – we had to report it for the hometown newspaper. Journalists hunger for overseas postings to write about dramatic events like the government-sponsored death squads murdering nuns in El Salvador, the Contra wars in Nicaragua, assassinations, and airplane crashes, not nuts-and-bolts stories to fill a column in the local daily.

I attended numerous "perp walks" of drug smugglers, traced the roots of a drug lord in Culiacán, and wrote about a bizarre satanic cult that murdered at least two dozen people as ritual sacrifices – some with machetes – and made jewelry from the victim's bones. I covered the Miss Universe pageant in Cancún, where Mexico's contestant was palpably shocked that she lost to Miss Holland. She was obviously accustomed to the privileges of Mexico's elite, where everything can be "fixed" to your satisfaction.

I enjoyed twisting backroads in mountainous Chiapas, the southernmost state bordering Guatemala; ambling through the lively public markets in Oaxaca; and the relaxed atmosphere in Merida, on the Yucatan Peninsula. My memories involve buying tasty warm corn tortillas from a street vendor, riding an antique polished brass-and-wood paneled Pullman rail car to Monterrey, climbing the Teotihuacan pyramid near Mexico City, browsing for crafts in Mexico City's historic San Angel neighborhood, attending the haunting Day of the Dead festivities in Mixquic, and listening to the battle of the horns with lively seven-piece mariachi bands in the somewhat seedy Plaza Garibaldi. That's the first place Mexicans go when returning from the United States and where I went last time I visited there. I play trumpet, poorly, but confess to sometimes fantasizing about joining a mariachi band. And my favorite Mexican expression is *para servirle*, literally "at your service."

The Yucatan Peninsula is chock full of Mexico's finest treasures. There we visited well-preserved Chichen-Itzá, the most extensive Mayan ruins, with dozens of structures still standing, a pyramid, observatory, temple, and a curiously reclining human-like statue called Chac-Mool. At Tulum, we clambered up from the beach in the early morning to deserted ruins atop a rock formation overlooking the Caribbean before they opened for visitors. Snorkeling at Xul-Ha, we marveled at the bright blue angel fish, zebra fish with black and yellow stripes, parrotfish and some strange-looking green fish. We rode bicycles to

Mayan ruins on Isla Mujeres and got caught in a thunderstorm. We found shelter under a straw roof as the fury of the storm was unleashed, whipped by frenzied winds. A taxi took us back to town over puddles so deep they splashed through the rusty holes in the floor that provided natural air-conditioning in our cab.

On days off, we relaxed in towns such as Cuernavaca and Taxco, which spills down steep mountainsides and is surrounded by silver mines, one of the best-preserved colonial towns in Latin America.

One last thing, by the way. While people all over Latin American call us *gringos*, Mexicans have coined their own word to describe their northern neighbors. To them, we are *gabachos*.

Chapter 19

Health Care in the Third World

My wife's father barely survived a close brush with death in one of Brazil's most modern medical facilities after escaping countless hazards in a far more dangerous place. José lived most of his life on the same patch of hardscrabble land in central Brazil, where he grew coffee, sugar cane, corn, bananas, oranges, and tended a small herd of cattle. In those parts, many people die from Chagas' disease or other maladies by middle age. Rattlesnakes and scorpions lurked about the farm, and a bite could prove fatal with no medical treatment nearby.

It took him five painful months to recover from an error during his gastric surgery. He spent his days and nights staring out the window in an apartment my wife rented for his recuperation. On good days, he would walk two blocks to the park and play with our then-infant daughter. But on his bad days, it was a strain for him even to eat, and his conversations revolved around pain and death.

We did not expect him ever to fully recover, but he lived another thirteen years until a heart attack felled him at age seventy-one.

A single glance out the apartment window in crowded São Paulo took in a larger swath of population than inhabits the entire vast, underpopulated region where he lived. City life did not suit him. He did not care for television or noise or traffic. He preferred to feed the chickens and cows, tend his crops, gather firewood, and chat with neighbors. He was an engaging man who easily made friends everywhere he went.

The life Maria struggled years to escape – eventually leading her to become a U.S. citizen – is the only one her father knew and loved. He owned about fifty acres, which put him a step above Brazil's millions of landless peasants. But he spent most of his life without electricity, running water, telephone or access to decent health care.

Millions of poor rural Brazilians flock to São Paulo, Rio de Janeiro, and other cities to seek a better life, but many end up in dangerous slums. The good life for my father-in-law meant hauling water up a steep hill from the stream several times a day or riding a horse for hours to the nearest town without care for all the conveniences we take for granted. He moved away from the simple farmhouse only once briefly and never liked living elsewhere. Even staying in the nearest town to visit his children and grandchildren was a strain; the village of about five thousand residents was too crowded and noisy.

José was gaunt after two operations, the first of which nearly killed him, the second to repair the damage from the first. He withered to a wisp of his former dynamic self, in appearance, energy and spirit. The impish glint disappeared from his eyes and took years to return. His health had decayed for years as Chagas' disease ate away his internal organs. The parasite – the biggest cause of death in rural Brazil – slowly eroded his esophagus, digestive system and heart. The operation was intended to repair some of this damage.

When we lived in Mexico, Maria went to Brazil to take care of her father and get him the medical treatment he needed. She is the take-charge person in her family, the only one with the organizational skills – let alone financial resources – to find an apartment, get a doctor and make the necessary arrangements.

But the surgeon my wife hired turned out to be negligent. He charged us three thousand dollars in physician's fees, delegated the operation to a student and left to play golf. This doctor, a member of the board of directors at São Paulo's best reputed private hospital, appeared to be a good choice. When the surgery was botched and her father nearly died from an infection, Maria was furious to learn from nurses that the physician himself wasn't even present.

Knowing this doctor's wealth could influence a judge, a lawsuit seemed futile.

While angry that a physician's unprofessional attitude had nearly killed this gentle man, we considered ourselves fortunate that he was still alive. If my father-in-law were wealthy, the surgeon would certainly have performed or supervised the operation himself. But because José was a poor farmer, he didn't count in Brazil's social scheme. The doctor – who earned enough money to attend medical conferences in the United States and Europe – apparently considered my father-in-law unworthy of his time or attention, while gladly collecting hefty fees for his services.

We found a way to exact our own justice on this doctor. I called the American Consulate and asked if they kept a referral list for English-speaking physicians. When I found out his name was on the list as a gastric surgeon, I wrote the Consul a detailed letter to make sure that the doctor's name was removed. Obviously, he would not have treated an American executive the same way, but that was not the point. How could the Consulate recommend someone with his dearth of medical ethics?

We were fortunate that my friend Flavio, with whom I had lived several years before, was a practicing physician and was able to arrange a doctor in Brazil's best public hospital to perform the second operation. The night the infection began and José suffered great pain, I took him to the hospital in a taxi while Maria stayed in the apartment with baby Juliana, who was named after her grandmother. I discussed his care with a doctor, who recommended he spend the night under observation. He was placed on a cot in a corridor with dozens of other people. I wanted to stay at his side, but he insisted that I go back to sleep.

All this was such a contrast to the health care my wife and daughter received at New York University Hospital. We were fond of the excellent, caring obstetrician who delivered Juliana. A resident assisted, but our obstetrician supervised every step of the nearly twenty-four-hour-long labor. Both mother and baby left the hospital happy and healthy.

José's whole ordeal cost us a great deal, financially and emotionally. I supported two households for half a year and longed for the company of my wife and daughter. I missed Juliana's first birthday and didn't see her first footsteps which I viewed later on videotape.

This doctor will never know the hardship his negligence cost one of the kindest people I've ever known. Had the surgeon performed the operation as promised, everyone would have gone home much earlier without suffering.

We were fortunate the story had a happy ending. José returned home in good health, and my wife and daughter joined me back in Mexico. Three years later, we were in Brazil on another trip, this time with our son, then seven months old. When he awoke in the middle of the night, Maria and I leaped to action. He cried loudly non-stop, his breathing was difficult, his forehead clammy. Joseph rarely cried except when he was hungry, had soiled diapers or needed to burp. Something clearly was wrong.

But calling medical help wasn't simple like dialing 911. In Maria's hometown there were few telephones at the time. The small local hospital was a mile from the family house up a hill steep enough to give some rough chugging to a San Francisco cable car. And the hospital was not staffed around the clock.

We had rented a car for the twenty-hour drive from São Paulo, where we had arrived from our home in New York. But one of Maria's brothers had borrowed the car to impress his girlfriend and had not returned by two in the morning. Fortunately, another brother-in-law, João, summoned a neighbor to drive us to the hospital. Once there, he walked around the corner to the doctor's house to awaken him.

Dr. José Barbosa arrived soon and led us into his office. It was spare, with none of the modern equipment you see in an American clinic. The clean white walls were bare except for a diploma, a few family pictures and some government posters urging childhood inoculations and how to prevent cholera. There was his desk, examining table and a glass-paneled cabinet containing medicines.

He followed standard procedure. He first listened to Joseph's chest with a stethoscope. Then he took the baby's temperature and examined him.

Most Americans trust a certain level of competence in our physicians that they meet rigorous professional standards. But this graduate of Faculdade de Medicina de Nova Iguaçu, an industrial city outside

Rio de Janeiro, didn't inspire the same confidence as did our family pediatrician, a faculty member of the prestigious New York University School of Medicine. All I knew about this doctor was that he had given Juliana, then three and a half, a health certificate required to swim in the local pool. For the usual five-dollar fee, he spent a minute glancing at her skin.

Years earlier, when a complication prevented Juliana from being born by natural delivery, the NYU team quickly shifted gears. An anesthesiologist came, and a little over an hour later Juliana was born by Caesarean section. Brazil, incidentally, has one of the world's highest rates of Caesarean births, not out of medical necessity, but vanity. Many Brazilian women mistakenly believe that delivering via natural childbirth stretches out their vaginas and renders them unable to please their husbands sexually. Brazilian physicians have tried in vain to set the record straight.

We heard about someone who had a difficult delivery at this same small town hospital where we waited and that the doctor sat on her belly to facilitate birth. I compared the action, which seemed crude, even dangerous, to squeezing the last bit of toothpaste out of a stubborn tube. I had pondered whether my wife and daughter would have survived the rigors of such a delivery if performed in rural Brazil instead of in New York.

I flashed back to José's botched operation a few years earlier. All these thoughts were crammed into my weary mind while anxiously waiting at this doctor's office in the middle of the night, worried about Joseph's weak gasps for air.

The diagnosis was a chest cold, pretty minor by any measure. The doctor administered some medicine and plugged in a vaporizer. Pretty soon, Joseph began coughing up phlegm and his nose started running. While we waited, we discussed differences in medical care and charges. Dr. Barbosa was incredulous to hear that it cost ten thousand dollars to have a baby in New York. He had one of the nicest homes in Virgem da Lapa, an expansive house adorned with colorful tiles and a huge patio. He drove a new car. Yet he probably earned no more than

Brazilians working illegally in the United States as shoeshine boys or parking attendants. His charge for us: thirty thousand cruzeiros, or fourteen dollars. While that may sound ridiculously low, consider that few people in the area even earned the minimum wage of fifty dollars a month.

We left the hospital an hour later, confident that our son was recovering from his first illness. We were grateful that he hadn't become sick at the farmhouse, an hour and a half drive over a rutted road that only a jeep or truck can traverse. There are no health-care services in that little farming village except a doctor who visits about once a month, no phones and no way to summon help. As rudimentary as health care is in Virgem da Lapa, it's nonexistent in the rural areas outside the town.

The next day, the doctor stopped by the house to check on Joseph. How many doctors in the United States have the time or the inclination to do that? The lesson here: the doctor with the prestigious credentials and fancy office did not have the ethics to do his job as promised, while the one with a simple office and ordinary degree performed when it counted, earning my respect.

After moving back to São Paulo two years later, we had no further problems with the medical community. For a pediatrician, a good friend recommended her cousin, who was top notch. For any other specialty we needed, Flavio referred us to friends whom he considered the best of breed, graduates of Brazil's finest medical schools. For an ophthalmologist or sinus specialist, he knew the right person. When I needed a urologist, Flavio's own father-in-law, a kindly traditional family doctor well into his seventies, provided excellent care. Except for one harrowing incident, I would generalize that the medical care we got in Brazil was as good as in the United States. Then again, I had excellent connections that are not available to everyone.

Flavio remained a cherished friend through the years even after I moved back to the United States. He became one of the most renowned sleep disorder specialists in Brazil, authored the definitive manual on the subject in Portuguese, lectured at medical conferences in the United States and Europe, and even appeared several times on Brazil's most-watched late-night talk show hosted by the witty, sarcastic ô Soares. Flavio and I visited each other numerous times and maintained frequent contact via email. At age 51, this doctor who did so much to improve the health and lives of others, succumbed to a massive heart attack after swimming laps, and I lost one of my dearest friends.

Chapter 20

Central America:
The Friendly Ticos

Costa Rica is the only place I have been besides Brazil where the enjoyment of life has reached an art form. The unofficial national motto of *Ticos,* as Costa Ricans call themselves, is *pura vida,* literally "pure life." This defines the *Tico* world view and is widely understood to mean "life is good," "take it as it comes," or even "thanks."

Ticos work hard, but work is not the cornerstone of their lives. Unlike workaholics in developed nations, they love nothing more than getting together with family and friends for meals and parties, where they whack at candy-filled piñatas, bask in the sunshine and enjoy the outdoors in their stunningly beautiful country. Most *Ticos* don't define themselves by their careers or material possessions. Successful people in the capital, San José, have nice homes but don't feel compelled to flaunt their wealth. It is certainly far more egalitarian and less class conscious than anywhere else I have been in Latin America. Citizens are intensely proud to be *Ticos* without being jingoistic or arrogant.

Even though Costa Rica is a developing nation, many consider it a paradise. Some describe it as the Switzerland of Central America, but that is a bit misleading. Costa Rica's GDP per capita is much higher than its peers, but only one-tenth that of Switzerland. Still, wealth is not the only measure of quality of life. For instance, the average life expectancy for *Ticos* is 79 years, a year longer than *norteamericanos.* The informal Happy Planet Index rates Costa Rica first in the world in life expectancy, well-being and environmental criteria, while the

World Database of Happiness rates *Ticos* as the happiest people on the planet. That's no surprise.

Costa Rica, understandably, is one of the most popular places in Latin America for foreign tourists as well as snowbird retirees because the people are friendly, infrastructure is functional, and the rate of violent crime is low. *Ticos*, however, need to make sure they don't let outsiders ruin a good thing. If gringos refuse to adjust to *Tico* ways, they'd better just clear out and not try to remake Costa Rica in their image. *Ticos* seem to have figured out that wealth and power can't buy happiness, so the "Ugly Americans" need not apply.

This nation, the size of Vermont and New Hampshire combined, has a surplus of captivating, diverse scenery: towering volcanic peaks, dense jungles, pristine national parks, playful wildlife, and palm-studded beaches on the Caribbean and Pacific. San José is a modern city on a plateau about three-quarters of a mile high, giving it pleasant weather year round, without temperature extremes. The sultry Caribbean is a couple hours away to the East, while the inviting Pacific is little over an hour to the West. There are no North American-style freeways or European bullet trains to whisk you around the country, but honestly, who wants or needs it?

How did Costa Rica become an enlightened society while its neighbors endured decades of war and strife? President José Figueres disbanded the army in 1948. Instead of catapulting between right-wing military coups and leftist strongmen, Costa Rica has avoided the extremes that have bedeviled its troubled neighbors by pursuing centrist policies. While Central America has wasted decades, billions of dollars, and countless lives fighting civil wars and neighbors, Costa Rica patiently achieved reconciliation. Some may see tiny Costa Rica as inconsequential in world affairs, but it achieved something that eluded the world's biggest powers: ending warfare in Central America. Then-President Oscar Arias won the Nobel Peace Prize in 1987 for brokering lasting peace accords.

Costa Rica earmarks public expenditures for health care, education, and basic infrastructure rather than the military. That has resulted in healthier, better-educated people and less poverty. Although crime has risen in Costa Rica – bars cover windows in San José as well as small towns – it remains far below rates endured by its neighbors. The rate of violent crime has surged in El Salvador and Honduras, committed by gang members, many of them covered head to toe with scary tattoos, who were deported from the United States after serving prison time. These children of undocumented aliens in U.S. cities such as Miami and Los Angeles have no marketable skills, no experience at honest jobs, and no knowledge of life in the home countries they left as youngsters. When dumped back into their homelands, these career criminals don't know how to do anything else.

Higher living standards, as well as strife in neighboring countries, have lured thousands of Hondurans, Salvadorans, and Nicaraguans to live and work in Costa Rica illegally. They blend in easily because they speak the same language and come from a similar culture. *Ticos* note that most shanty town residents are from neighboring countries, the same way Argentines point out that Buenos Aires' slums are inhabited by swarthy-complexioned illegal aliens from neighboring Bolivia and Paraguay. Immigrants from Central American neighbors commit a disproportionate number of crimes in Costa Rica.

For decades, the Caribbean coast was cut off from the rest of Costa Rica, Honduras and Nicaragua by poor transportation and communications. The black English-speaking coastal residents were descendants of Jamaicans and other West Indian islands imported to work on sugar cane and banana plantations. They lived mostly in isolated pockets or on islands, and had little contact with their Spanish-speaking countrymen. Now that highways and modern telecommunications have linked many of those communities to the rest of the country, residents are learning Spanish. Still, not many of them have moved inland, and few highlanders have migrated to the Caribbean coast. Some Caribbean coastal communities still seem like separate countries in terms of language, culture, music, and food.

I have gone three times to Costa Rica, where I stayed with my uncle who retired there. Affable Uncle Jim seemed to not only know everybody in the nation of 4.8 million people, but appeared to have made friends with each one.

Costa Rica is charming, but it is mind-numbing to find your way around. Street signs are scarce, addresses rarely have a normal street name and number, and directions are convoluted. A typical address might be something like "Sr. Don José Brenes, 25 mts. Norte de la Escuela Common y 350 mts. Este de la Plaza de Futbol, La Hermosa del Sol, Perez Zeledon, Costa Rica, America Central." Addresses usually describe the direction and distance from a landmark, even if it no longer exists. This may sound perplexing, but it tells a visitor precisely how far to walk north of the school and east of the soccer field. If you, like most outsiders, get lost with these discombobulated directions, friendly *Ticos* are glad to show you the way. More than once, someone grabbed my hand, or gently took my arm to lead the way.

Driving is a headache with such crazy directions and lack of street signs, confusing even the locals, so I am always happy to ride with someone else in Costa Rica. Our friend Gonzalo, who goes by Chalo, was taking us to the beach when a truck traveling the wrong way on a narrow highway onramp nearly plowed into us; he muttered *cabrón* as he veered. And every time Uncle Jim asked how long it took to get somewhere, he got the standard *Tico* response: "Five minutes," no matter how long it took.

While rice and black beans, usually with some kind of meat, accompany most meals, *Ticos* enjoy a wide variety of food. Fresh fruits and vegetables, fried plantains (a type of banana) and corn tortillas are popular, as is seafood. Watch for pungent *culantro* (similar to coriander), sprinkled on everything. Wherever we went, Uncle Jim said, "No *culantro por favor.*" When hungry or thirsty, you might stumble across a *Soda*, which is not a soft drink but rather a small, family-owned restaurant or lunch counter.

Costa Rica can be unintentionally amusing. For instance, when San José got its first automated carwash, everybody came to marvel as if the circus had rolled into town. *Ticos* were transfixed by the spigots that whooshed water onto the car, the soap that squirted out, the colorful whirling pads that scrubbed off the dirt, the frilly chamois that danced over the car to sop up water, and air jets that dried it. Few *Ticos* can afford a new car, so the practical minded take their family jewel, imported from the streets of Miami, for a manual, family car wash to nearby rivers and streams. Most nations in Latin American have mobile car washes by people who gladly wash cars for a pittance. These unskilled, unemployed workers mysteriously appear while people park their cars, charge to "watch" the car and also offer to wash it from a bucket.

My travels around Costa Rica are always enjoyable. Uncle Jim took me to the rustic Turrialtico lodge in the cool mountains near Turrialba volcano, waterfalls and chirping birds. Wool blankets warmed us at night in a cabin outside Fraijanes, six-thousand feet up in the mountains on the edge of 8,871-foot Poás Volcano. However, the national park, with steam and occasional volcanic eruptions, was closed by a human barrier of rangers out on strike. Years later, I was turned away from another volcano, 11,260-foot Irazú, by Mother Nature, which wrapped the mountaintops with impenetrable fog. Near the Pacific, people stop at the bridge over the Rio Tarcoles to gaze curiously at the *lagartos*, crocodiles who look quite harmless – from a distance – doing exactly what tourists do in Costa Rica: swimming and lazily basking in the sun. Monkeys swing from branches and pilfer food at Punta Leona's beaches, where a gecko tickled as he ran around my bare back while I dined in an open-air restaurant.

Costa Rica had the wisdom to preserve Manuel Antonio beaches in a national park where jungle creeps up to the Pacific shore and agile White-headed Capuchin monkeys frolic. The first time I went in 1985, just a few simple hotels existed, and backpackers slept in tents which were pelted by the skins of fruit discarded by the monkeys. Five years later I returned with Maria and toddler Juliana. In that interval, some monstrosities had been erected, including a cement block hotel, standing as a sore thumb amid the older simple wooden structures. Juliana and I strolled the beach early one morning, watching seabirds and listening to waves, when the ground trembled feverishly beneath our feet. Aware that earthquakes can trigger tsunamis, I grabbed her and ran inland. Fortunately, no killer waves ensued, and the good-natured locals smiled gently and knowingly.

Decades later, I visited for a third time. Juliana was now twenty-five, scores of hotels, most of them expensive, dotted the landscape, and crowds rivaled Yosemite. Costa Rica's crown jewel had lost some of its luster. The monkeys migrated to the heavily touristed areas outside the park. People now must trudge two miles out of their way, past cheesy tourist trap shops and up a steep trail through the jungle – with few benches – before finding a beach. Scant wildlife is visible without binoculars, other than a few electric blue or lavender butterflies nearly the size of my hand. The old entrance was just a couple minutes' walk. This was an unnecessarily tough ordeal for Uncle Jim, now in his late 80s. Near the exit, a sign warns visitors to steer clear of a crocodile-infested pond, yet, a minute later, they are forced to ford a knee-deep stream connected to that same pond.

Nearby we enjoyed tasty meals at El Avión Restaurant, where a Fairchild C-123 serves as a bar. The aircraft was downed in 1986 over Nicaragua while on a clandestine CIA mission to help Contra rebels battle the Sandinista government. The airplane later was shipped to Costa Rica, where it now overlooks the Pacific. There, watching the sun as it was devoured by the Pacific, we toasted Costa Rican independence and neutrality.

I would be remiss to depict Costa Rica as a Shangri-La. There remains too much poverty, ignorance and corruption. While Costa Rica is laid back, it's not an anything-goes kind of place. Even in the 1980s, a female tourist dressed in modest walking shorts could be hooted off the streets by matrons who objected to what they considered improper public attire. Uncle Jim once saw an intoxicated woman accosted by men who pulled up her dress and yanked down her panties. He ran to get a police officer, who refused to intervene because "it was the woman's fault for being drunk."

Even basic necessities like lifeguards at crowded beaches get ignored. In the 1980s, an empty, rusted lifeguard station stood as a silent sentinel near Quepos, the closest town to Manuel Antonio, with no signs warning swimmers of the dangers. The rate of drowning in ferocious riptides was alarming, but authorities always just said the dead swimmers were drunk. The simple fact that *Ticos* worried about drowning more than civil war in the 1980s was a powerful statement about its tranquility: *Ticos* perished in pursuit of pleasure at a time its neighbors were routinely butchered by warfare and political violence. During my latest trip I saw a few signs warning about riptides, but still a lack of lifeguards on public beaches.

As I traveled far and wide in Latin America, I have seen numerous American and English schools, quite a few French schools, and even a German school or two, but Quepos had the strangest one yet: a Korean school.

Even though most *Ticos* are exceedingly friendly and generous, there are a few bad apples. One scam targets absentee property owners, mostly snowbirds from the United States and Canada who visit during winters or less frequently. A *Tico* posing as the property owner conspires with a lawyer to sell the property to a third party who is also part of the plot. Under Costa Rican law, the third party is held harmless and lays claim to title on the property. The unwitting landowner, who may speak little Spanish, is far away and may not discover he's been cheated until it's too late. His only recourse is to prove the first two knowingly took his property, if he can even find them. It's a costly and difficult process, especially from a distance. Since the third party can claim good faith, recovery is a long shot. Absentee owners must take extraordinary steps to prevent being swindled. They need to find a local lawyer and grant power of attorney to obtain a mortgage for a small amount of money since the title on mortgaged property cannot be transferred. Similarly, Uncle Jim was powerless to stop criminals from taking over his cute little beach house, nestled amid swaying palms in Cahuita on a Caribbean beach, after his caretaker died. Throughout Latin America, squatters obtaining title to unoccupied property is a major problem for absentee landowners.

Other unscrupulous *Ticos* operated a prolific Ponzi scheme which bilked thousands of people, many of them foreign residents. Investors with at least ten thousand dollars earned three percent monthly interest, and it paid well for years. The Villalobos brothers operated a legitimate agricultural aviation business, and customers made investment transactions at their modern office in San José. Deposits and withdrawals were entered by hand in a ledger. I went with my uncle, who knew many people who had stuffed money into this "golden goose." Anyone who deposited a hundred thousand dollars, for instance, could live quite well in Costa Rica off the three thousand dollars they collected in monthly tax-free interest without even touching the principal. Word got around, and people were ushered in by trusted friends who raved about the simplicity of their fat profits. The English-speaking brothers were an agreeable pair, as are most con men. After the scheme collapsed in 2002, one brother was sentenced to a long prison term for fraud; the other one is still on the lam. And, this was only the biggest among numerous similar scams. Even today, many people believe that high-level government officials were involved. My uncle's friends lost money in Costa Rica, but I never put my money into something so risky. Instead, I invested in a highly regulated safe haven, the New York Stock Exchange, where I lost even more money in a much worse swindle. Remember Angelo Mozilo and Countrywide during the U.S. stock market crash in the fall of 2008?

That stock market and real estate collapse had a disastrous impact on Costa Rica. Coastal towns are now littered with the unsightly hulks of partly constructed projects abandoned when financing evaporated.

The National Museum in downtown San José occupies an old fortress with bullet holes. It has artifacts from primitive people, as well as various sizes of rock spheres which are found around the country. Their origin remains a mystery. Some are small enough to hold in your hand, while the biggest is eight feet in diameter and weighs twenty tons. Costa Rica, however, lacks enchanting colonial towns and major pre-historic ruins. Such features are more easily found in Guatemala.

The airline ticket agent in Mexico City, when I told him I was flying to Tapachula, in southern Mexico, to visit Guatemala and Costa Rica, responded: "There is nothing to see in Central America. Don't bother to go there." On the first leg of that journey, a baggage handler in Tijuana misplaced my backpack, the same one that got waylaid a couple of years earlier in Lima, so I was unexpectedly stuck overnight in Mexico City instead of only a couple of hours between flights. The following day I flew to Tapachula, minutes from the border. At the Guatemalan border, the guard sent me back to Tapachula to get a visa at the Consulate, where I met one of the most amusing people.

The Consul himself, who worked alone, helped me. He was of Chinese heritage and drove a rusted sixties vintage Chevy with long-expired Illinois license plates that he had purchased while working at the Guatemalan Consulate in Chicago. After stamping the visa in my passport, he drove me back to the border and talked non-stop about life in Chicago, which he loved, compared with messed-up Guatemala.

By this point, I was amused by the slowdowns instead of annoyed. I had been back living in the United States for a few months, helping my parents on the family orchard and job hunting. This was a comparatively short trip lasting just a month to travel around Central America and southern Mexico with Uncle Jim. Until I met the Guatemalan consul, I seemed to have lost the tangled skein that brought me back to myself, to my sense of adventure, my lust for discovering the unknown and viewing the unseen. I needed to get back to the rhythm of the road, the separate reality of dealing with the unforeseen. I realized that it's not the nuisances I like, but overcoming them. There is a certain sense of exhilaration, after thinking you won't be able to get somewhere, to finally somehow arriving anyway.

And what a rhythm of the road it turned out to be! The Guatemalan bus driver raced kamikaze-style along the steep winding highway, as the flat border burst suddenly into jungle-clad hills. This was an old school bus from the United States, seemingly with renegade students driving, and it reminded me of trips through the Andes. The driving was just as perilous, but at least the paved roads were an improvement.

Another bus was pulled over on the highway: the fare collector was face down on the ground with a plastic-wrapped machine gun pointed at him. Our bus just sped by, powerless to help. Had I not been delayed at the border that morning, I likely would have been robbed on that earlier bus instead.

Later we stopped for a bus stalled in front of us, whereupon the passengers got out and pushed the bus uphill. Immediately a flock of vendors swarmed our bus, pouring soft drinks into plastic baggies and selling them to straw-slurping customers.

The bus dropped me off, not at a terminal or station, but in the middle of the city surrounded by Chinese restaurants. Guatemala City was poorly lit at night, reminding me of the former Eastern Bloc in Europe, where houses were illuminated only by a single twenty-watt light bulb.

After finding a room, I went to eat. Through the restaurants flowed a constant stream of beggars, scraps on life's table. Abandoned children ate leftovers from customers' plates. Despite the face of poverty scratched into this city, there was a lively, animated, joyous spirit that I never saw in Mexico in the nearly two years I lived there and numerous visits.

For all its poverty and history of political oppression, Guatemala is still one of the most interesting countries I have ever seen. My uncle and I went to Antigua Guatemala, with a grand white church as well as crumbling ruins of colonial-era buildings knocked down in the 1967 quake. We stayed in a hotel converted from a stately old home and ate in a restaurant sculpted from the ruins left by the temblor. The plaza was squared off by covered sidewalks on all four surrounding streets, and the enchanting town was full of gringo tourists and expatriates.

At Panajuachel, on the shores of Lake Atitlan below a towering volcano, our hotel had an opulent courtyard, overgrown in a rainbow of flowers. The sun set in a bright, glowing orange behind the lake. Wherever you travel, your eyes take a thousand keepsake snapshots of God's wonders and the wonders that beggarly peasants are waiting patiently for God to perform for them.

In front of the church in Chichicastenango, Indians from the mountains, dressed in colorful native costumes, danced and prostrated themselves, seemingly mesmerized by the sweet incense permeating the marketplace. Children stole fruits and vegetables spread out on blankets alongside wooden coffins. Not in need of a casket at the time, I selected an authentic old wooden mask, the kind worn during Carnival. I also bought a colorful woven square collar – sewn onto dresses worn by tiny women with round faces – to use as a picture frame.

Guatemalan men wore straw cowboy hats and finely embroidered shirts. At an outdoor bus station in Los Encuentros, a sign warned people not to relieve their bodily fluids outside.

We rode to the Mayan ruins of Tikal aboard a bus on which the collector, agile as a spider monkey, clambered up and down the roof to collect fares from passengers seated on top amid crates of chickens, ducks, rabbits, songbirds, and not a few children as the bus slid through mountain roads; he then shimmied in a window or lumbered through the back door. He assured us that we needn't worry about the youngsters; they were tied down on the roof.

Plowing through the jungle, we saw little more than dense vines and an occasional quetzal – Guatemala's resplendent green-and-red national bird with a fluttering tail triple the size of its body – until Tikal's crumbling pyramids began to poke through the thick foliage in the distance. The pyramids, some built hundreds of years BC, appeared dramatically amid the overgrown green vegetation, where colorful long-billed toucans flew, lizards scampered, and monkeys littered the ground with leftover skin and seeds after munching the fruit they grab in trees. We learned the test for clay artifacts: if authentic, water beads up; if imitation, it immediately soaks up liquid.

The great ruins of Tikal were open at night only once a month, during full moon, which gave us the opportunity to gaze at the moon rising and bathing the ancient pyramids in an enchanting shimmering light.

Leaving Tikal, we crossed from Guatemala into Belize. The capital, Belmopan, was an ungainly clump of cement slab buildings plopped down in the jungle. Down the road a bit farther was uncrowded Belize City, a coastal town sliced by canals and houses on stilts to survive hurricanes. When the British turned liberty-loving Belize back to its original citizens, they took everything British that wasn't nailed down. Now you have to ask a drug seller to make room for you at a restaurant table, if he is inclined to move over. To get away, we rode a boat to one of the islands, Cayo Ambergris, skimming over water only six feet deep in some places and watching bright coral beds through translucent aquamarine water. Next, we headed to Mexico.

I haven't forgotten poor Honduras. I flew into the capital, Tegucigalpa, called *Tay-goose* by locals. Rather than a big, spidery city with tentacles spread outward, it resembled a collection of adjacent small villages which have slowly filled in the gaps and merged into a single spread-out, but unspectacular, small town. From there, I traveled with colleagues overland to Tela, on the Caribbean, for a Central American peace conference to end the rampant violence in El Salvador, Nicaragua, and Guatemala. Costa Rica's President Arias, with his putty-like face and droopy ears, resembles a cartoon caricature. He arm-wrestled his neighbors to stop aiding insurgents in each others' countries, which forced governments to negotiate longstanding grievances with their armed opponents. I asked Sandinista leader Daniel Ortega about political prisoners. He jabbed his forefinger repeatedly and forcefully into my breastbone to emphasize, "There are no political prisoners in Nicaragua. None." I couldn't help but wonder how safe I would have been if pressing these same tough questions about his revolution back in Nicaragua instead of Honduras. In fact, all the nations at that conference, led by right-wing or left-wing regimes, held political prisoners, with the lone exception of democratic, centrist Costa Rica.

Chapter 21

The Illegal Alien, Part II

I had crossed into Brazil illegally, albeit accidentally, the first time I entered the country (Chapter 11). A decade later, I was doing it again. My job as Dow Jones bureau chief consumed long hours. I frequently started work at seven in the morning and often was still working at midnight. The government would release important data before dawn or announce the firing of a Cabinet minister long after midnight. My employer was not a newspaper with a once-daily deadline for all the news that's fit to print. Instead, I worked for a wire service that put out news twenty-four hours a day around the globe. When the rest of us are sleeping, it is morning in Asia, and the news there is active. It was my job to not only to report events that happened at any hour, but to get it before my competitors knew.

I was not alone in this effort. I supervised correspondents in São Paulo, Rio de Janeiro and Brasília. They all had standing instructions to call me at home any hour if the news warranted; I was rarely awakened unjustifiably.

Occupied with my work, I forgot to renew my visa. This came to my attention through our cantankerous landlady. When Brazil adopted a new monetary plan to end years of hyperinflation, the government specified how to convert the old money into the new currency. Detailed tables showed how to adjust rents, pensions, taxes and everything else. We used a government-issued chart to convert our rent, but the landlady arbitrarily and unilaterally decided to quintuple our rent in dollar terms, and took us to court when we disagreed. Her lawyer sent a letter to our lawyer saying that I was in the country illegally and this could have bearing on my legal standing.

I was baffled by her statement, but my lawyer suggested that I look at my passport. Sure enough, when I checked, my visa had expired a month earlier. How on earth had my landlady or her lawyer gotten this confidential information? In any event, it put me in a bind. I had to get legal again as soon as possible. If I had to leave the country for some unexpected reason, I would not get back in because my visa had expired. And part of being a foreign correspondent is to expect the unexpected.

Because bureaucracy can be burdensome, Brazil's Foreign Ministry had a full-time official in charge of overseeing foreign correspondents so they were able to do their jobs. It is quintessentially Brazilian to make outsiders feel welcome, whether on a brief visit or as incoming immigrants.

I phoned my Foreign Ministry handler, who informed me that renewal was more complicated than I expected. Had I renewed the visa before it expired, it would have been a no-brainer, but expiration required that I renew it outside Brazil. I imagined the time and expense of flying back to the United States for something as silly as this. He had a much easier solution. I could take a short trip to a bordering country and get my documents there. The closest was Paraguay, where I had first entered Brazil twelve years earlier, a simple sixteen-hour bus ride from São Paulo. We set a date for the following Monday because it would involve the least time missed from work.

The Foreign Ministry sent my visa documentation to the Brazilian Consulate in Ciudad del Este, the new name for Ciudad Stroessner after the dictator was toppled, just over the border from Iguaçu Falls. All I had to do was show up with my passport.

I don't sleep well on airplanes, trains or buses. Noise, light, and the inability to lie down make me uncomfortable. Brazil has a great alternative for long-distance bus riders called the *leito* (berth), a first-class bus in every sense of the word. There are only half as many seats to provide more room for backs to decline, and tickets, accordingly, cost double the standard fare. During my bargain basement traveling days I had never been on one. But times were different. I was earning good money, which made me rich compared with the vast majority of Brazilians.

Paying a hundred dollars for a round-trip ticket instead of fifty dollars was worth it to be able to sleep, especially considering that I would spend two consecutive nights on a bus. Not only were the seats comfortable, there was a hostess like on an airplane. She brought passengers a beer, soda or snack whenever they wanted. At night, the lights were out and it seemed that everybody but the driver slept. There was none of the loud music or mindless chatter that I had endured on cheapo bus and train rides.

My bus left São Paulo on Sunday mid-afternoon and got us to the border by Monday morning. I had to get stamped out of Brazil and into Paraguay to show that I was legally outside of Brazil, even if it was just a few blocks away. In fact, I arrived before the consulate opened, so I got in line outside. Once inside I was given the royal treatment and dealt with the consul herself. I only had to fill out some forms, show my passport, pay the fee and get the new visa stamped in my passport. I was done in less than an hour.

In fact, I finished too early. I left the consulate by ten, and the first bus back to São Paulo would not leave for another five hours. That would get me home about seven the next morning. It left me with five hours to kill. That was not enough time to go to the falls and see anything. So, I wandered around Ciudad del Este.

I marveled at the sharp contrasts between Brazil and Paraguay. While living in Brazil, I compared life to the United States, not worse-off neighbors. I tired of the chaos, poverty, crime, and indifference to it all in Brazil. But from here, across the bridge from Foz de Iguaçu, Brazil looked neat and tidy by comparison. Ciudad del Este is a big open-air bazaar with lots of Arab merchants, and seemingly, anything goes. Brazilian authorities say that most of the cars stolen in Brazil end up in Paraguay with phony registration documents obtained by bribery.

Ciudad del Este had grown beyond the sleepy little burg I remembered a dozen years earlier. More streets were paved; more shops now had glass windows. It seemed that everything cost less than in Brazil and almost everything was imported, mainly from Asia. Brazil was starting to get cheap imports from China and Korea, but most items were still made in Brazil when I lived there. That has changed rapidly in the intervening years, with Brazil opening the floodgates to imports.

Brazilians went to Paraguay to buy goodies that were either unavailable or much more expensive at home. Buses were full of border runners called *sacoleiros,* or bagmen. People made a living buying DVD players or laptop computers in Paraguay and selling them at a profit in Brazil. Paraguayan shops sported signs reading, *Fala-se Portugûes* (Portuguese spoken).

After returning from this trip, I learned that bandits hijacked buses late at night coming from Paraguay, this exact route, knowing that passengers were carrying either contraband or cash. The assailants dressed nicely, looking like any other middle-class passenger; they bought tickets, then pulled a pistol on the driver in a dark, deserted spot. Their gun-toting confederates waiting at the appointed place would swarm the bus once it stopped. Luckily, this did not happen to me, but I had run this risk unknowingly.

Between Paraguay and São Paulo is mostly rolling green hills and bright copper-red soil. My life sure had changed from the days when I rode on the back of trucks and endured a fine film of choking dust everywhere: my teeth, eyes, ears, every crease in my clothing, socks and even a residue coating each pocket. Now I watched Brazil roll by from my bourgeois cushioned seat on this air conditioned bus with a clean bathroom. It struck me that finally, I had truly *arrived.*

The bus got in early enough for me to ride a subway home, shower and get to work on time, refreshed after a good night's sleep, and a legal resident of Brazil once again.

Chapter 22

Voodoo Economics

Many Americans remember the nightmare when inflation in the late seventies and early eighties shot up to double digits. Sky-high interest rates made it prohibitive to buy a house or finance a car. Unemployment was on a rampage. Americans did not know how to react because they had not experienced that level of inflation for generations. Economic malaise labeled "stagflation" largely explains why neither Gerald Ford nor Jimmy Carter won a second term as president.

What would Americans have done if instead of 13.5 percent, inflation was four digits? In the 1980s, numerous Latin American nations suffered from hyperinflation. Among the worst was in Brazil, where it topped out at more than two thousand percent (some calculate it above five thousand percent) in 1993.

The most immediate impact of runaway inflation is that people do not hold onto money, which means that stores often carry no change for customers. Nobody squirrels cash under a mattress. They spend their paycheck as soon as they get it. If not, inflation erodes it daily, unevenly and unpredictably. Prices didn't increase by a few percent a day. They would suddenly shoot up fifty percent, or even double.

How did people cope with such chaotic, unpredictable conditions? In Brazil, everything was indexed. Prices of cars, interest rates, salaries, bus fares, rent, and everything else was adjusted according to complicated charts devised by government economists. These tables were printed in newspapers and posted on walls in offices and businesses.

This forced people to seek anything with real value: dollars or some tangible item. The wealthy speculated in real estate, invested in the lucrative, high-interest "overnight" financial markets, and stashed assets outside the country. Middle-class people with less disposable income bought jewelry and vehicles. In fact, when I met my wife, she sold jewelry as a sideline. Others devised desperate schemes such as buying cars, only to sell them a few months later. When I was car hunting, it got too complicated having to compete with speculators for a decent used car. In the end, it was easier just to buy a brand new "popular car," a little thousand-cc Fiat that was peppy, easy to park and got great mileage. One odd investment was a telephone line. Before telephone privatization, there was a chronic shortage of phone lines and long waiting lists, so a phone line was worth thousands of dollars and was a solid investment. Brazil had stockbrokers, real estate brokers, and .... phone line brokerages.

Even though high interest rates compensated for inflation, people didn't trust banks after the government froze bank accounts under one disastrous economic plan. If you can't get your money when you need it, a savings account becomes worthless.

Dollars were secure because the exchange rate was readjusted daily. On Monday, I might get two thousand cruzeiros to the dollar, on Tuesday two thousand fifty per dollar and by Friday it may be two thousand two hundred. This made for a speculation game to get the best exchange rates for dollars, hopefully right before prices go up. There was no way of knowing when the item you want would sport a higher price tag. Let's say you are buying rolls of film. If you wait a couple more days, you will get more cruzeiros for your dollars, but you also run the risk of the film prices doubling. That meant you usually changed small amounts of money at a time so you would not lose to inflation and forced nerve-wracking snap decisions about purchases.

For a traveler it got even more complicated because outside the major cities or heavily touristed areas, money changers become scarce, and the exchange rate was abysmal. In big cities, there was a thriving black market because people were limited in the amount of dollars they could legally buy at banks at the "official rate" for an overseas trip. Brazilian travelers had to buy additional dollars because they could not exchange their local currency in any other country. Middle-class people bought dollars as a safeguard. Even if they sold the dollars back a few weeks later, at least they were protected from inflation. Most people in small towns did not have this luxury. When I traveled into the hinterlands, I often changed enough money to last me weeks, so I lost to inflation.

Argentina and Bolivia suffered the same woes as Brazil. At one point, the largest bill in circulation in Bolivia was worth about a nickel. If you exchanged a hundred dollars, it required a grocery sack full of banknotes and panicked memories of the Weimar Republic.

The biggest banknote I ever held in my hands was a million pesos in Argentina, at the time worth about ten dollars. Most countries erase zeros long before they tackle the root causes of inflation. Argentina, Brazil and Bolivia, for instance, lopped off multiple zeros and renamed the currency. Argentina decreed that a million pesos would become equal to one "new peso" at the equivalent of one dollar. Of course, that new peso's value began to erode as soon as it entered circulation.

For years, Brazil lurched back and forth from cruzeiros to cruzados to "new" versions of those currencies. After numerous failed plans, the government finally vanquished inflation in the mid-nineties. President Itamar Franco appointed Foreign Minister Fernando Henrique Cardoso as finance minister. The Sarbonne-educated sociologist was not an economist, but he shanghaied the sharpest brains among Brazil's economic elite, many of them educated in the United States and Europe, and equipped them with ammunition to go gunning for inflation. It worked. For the first time in a generation, Brazilians could count on price stability. No longer did they need to adjust prices all the time. The success of the "real plan" was so popular that it propelled Cardoso into the presidency in 1994. And, even after his two four-year terms were up, his successor, leftist and former union leader Luiz Inácio Lula da Silva, maintained much of the economic structure put in place by Cardoso and held inflation to single digits since then.

That same currency, the real, has now lasted two decades. That made things much easier for everyone except foreigners, whose hard currencies no longer had speculative value, and Brazil became much more expensive for them. It's great for Brazilians, whose overvalued real buys a lot of dollars, euros or pounds, and travel to North America and Europe on the cheap. When my wife and I went to Paris a few years ago, we ran into more Brazilians than Americans.

Some strange economic distortions accompanied the death of inflation. Prices for goods stabilized, and many declined, as imports competed with locally made products. But the price for services, which could not be imported and were not subject to government guidelines doubled, tripled, or quadrupled overnight. Suddenly, it cost a whole lot more to get your hair cut, hire a mechanic, consult a barrister, or see a doctor. Jaded landlords left rental properties vacant as they took a wait-and-see attitude. Only existing rental contracts were subject to the official conversion formula, while the scarcity of available apartments caused rents to skyrocket. Many landlords demanded three thousand dollars a month for apartments that would have rented for a fraction of that price in dollar terms a few months earlier. In some sort of perverse backwards Latin logic, some landlords thought they would lose money to rent for less than the price they demanded while believing they were making money by allowing their property to sit vacant.

One result of economic disorder is labor unrest. It seems that some workers somewhere in Latin America are *always* on strike. In Brazil, the oil workers had been out for a month in June 1995, and fuel supplies were dwindling. Following a rumor that President Franco was negotiating a settlement, my colleague Stan and I learned the president was in his hometown, Juiz da Fora. We called directory assistance and got numbers for the best hotels and restaurants in that lovely colonial city. When I reached the right restaurant, I requested the union boss by name. They took the phone to his table, where he confirmed that the strike was ending. When I asked for details, he responded, "If you'd excuse me *senhor*, I'm having lunch with the *presidente* now." It took many hours before any rival could match this scoop, one of my best and most memorable ever.

On another occasion, I covered a speech by Finance Minister Pedro Malan, a brilliant economist who received his Ph.D. at Cal-Berkeley. When I learned that Malan had barred the press from entering, I broke away from the herd and sought a way inside. I sneaked in a side door to the ballroom but was spotted by a Malan toadie and escorted out. Undaunted, I then found an air shaft where I could listen to the speech, albeit faintly. As Malan spoke, it became obvious why he did not want pesky journalists to listen: he told the audience of business executives the direct opposite of many statements he had been making in public.

Over the years, in different countries and varying economic conditions, I both won and lost money from inflation. In Venezuela, I got whiplashed by unexpected chaos in the economy and lost one thousand three-hundred dollars as a result. Considering that my entire budget to travel around the world in two years was ten thousand dollars, thirteen percent of my grubstake evaporated overnight.

During my two years in Caracas, the official exchange rate never wavered from 4.3 bolivars per dollar. There was no black market because the government let its free-spending, profligate citizens buy as many dollars as they wanted to waste. Wealthy Venezuelans exploited the proximity to Miami, where they filled their suitcases with every latest gadget. The local saying in Venezuela was, "It's so cheap, buy two." And so they did. They also bought condos and lived like royalty in Florida, thanks to a ridiculously overvalued bolivar. The currency was tied to the petro-dollar, so this major oil producer could afford to keep its own money artificially high for years.

But economies and currencies that rise with oil prices inevitably fall when oil prices collapse.

That's what happened in 1983 on "black Friday," when the government allowed the bolivar to float. But instead of floating, it sank to Davy Jones' Locker. Overnight, it cost Venezuelans thirteen bolivars to buy a dollar instead of 4.3.

For people with dollars in their pockets, devaluation is a godsend. But for Venezuelans buying dollars with their suddenly cheapened bolivars, it was misery. While living in Caracas, I moonlighted for the British Chamber of Commerce. I spent my free time for a couple of months editing their annual yearbook for an agreed-upon price of five-thousand five-hundred bolivars, knowing that was 1,280 dollars and would support me on the road for a couple of months. The only hitch was that the chamber was short cash upon my departure in December, so they were supposed to wire me the money later. The chamber waited and waited, and by the time I got my money the devaluation wiped me out. I finally got 425 dollars, so I lost more than 850 dollars in that devaluation. I returned to Venezuela a year later and argued my case with the chamber leaders, to no avail. The chamber president simply said that everybody had lost in one way or the other by the devaluation.

The same thing happened when I worked for Exxon. I wrote a biweekly newsletter for them for which they owed me eight hundred dollars when I left Venezuela. My roommate, Jean-François agreed to pick up my last check. Instead, they dragged their feet. By the time they paid me, that same amount in bolivars was worth only 265 dollars. Jean-François said that everyone with deep pockets in Venezuela pulled this same trick and got their own money out of the country before the devaluation. Then they brought their dollars back after the devaluation and paid debts.

Even outside of major events like devaluations, dealing with foreign currencies was complicated. When I lived and traveled in Latin America, I changed money often. I learned quickly that a bank is usually the worst place to exchange currency. They often pay the lowest rates and tack on fees. As well, banks operate at the official rate, so if there is a "parallel" or black market rate, you can do better elsewhere.

If not banks where to go? Black market operators were common all over the region, usually in nondescript offices. Otherwise, travel agencies typically were good source, or could recommend a black market dealer. Travel agencies needed dollars to sell to local residents planning a trip. In smaller towns without travel agencies, jewelry shops might buy dollars. It made sense. In unstable economies, people without foreign bank accounts often invest in precious metals, gold and silver, which withstand inflationary pressures.

At border crossings, money changers usually roamed the streets trading currencies. When Bolivia suffered from hyperinflation, it seemed that every shop and street vendor in La Paz was also trading dollars, not to get rich, but simply to survive. A year later I was in Bolivia again. The economy had stabilized somewhat, and the price of everything cost more than double in dollar terms because the black market had abated.

My strangest experience exchanging dollars was with a money changer at a funeral parlor in Salvador, Brazil. Along with the coffins for sale, prostitutes who worked the plaza outside sat among the stiffs catching up on the soap operas as they sucked away on their cancer sticks.

Chapter 23

Happy Birthday
is Serious Business

Brazil is the only place I've been where people take their birthday cards and greetings seriously. I mean, *really* seriously.

Most Americans tread lightly with regards to birthday cards, almost as an afterthought. When we shop for a card, we might spend five or ten minutes perusing the card rack to find one that closely approximates our feelings, mood or personality and those of the recipient: usually funny, serious or spiritual. Also age appropriate. The card with flowers we send to grandma is different from the one with cartoon characters, animals or balloons we pick out for a child. But few people give much thought to the dime store greeting written on the card, unless it is funny or extremely clever, which is a rarity. The card has visual impact, a brief and warm or perhaps funny message to the recipient, but overall something to pass over quickly on the way to a present. If there is no present, it is just a pleasant reminder that "I'm thinking about you" and not much more, something like a quick shot of whiskey that briefly warms the cockles on a cold night.

In Brazil, on the other hand, a birthday card is something to be savored, like elegant crystal holding fine brandy. Swish around the snifter, whiff its bouquet, take a sip, a tiny amount, and slosh it around your mouth before you finally swallow. Nothing like gulping a shot of whiskey.

A Brazilian who receives a birthday card will first look it over, appreciate the cover drawing or photograph, then open it up and read slowly, savoring each word, letting the cadence roll over his or her tongue and consider the meaning of each word. It might be dime store philosophy to many people, but Brazilians take it seriously.

But that's not all. The card doesn't come close to the effusive, occasionally eloquent, birthday message delivered in person. Spoken in the ornate, flowery language of a crooner delivering a love song, a typical greeting might go something like this: "I wish you the greatest birthday, I wish you peace, I wish you success and prosperity, I wish you love and harmony." It might go on for five minutes with everything the friend or relative is feeling and wishing to the celebrant. It's almost a eulogy that you get to hear while you are still alive, a sincere moment of communion between two people.

It all boils down to culture. I don't know the roots, if it was a tradition brought over by the Portuguese or a home-grown custom that sprouted in the New World. It is an essentially Brazilian form of interpersonal intimacy. To an American accustomed to a simple and cheerful "Happy Birthday" greeting, it might seem overblown, saccharine and perhaps even pretentious. But it assuredly is not. It is a very soulful experience in which the giver of the message connects to the recipient on an emotional level, and they share these warm sentiments together. It makes the birthday truly a special day for everyone involved.

Think of it from another perspective. To someone who is accustomed to such flowery sentimental expressions, a simple "Happy Birthday," while it may be heartfelt and genuine, comes across as coldly blunt and unsentimental, the identical two-word greeting given to a near-stranger or to a spouse of half a century. Short and sweet or *curto e grosso?*

I have heard the "Happy Birthday" song in various countries. In Mexico, it is not even the same tune Americans know. Instead, Mexicans sing *Mañanitas,* or "little mornings," in a flat, tedious and almost mournful tune. Then again, maybe birthdays should serve as a sorrowful reminder that they come in finite numbers.

Brazilians sing *Parabéns Pra Você* (Happy Birthday) to the same tune as Americans, but in a much more lively, festive way. Accompanied by hand clapping, the song is repeated several times, each time faster han before. Partygoers might poke fun of the celebrant or speculate on future romances before ending with loud cheers.

Any Brazilian who can afford it celebrates a child's birthday at "party salons," with brightly colored rooms and entertainers (and no cleanup mess). The first birthday is a major event that often involves formal clothing even though the child is too young to know what's going on. For an adult's birthday, they usually throw a bash for the whole neighborhood, along with every friend, relative and work colleague. It's easy to guarantee a big showing because guests flock to the open bar, stocked with liquor, liqueurs, wine and beer.

Birthday parties aren't segregated events just for kids, or adults only. Anyone who puts on a party for a child assumes that parents will also attend, so they buy booze and food for the whole gang and assorted hangers on. This was difficult for me because I drop off my children at birthday parties and have no interest in staying. I also found it offensive that the parent of a playmate would use my child's birthday as an excuse to get drunk, on my dime. However, in Brazil, you have to realize that everybody is invited: family, lifelong intimate friends, and maybe even the new acquaintance just met on the way to the party.

Brazilian get-togethers expose the wide gulf in the concept of extended family in Latin America compared with North America. Most Latins would argue that Americans tend to be cold, individualistic and overly obsessed with privacy.

My wife complains that our children are too "Americanized," meaning that they spend their free hours with peers instead of with us. I understand that is part of the socialization process as they become gradually more independent and did the same thing at their age. When I am in Brazil or elsewhere in Latin America, I see teenagers hanging out at parks, fast-food restaurants, malls, and movie theaters with other teens, in other words, doing the exact same things their American counterparts do.

My wife may not realize it, but she appears to be talking about degrees, the amount of time youth spend with friends versus family.

In the United States, Italians and Greeks, for instance, are known for big family shindigs that include cousins, aunts, uncles and anybody faintly related. Welcome to *My Big Fat Greek Wedding* in Latin America.

Especially in Brazil, I found that I had little free time to myself because of the togetherness of life there. People think nothing of dropping in unannounced, be it friend, family or neighbor. You see a neighbor on the street or at the corner grocery and they want to chat or invite you for a beer. Similarly, on the road I often had company. I always carry a book or magazine while traveling, enjoy the scenery, and don't socialize so I don't get stuck with no escape listening to a know-it-all Cliff Claven windbag. In Brazil, that level of privacy is almost impossible. Someone nearby will usually start up a conversation, and once they spot an accent, will have a dozen questions about your life and background. That can be both a blessing and a curse. While it is heartening to be in such friendly surroundings, it is much more diffi-cult to read if that is your preference. But how can you fault people for being naturally friendly, courteous and curious? There might be an invitation to share a beer or *cafezinho*. As well, it's easy to make friends on the road and get invitations to visit when you are in someone's home town. These are authentic invitations; they really are happy to see you when you show up on their doorstep. Time and again, I was invited to a party, beach excursion, or some other enjoyable activity. There is always room for one more. In Brazil, nobody is excluded, unless, of course, they belong to a lower social class.

But the friendliness is accompanied by harsh judgment. Brazilians are prone to criticizing an acquaintance's wardrobe or hairstyle as *cafona* (gauche), comment on his *suvaco* (literally armpit, but meaning body odor), *bafo* (bad breath), or *chulé* (smelly feet). If your appear-ance or mannerisms fall short, you might be labeled *caipira* (hick). And, God help you if you accidentally fart – which will earn you the malodorous fame of *peidorreiro* – or need to blow your nose in some-one's presence, especially if they are eating. Such unwelcome com-mentary is called *palpite*. Because Brazilians seem almost obsessive about appearance, it's baffling to understand how they admire France, where less attention is paid to bathing, or vice-versa, how the French could enjoy a place that puts such a high value on personal hygiene.

Brazil is the only place I ever saw where strangers were treated almost as family. The lines are blurred between family, long-time intimate friends, and casual acquaintances. They even have a word, *concunhado*, for your sister-in-law's husband, who is considered a relative in Brazil's extended family. While they spend a lot of time with family, get-togethers are often chaotic and frequently the scene of strife. It sometimes seems that Brazilian families gather to argue over petty matters rather than revel in harmony. Brazilians who live in the United States complain Americans are superficial and mask the deep disagreements to maintain a semblance of family harmony, unless they are dysfunctional and that is the only way they can communicate.

Brazil is less segregated by age. Several generations often live under one roof due to economic necessity. Grandma doesn't play cards just with other senior citizens. Junior doesn't play soccer only with other kids his age. In this social setting, people have a greater sense of belonging because they are part of the wider group. You see fewer solitary people anywhere. Someone without family will be invited to spend time with neighbors, in small villages or big cities. Children who lose parents are taken in without hesitation by distant relatives or friends, with or without formal adoption. A metropolis in Brazil is not as anonymous and alienating as its American counterpart. People get out into the streets on foot and circulate, walk around town with no particular destination, something my grandfather complained was lost from his youth when he saw Americans barricade themselves behind their doors and plant themselves in front of their televisions.

When I visited my friend Flavio for the first time in São Paulo, I intended to stay just a weekend and head off to Rio on Monday. But I kept meeting people who invited me to stick around a few more days to do something with them. The days rolled into weeks and months. I left and came back numerous times. There was just too much to keep me there, especially a girlfriend, who eventually became my wife.

Chapter 24

Preta: A Bird's Eye View of Complicated Race Relations

Shortly after my family moved to São Paulo in 1993, Preta came to stay with us as a live-in maid and nanny. She was of pure African descent, not lighter-skinned mixed race like many blacks in the United States or *morenas* in Brazil. She was eighteen and walked with a limp from a polio attack as a child. One leg was longer and more muscular than the other, so she walked on the toes of one foot to compensate. She was simple, pleasant and humble, with only a grade-school education, a shy smile and easy manner. She had street smarts and was not stupid. I did not care how well she cooked or how clean she kept the apartment. My main concern was her reliability. Could we trust her with our young children? I worked long hours, saw too little of them and needed to be sure they were protected under her wing.

Her nickname bothered me, and I told her that the first time I met her. Her name was Maria Isabel, but everyone called her Preta, literally "black." Having supported civil rights struggles during my youth in the turbulent sixties, when as a ten-year-old I challenged adult racist neighbors who said "give 'em an inch and they take a mile," it was offensive to nickname someone "black." But it's just a cultural thing in Brazil, where people are often given a nickname to describe the shade of their skin or even a disfigurement. I once ate at a restaurant called *Raimundo Sem Braço*, literally "One-Armed Raymond," the owner's nickname. In college, I was given the nickname "zoomer" because I was a go-getter who zoomed from one place to another in the age of laid-back hippiedom, but the label never offended me because it was a hundred percent accurate. I still am a zoomer.

Maria had brought Preta back from Araçuaí, near her own home town. Hiring her was a smart move because she had worked in the home of an extended relative. Many people in São Paulo are suspicious of household help for fear of crime. Consider the ingredients: an impoverished background; miserable salary; access to a household with money, jewelry or other valuables; knowledge of when the family will be home or away; intimate coexistence with an enviable lifestyle out of reach; and lingering resentments about shabby treatment. Many are treated like second-class citizens. Some people keep servants locked in their apartments when they are away so they can't steal (locks in Brazil require keys inside and out). That also means the servant has no escape in case of emergency, and newspapers have carried grisly stories about maids who perished in fires while locked inside.

Preta could not steal from us because a sister-in-law knew her family. If she did something wrong, we would know where to find her. I felt safe with this arrangement. I worried little about the theft of money or valuables (I had little of either). My overriding concern was the safety of our family in a high-crime city. If there was a kidnapping or violence against a family, hired help was often involved. I dreaded something like this because to a slum dweller, we must have seemed like Bill Gates by comparison. Someone could snatch one of the kids and make outrageous demands we could never meet and as a result they might be harmed or killed. It was not an unreasonable fear, knowing the violent crime rate in major Brazilian cities and the frequency of kidnapping for ransom, with the victims often turning up dead or never found, whether or not ransom was paid.

Nearly everyone in the middle class had an *empregada*, or maid, but only families with young children had a *babá*, or nanny. What distinguished us from the wealthy is that we had only one person who filled both roles. Those better off than we were had an *empregada* and a *babá*, as well as a *motorista* to drive them around.

Preta worked six days a week, often twelve hours a day, and earned about fifty dollars a month, the minimum wage at the time. Like most servants, she got free room and board. Nearly all apartments and houses in Brazil have a maid's room the size of a closet, big enough for a narrow cot and not much else. She hung clothes on the wall and had shelves for her few other belongings. Her room – next to the laundry area behind the kitchen – did not have an outside window. Her cramped bathroom lacked a separate shower stall; the shower spigot was simply overhead in the bathroom, next to the toilet. It reminded me of the tiny bathrooms in motor homes or boats; some of the cheap hotels where I stayed during my traveling days had this same configuration.

Room and board was necessary because it would be difficult to live on a maid's meager earnings. I encouraged her to save money for the future, since she had few expenses. My reaction was probably typical of an American living in Latin America because most people from my middle-class background are not accustomed to full-time hired help. For that reason, my countrymen usually are a bit embarrassed by having a maid and end up treating her much better than do locals who grew up with servants. My own wife thought I was far too lax with Preta and that this would make her lazy and arrogant.

Some Brazilian friends confessed that their first sexual experience came at puberty with the maid who lived and worked in their home. It makes sense when you consider: servants do as they are told, have little opportunity to meet suitors because they work long hours and don't get out much, most are young single women, and there are opportunities when nobody is home other than the lonely servant girl and a hormone-charged teenage boy.

A naive impoverished girl could see the boy as her meal ticket. She might fantasize that if she married him, it would allow her to live this enviable life she watches every day from the periphery. This same notion also leads to affairs between the man of the house and the maid. Confession of such transgressions to the lady of the house would almost certainly result in dismissal. Variations on this scenario, in fact, are a common theme in the sizzling nightly *novelas*, or soap operas, that people from all social classes watch. A typical hackneyed formula involves a kindhearted, beautiful but naive young maid; a shrewish housewife; and a husband who seeks companionship with a woman who "understands" him.

If a maid gets pregnant, abortions are illegal in Brazil and most of Latin America. Qualified doctors, however, are willing to bend the rules if they are paid well enough by a family with means. Poor girls who seek abortions on their own throw themselves down stairs, squirt soft drinks into their vaginas or tell someone to kick them in the uterus. If that doesn't work, they might pay someone in their neighborhood with no medical training who moonlights as an abortionist. Death rates from botched illegal abortions are frighteningly high in Latin America.

I never had an affair with Preta or any other household help during all my years in Latin America. Luckily, my son was too young for such dalliances. He was in diapers when we moved to Brazil and a kindergartner when we returned to the United States.

From my viewpoint, we treated Preta quite well. We took her to the beach and let her eat the same food we did. Many families give servants only rice and beans and would rather throw away leftover meat or vegetables than to let the hired help eat it, so as not to "spoil" them. Preta had many reasons to feel envious. When we went somewhere, she had the chance to ride in a car rather than an overcrowded bus. But, with her income, she could never afford to buy one. She walked our kids to ballet and swimming lessons, another taste of a life she had never seen before and could not afford. She walked them to get their ride to a private school her children would never attend.

Most people think it would be great to have servants and be freed from washing dishes, doing laundry and cleaning the bathroom. I agree, but another consideration is privacy. The servant has little privacy because she inhabits a cubicle the size of a jail cell. But this person has access to the whole house, so neither does the *patrão* have privacy. A servant is well aware of the dynamics in a family, disagreements, and what you truly think about your neighbors. The hired help is invisible. I befriended numerous neighbors in our apartment building, but I don't remember anyone's servants, though most everyone had a live-in maid. One way of keeping the maids in "their place" was that buildings have so-called service elevators in the back. They are intended for moving furniture or carrying groceries – and servants. The hired help does not ride in the "social" elevator unless she is accompanying the family.

Because servants have only one day off and not much of a private life, most of their free time is spent socializing with neighbors' servants and their main pastime is gossip. From our viewpoint, it is certainly not a life we would envy. But high and low status are relative. Some of my Seattle neighbors are envious of those who live on the lake in multi-million-dollar homes a few blocks away, yet someone in a slum would be envious of my decidedly middle-class surroundings. Household servants with little education and no marketable skills have a better life in a puny room in a middle-class home than a slum or back in their hometowns unemployed. My wife comes from humble beginnings, and I am proud of how she worked her way up to a middle-class career. Among Brazilians, however, her rural background is something to hide out of shame, despite her self-made success and prosperity.

Preta sent money to her parents, who bought a house without a roof. While that seemed bizarre to me, it makes sense from a Third World perspective. When inflation was out of control, people bought what they could afford at the moment, because if they held onto their money it would lose value and that same item would be out of reach. Preta's parents could always put a roof on later when they had more money.

Flirting would be too strong a description, but Preta sought the attention of my friends who came over, whether other gringos or middle-class Brazilians. She wore low-cut revealing blouses when she knew we would have company. Though we spoke mostly Portuguese at home, she picked up snippets of English she heard.

I'll admit I got spoiled having a maid. For three years, I never washed a dish, swept a floor or cleaned a bathtub. Often, I worked such long hours that I would not have had time for such household chores anyway. Now that I have to maintain a two thousand, two hundred-square-foot home and quarter-acre yard, I think back with fondness to my freedom from the drudgery of household duties.

I knew that it would change when I got back to the United States and my charmed life would abruptly end. Yet, it did not. Maria took

Preta to the American Consulate, looked up someone we knew, and got a maid's visa. At first, I did not want her to come back with us. I like Preta, but I wanted more privacy. That's the gringo in me.

I had envisioned moving back to Seattle, buying a house and living as a family unit. Luckily, the house we bought was ample enough that Preta could sleep in a corner of the rec room, which was at least ten times bigger than her room in Brazil. Once again, I was saved from most household chores. Having never owned a home, I was not prepared for the amount of time required to maintain the house and yard.

Preta had never experienced life in the United States, nor had she seen snow or sub-freezing temperatures. Neighbors didn't quite know quite what to think about a servant in their midst, though everyone was courteous to her. One recommended an English class for foreigners. Seeing that we had a good thing, some neighbors invited her to clean their houses on the side.

With her increased earnings and lack of household expenses, she soon banked savings in the thousands of dollars. When she went to work for us, it was the first time Preta had ever earned even the legally required minimum wage.

Unfortunately, we discovered that she had lied to a neighbor by saying that we did not pay her, prompting the neighbor to seek legal representation. After hearing about household help who had sued their employers, we decided to send Preta back to Brazil. I bought her a one-way ticket to São Paulo and accompanied her. Upon arrival in Brazil, I took her to the bus station, put her on a bus for Araçuaí and gave her traveling money. To avoid the risk of robbery, we sent her money via bank wire transfer to a relative who then gave Preta the money when she got home. She went to live in her parents' new house, which had a roof by then, while I spent one night in São Paulo before flying back home the following day.

My proximity to Preta allowed me an in-depth view of race relations. Brazilians deplore racism in the United States and call their country a true racial democracy. But Brazil has never had a black president, and some states with black majorities have never elected black governors or senators. The caste system remains intact in Brazil (and throughout Latin America), little changed from colonial days. Class and income levels are more important than race, but blacks and native Indians occupy the lowest social and income scale. Many whites in Brazil call blacks *pedaços de asfalto* (chunks of asphalt) or *negão*. That's not racist?

More outrageous was how lower-income people sided against their own kind to flatter their economic betters. A black doorman in a building must enforce the rule that servants, most of them black, must ride in the service elevator.

On the way to work one morning in São Paulo, I noticed a well-dressed man sitting in a shiny new Mercedes. But his car was stalled and he was holding up traffic, with horns blaring behind him. He got out and beckoned pedestrians dressed in ragged clothing to push him out of the way. It wasn't long before several obliged. They huffed and puffed, breathing heavily, straining their backs, and pushed the Mercedes to the side of the road. The driver probably spent more on his Mercedes than any of them would earn in a lifetime. What did they get in return? A quick thank you. No money. No offer of a ride. The driver did not even get his hands dirty or strain a muscle. He acted as if they were obliged to rescue him. Why did they bother? What's in it for them? Brazilians can't answer the question, except to say that the poor have been humbled into hoping that the rich guy might toss them a bone (hint: they *never* do).

When a low-income person driving a rust heap in Latin America is involved in a traffic accident with someone driving a shiny new car, eyewitnesses inevitably pop out of the woodwork, whether or not they saw anything, to assert that the poor man was at fault. Their fellow poor guy has nothing to offer them. In the end, it does not matter who was to blame. The rich are rarely held responsible for anything, and the poor let them get away with it.

Chapter 25

Getting Away From it All
in the Search for Paradise

When I first went to Latin America in 1981, I was searching for adventure and, at least perhaps subconsciously, my own vision of paradise. No sane person would call the super-sized, disorderly behemoth cities where I lived – Caracas, São Paulo, and Mexico City – paradise, but I expected them at least to offer proximity. Palm trees, fresh sea breezes, tropical beaches, beautiful girls in skimpy bikinis. It was just a matter of finding those amenities.

Can paradise coexist with the modern world? We assume that basic services are going to function: electricity, telephones, water, roads, hospitals and the like. In fact, we consider the reliability of these services part of our birthright in the United States.

Yet, when the frenetic pace of everyday life becomes the master and we, the slave, we sometimes yearn for a far different, idyllic existence. Who has not fantasized escaping to a tropical paradise? Take One: a cornucopia of stars spilling over a night sky befitting Van Gogh. Take Two: palm trees whispering secrets in a soft ocean breeze. Take Three: gentle waves stroking strands of sugary sand. We all know it well, all the good stuff that Hollywood, and our own, dreams are made of.

No screaming car alarms, blaring horns or squealing tires to drown out the twitter of tropical birds. No stench of hot asphalt roads or belch of catalytic converters to overpower the fragrance of mimosa or night-blooming jasmine. No mind-numbing TV, neon lights, or loud music to detract from Eden's splendors. In heaven's lap, there is no need for the marvels of modern life. In a tropical paradise, you've got it all. Or do you?

Are you really prepared to give up twenty-four-hour cable news, the Internet, the World Series, or the ability to use your cellular phone to text messages or take digital pictures and send them to everyone instantly? You may become mesmerized by the hypnotic rhythm of distant native drums – for a while anyway. But won't you tire of the incessant lapping of waves on the shore, the cacophony of unseen nocturnal birds, the unintelligible gibbering of native speech? Won't you begin to long for Mozart or the Beatles (or even Muzak)? Something, anything, familiar? No electricity means no fridge, and we all know what that means – NO COLD BEER. No ice cream either. Face it, this might be a great vacation for a week or two, but it won't be long before most people get antsy and start missing the civilization they worked overtime at two jobs to escape.

In my travels, I have encountered many so-called primitive paradises, but I never met a Paul Gauguin. Rather, I found many social misfits and dropouts, a variety of alcohol- and drug-induced pursuers of far-fetched schemes and dreams, and a good number of American expatriates quick to proclaim that they are "mad as hell" at the mismanagement of America and are "not going to take it anymore." So, they opt out in favor of their Garden of Eden.

High in the crisp Andean air of Bolivia and Peru, I encountered endless dingy, dreary hamlets where the inhabitants swept the dirt floors in their mud huts with bundles of dry grass, cooked in earthenware pots over open fires, and dimly illuminated the dark recesses with the sickly glimmer of kerosene lanterns. Perhaps ungraciously I declined the hospitality of my hosts to join in their meals, wary of evil-smelling sauce and dubious ingredients.

I visited tiny Indian villages in Venezuela's Amazon rain forest where adults wore loincloths and didn't speak Spanish. So I called on the children, who had learned Spanish from missionaries, to interpret for me. Sometimes I could only communicate my thoughts via the universal language of gestures, grunts and charades.

The warmheartedness of many native peoples is well known. They want to be helpful and try ever so hard to please. So badly, in fact, that f they don't know the directions for you to follow, they will cheerfully nvent directions.

As I sought temporary refuge in Shangri-Las, I questioned whether they existed except on the silver screen. The eighteenth century French philosopher Jean Jacques Rousseau theorized that primitive peoples live in peace and harmony with nature. But in what sense are malaria, yellow fever and river blindness harmonious with nature?

The "back to nature" movement seems charmingly curious, if not archaic, in the United States, where President Franklin Delano Roosevelt's Works Progress Administration (WPA) left few Americans untouched when it electrified rural America in the Depression-whacked thirties.

The thirst for electricity and its benefits has so crazed inhabitants in Third World countries that it's not unusual for slum residents to be electrocuted while illegally tapping overhead high-voltage power lines. I once saw a homeless man living under a bridge in São Paulo with few possessions, watching a television powered by bare wires pirated from a nearby line. These tragic electrocutions are so commonplace, in fact, that they merit no more than a three-inch filler in local newspapers. In a developed country, such an anomalous event would be major news.

Before I visited the family farm where my wife grew up, I had seen similar places in Brazil and throughout Latin America. Early in our romance, here is how she described it to me in a letter: "I'm sitting on the porch in front of my house looking at the moon and the stars. The sky is clean and the air is pure. Nature is ever-present in this place. The houses are made of mud with tile roofs. Inside the houses, the carpet is made of earth. There is no electricity. Light is from kerosene lamps. The oven is cement and food is cooked with firewood, which makes the pans black. There is a creek where we take a bath. The water is cold in the morning, but in the afternoon it is warmed by the sun and you can bathe comfortably. There are no doctors or medicine. Most of the people are born and die of diseases without knowing the causes."

The first time I visited the family farm I was startled when a snake lurched into my path, believing it had targeted me to coil around my neck and choke me to death or puncture my veins with razor-sharp teeth and inject lethal venom. My father-in-law laughed; it was just a harmless garden variety they called a "two-headed snake," which he dispatched with a shovel, cleanly cleaving it in half.

Even though we had kerosene lanterns, we still went to bed by eight in those days. One night, I got a real taste of our remoteness. Maria was sorting through sheets, blankets and mosquito nets, making sure to find a bedpan so we wouldn't have to stumble over the rocky path to the outhouse at night, when encountering a tarantula was an unseen danger. I sat on the corner of the double bed and it gave way, dumping the mattress and me with it to the floor.

We lifted the mattress and support rack only to find that the thumb-sized wooden pegs that underpin the mattress were fastened with thin nails not fully pounded in. One had snapped off, and another was loose and ready to give way. This needed immediate carpentry surgery.

If we were back home in the United States, we could go out and buy the materials to fix the bed, with the 24/7 culture, the all-the-time economy, to fall back on. Light bulb burned out? Hungry for Ben & Jerry's? A nearby supermarket is always open. Computer crash when you urgently need to send an e-mail? Send a text, call twenty-four-hour tech support or send a fax from Kinko's. Do you need a hammer, nails or a piece of wood to repair a broken bed? Head for a twenty-four-hour home improvement store.

None of the above applied. The closest phone, or store of any kind, was an hour and a half away over a dirt road that shakes loose your entrails and fills your nostrils with clouds of fine red dust.

Even if we ventured into town, the hardware store would be closed. The only places open at this hour would be bars. When my wife was growing up here, she used to walk six hours into town carrying a basketful of eggs, sell them for a few coins, then maybe buy some flour or cooking oil and carry it another six hours back home. She now complains about the hardships of running her businesses, keeping up with the Microsoft millionaires in our midst, and upkeep of a big house and yard.

Despite all the conveniences to which we're accustomed back at home, I probably wouldn't even bother to fix a broken bed immediately if I were tired. I'd simply throw the mattress on the floor and snooze comfortably. But you can't do that in remote Brazil. Sleeping on the floor would leave you vulnerable to the vector which carries Chagas' disease. The fingernail-size insect inhabits cracks in the red tile roof and adobe walls. It attacks in the silence of night, burrowing into the skin and laying eggs. The offspring hitchhike through the bloodstream and invade the heart and other vital organs. It might kill you soon or thirty years later. Or the illness might simply lay dormant and never cause damage. Most rural people in Brazil and other countries in the region have been exposed.

We had to fix the bed. My father-in-law couldn't find his hammer. It was probably at a son's house. Going elsewhere would be arduous, and there is a real danger of stepping on a rattlesnake at night.

That means we had to fall back on a different 24/7, what in Brazil is called *jeitinho* (zhay-TEEN-yo), which means improvisation, to make things somehow work and rely on your own ingenuity. My father-in-law found a fist-size rock outside, a few rusty nails in the shed, and we went to work. We stripped the frame, pulled out the broken nails and pounded in the longer, albeit rusty ones. It took a few attempts, replacing ones that bent, before we had the new supports firmly in place. We put the bed back together, complete with fitted sheets brought from the United States and a mosquito net to protect us from minuscule enemies.

A few years later, in the 1990s, electricity arrived, and I experienced firsthand what happens when a Third World community becomes electrified for the first time. Before that, I loved spending vacations in the wilderness, chirped with a good-night lullaby by the invisible creatures of the darkness: crickets, cicadas, frogs and punctuated by the occasional bark of a dog or mooing cow. The only night illumination in this overwhelming void was generated by an occasional kerosene lantern or flashlights while fireflies performed their glorious dance under a magnificent blanket of stars brushed across the jet black sky.

Before the power lines were strung, people passed evenings chatting or playing cards around candles or kerosene lanterns, sharing dried homemade biscuits, sipping thick coffee or bravely ingesting shots of a fiery, potent sugar-cane liquor called *cachaça* (ka-SHAH-suh).

The tapestry of the night's gentle noises would be interrupted occasionally by the crackling of a battery-powered or hand-cranked radio. But the old customs lost ground to the modern onslaught as the power lines arrived. Today there are even a few streetlights to illuminate the rutted dirt roads. This singular event changed life profoundly and rapidly. The night's gentle noises were replaced by the shouting, histrionics of nightly television soap operas, as the mesmerizing glowing tube accompanied electricity to outlying areas thanks to relay towers and satellite dishes.

People cluster silently, almost reverently, in front of TV sets to watch *novelas*, which networks beam from the remotest depths of the Amazon to the pampas along the Argentine border. In the seemingly endless trysts, couples argue and flail their arms, lovers coo, lovers find new lovers. Those without electricity or television visit neighbors who do.

For millions of poor Brazilians, life is a struggle that seems to improve only marginally. But the arrival of electricity is changing life for many all over Brazil. The 2010 census found 98.7 percent of Brazilian households with access to electricity, up dramatically from sixty-eight percent in 1980.

There still is no telephone service in many outlying areas, and residents often travel for hours to reach a phone in town.

Most of the land in this arid region is devoted to grazing livestock. Bananas, mangos, coffee, oranges and peanuts are cultivated on small plots irrigated by hand or pipes fed by a well. Sugar cane grew along the river bank before it dried up. A surly neighbor threatened to kill my father-in-law if he did not allow him to take more water from a well on my family's property. Using electric pumps to irrigate the dry soil makes the land more productive, but power service remains irregular.

"I'd put in a pump and plant lettuce, tomatoes and coffee," one neighbor told me, but he couldn't. The power line is half a mile away from his farm.

The rural exodus to the crowded cities continues and probably will not be reversed. Seventy percent of Brazilians lived in the country in 1950. Now eighty-four percent are in urban areas, many of them in slums.

"Every day, the bus leaves full of people going to São Paulo to work in the factories," Diogenes Timos Silva, the former mayor of Virgem da Lapa who electrified the nearby villages and then became a state legislator, told me. South America's largest metropolis is seven hundred seventy-five miles to the south, a twenty-hour bus ride.

In this poor region, electricity is also a means of combating illness and ignorance.

"Light scares off the insects" that carry Chagas, Silva said.

His late father, who also served as mayor, was among the millions of victims of the disease.

As for television, Silva said it was "projecting vital information people need to improve their lives."

Not everybody agreed that such a basic service was worthwhile. One neighbor griped: "What is this good for? People here can't even afford televisions. They should put in a telephone instead so I could call my children in São Paulo."

One might wonder why anyone would endure such a hard life. For most people, there is no other choice. With no skills other than tending cattle or raising subsistence crops, many people are hard pressed to earn a living in town. Among the seven siblings in my wife's family, only one remains on the family farm, and he teaches school at the nearby village. The rest moved to Virgem da Lapa, the closest town, or to São Paulo. My in-laws did have a choice. They owned a house in town Maria bought for them. But every time they went into town – the municipal government sends a truck once a week for farmers to carry their wares into town and purchase staples – they couldn't wait to get back. It's too noisy, with honking horns and loud TVs and radios.

"I'm free to walk around in silence here, completely free," my mother-in-law likes to say. Even though she must endure a long, uncomfortable ride to faraway Belo Horizonte to seek treatment for her various ailments and get her pacemaker calibrated, she feels secure from the trappings of modern life in her little corner of the globe. From her own version of paradise, she visits the outside world as rarely as possible.

Chapter 26

Danger in the Streets

It's widely believed that hired killers in Brazil don't shoot or stab or poison their victims as often as they just plow them down in the street. Because the rate of car crashes and pedestrian fatalities is stratospheric, a hit-and-run raises few questions. Gunshots and knifings are suspicious; dead pedestrians, tragically, are all too common.

Translation: Be careful. Whether you are a pedestrian, a driver, or a passenger, watch out!

While driving on Brazilian highways, I often encountered cars heading straight toward me on blind curves. Expecting someone might be aiming right at me, I was always prepared. That thinking saved my life more than once. In Brazilian cities, nobody turns on their headlights at night. Instead, they use only their running lights, with drivers and passengers leaning their seats back 45 degrees. Because of this, people frequently die of a broken neck when minor traffic accidents toss them into their own seat belts. And, when traffic bogs down, drivers routinely use the shoulder as an extra lane, then cut back in front of other cars without warning as soon as they can.

Such harrowing experiences are commonplace all over Latin America. Panamanians love to say their fellow citizens must all be illiterate because nobody reads the stop signs. I adapted to the Panama style of driving right away; otherwise, I would have been eaten alive by the aggressive drivers.

And it was even more frightening in Colombia, crossing the Andes by bus. The Pan-American Highway was largely unpaved and winding, with hairpin curves, often with no guardrails at the edge of cliffs hundreds of feet deep. Drivers skidded around blind curves, honking furiously, playing loud *salsa* or *cumbia*, and chatting amiably with the ticket taker while eyeing the curves of sexy passengers more than the curves in the road. This had all the elements for disaster: poorly graded, badly maintained highways; jalopies in a perpetual state of disrepair; inattention by the driver; and a potent dose of testosterone-fueled machismo. The hapless passengers had no control over anything. Buses almost always had a Virgin Mary statuette on the dashboard or a Jesus sticker on the windshield, along with local patron saints. The drivers habitually made the sign of the cross when departing, but there was no protection if your number was up, when fate and the elements conspired against you. I traveled around Colombia twice and read the newspapers regularly. Almost every day I came across a story about a bus accident killing a dozen or more people. It never surprised me.

Bolivia's roads were even worse. The scenery was majestic, lowland jungle, arid altiplano (high plateau), and stunning gradations in-between. Its territory combines the elements of several elevations and climates, and you get to see it because you travel slowly. The roads are so bad and the vehicles are in such disrepair, that you never whiz by anything. Furthermore, you are almost guaranteed to break down whenever you travel. Like a motorized lame horse, the buses and trucks wheeze forward, chugging and backfiring. How far can they go in that condition? Not very far. They always have bald tires, looking as if rats had chewed the tread, which dangles from the side and flaps while in motion. And they never carry a spare. When a tire goes flat, the driver leaves to get help. He might be back in an hour, or the next day. While waiting, passengers can explore the countryside or some village with mud huts. There is no sense in getting upset; the delay is inevitable, and it is just part of the adventure. Breakdowns offer opportunities: hawkers sell oranges or bananas to the stranded passengers. They build a fire by the side of the road and start cooking food they are carrying. I often rode on the back of uncovered flatbed trucks, sprawled across sacks of potatoes (not comfortable), or sat atop bags of flour or sugar (less uncomfortable). If it rained, passengers pulled tarps over themselves. Without sanitary facilities, I bathed in cold mountain streams. I met elderly passengers wearing colorful blankets, a felt hat – each village has a different shape or color headband – and multiple hooped skirts for the women. They often spoke only Quechua and no Spanish, so I conversed with them through grandchildren. They were quiet, shy and not very curious about why this strange gringo was sitting next to them.

On the back of a truck I passed through part of the Andes the locals call Siberia, where it was parched, then around a corner was mist-draped jungle, like a Siberian rain forest and seemingly just as cold. Traffic stopped all day for road construction near a house with a flattened oil drum as a front door. Passage was allowed only every other night; police said the gate would swing open between four and six in the afternoon, but suddenly it opened at 2:40, and people ran to jump on the lumbering trucks pulling away with or without them. A couple of hours earlier, a mob nearly lynched the policeman because buses had been allowed to go through on the allegedly closed road. The dust made me sneeze for the whole long ride.

After enduring these conditions, it was a luxury to ride the bus in Brazil. The quality of buses was not as good on the backroads, but still far better than anything I encountered in the poor Andean countries.

Brazilian passengers feel at home on the buses. Before leaving the station, drivers come back to the passenger section, introduce themselves, announce how long it will take to reach the destination and when travelers will get a rest stop. On long routes, when they switch drivers, the departing one says goodbye to the passengers and the new one says hello.

Roads in Brazil span the full range from divided paved freeways as good as any in North America down to rutted dirt paths that were impassable. One indication of inferior roads is the omnipresence of tire shops. Potholes and ruts regularly blow out tires. These little shops seem to appear every few miles nationwide, even in the most desolate spots, to sell an inner tube, patch a tire, and get you running again with a smile.

During one trip, the highway connecting São Paulo to Belo Horizonte, two of the biggest cities, was so bad that the bus driver had to slow down to barely ten miles per hour numerous times to traverse the treacherous potholes. Yet other sections of this same highway were newly paved and remarkably smooth.

Getting to my wife's family farm is a different matter. I've broken down twice on that bone-jarring route, about an hour and a half from the closest town. One such trip started fortuitous. Rains had recently arrived, so it was no longer dusty. The road had been scraped a year or two before to even out ruts, so we could travel at about thirty miles per hour in the truck driven by Zé, a neighbor, family friend, and member of the town council. The truck carried two passengers in the front and two others in the back, hiding beneath a tarp to avoid the intermittent rain. Zé had a thin face, always sporting a few days' growth of beard stubble, and rounded leather cap common in these parts.

The sun gradually descended into the *chapada,* the surrounding plateau, giving us a short-lived brilliant red sky with thick clouds. The copper-colored earth became a vibrant deep rich red, and the brown scrub sprouted bright green shoots. An occasional frog crossed our path, and Zé was cautious because flattening a frog is believed to bring years of bad luck. Frogs appear in this arid territory only during the rainy season.

The scraggly trees and fence posts harbored muddy nests. The larger ones, some as big as soccer balls, house termite colonies; the smaller variety is constructed by enterprising birds which use mud rather than straw as building material. Other than languishing cattle and occasional goats, there are few other signs of life.

Darkness quickly swallowed the remaining light. We turned off the main road to one even narrower, deep and winding, to take a passenger home. When she got out, there was nowhere to turn around, and the road became a swamp. When Zé tried to back up, the wheels spun endlessly to the smell of burning rubber. There were no tow trucks, and no phones to make a call. But failure was not an option. We had to rely on *jeitinho* and somehow improvise. We yanked out plants in the dark and threw them down to improve traction. The four of us spent a half hour pulling out reeds and weeds, making a dozen futile attempts at progress. Two relatives of the passenger came to our rescue. One of them dug fresh dirt with a hoe to cover the mud while the other gathered more plants to throw in the road. Zé made another try, and one of the men hopped onto the rear bumper to provide more weight and traction. After more slipping and sliding, the truck finally passed the muddy patch to reach solid dry ground again.

By now, it was pitch dark except for our headlights, and clouds blocked the usually brilliant tapestry of stars dominated by the Southern Cross.

We needed only another fifteen minutes to arrive at the family farm. We heard crickets chirping, cicadas clicking and frogs croaking over the loud engine. We reached the small settlement of about twenty homes that comprises Santana, which has a tiny church where my father-in-law was buried, a primary schoolhouse, and a crude bar, but not even a general store. The staples of life, rice, beans and other necessities, are available only in town.

In the final stretch of road, the truck once again bogged down. This time one of the wheels fell into a rut up to the axle. We were near our destination, and it was late, so we would just dig it out in the morning.

We were about a half kilometer from the family farm and had to carry our provisions the rest of the way. Because water on the farm is muddy, we brought bottles of filtered water from town, six to eight liter bottles apiece, stowed in two canvas bags. It's a good lesson in life to carry the water you drink. We think of water as turning on a tap, but here potable water was not always available. My wife and other members of her family used to carry water buckets on their heads up a steep trail before the formerly rushing stream withered to a muddy trickle during the rainy season and bare the rest of the year.

We finally arrived at the farm, late, tired, dirty and hungry. I greeted my mother-in-law, Juliana, for the first time in five years. The last time I came, my father-in-law had bid me an emotional farewell, as if he knew it would be our last encounter. I missed his simplicity, his open heart, his soft voice and always-twinkling eyes.

Juliana wears her hair pulled back with a scarf and a faded, tattered dress; she refuses to wear newer clothing we bought her. Her leathered face reflects a stoic, quiet dignity. She complains of chest and joint pains, her legs hardened with crystallized varicose veins. But she won't leave the harsh farm life for an easier existence in town where she would have nothing to occupy herself. Backbreaking work on the farm gives her life meaning.

We entered the house infested with knee-deep termites scampering about the cement floor, calling up visions of biblical plagues. To get rid of them, we shut off the inside lights and turned on the outside lights to attract them. Then we swept the floor and brushed piles of them into a dustpan, which we dumped in the chicken coop. Nothing goes to waste in these parts. Before going to sleep, we had to sweep the bed for bugs, then spread out the mosquito net. Insects are a constant in this environment. Flies buzz all day, while various types of mosquitoes and other pests flit about by night.

Some years earlier, in town, danger unexpectedly roared toward us and nearly killed my son, who was eight years old at the time. Right after sunset, my wife, her sister, our children and their cousins were walking home from the local athletic club, where we had spent the afternoon playing soccer and billiards. The club is on the outskirts of town, where the paving stones give way to a dusty copper ribbon that winds through the hills to hardscrabble ranches where cattle graze on parched sagebrush. The walk back home wasn't far, just a few blocks of mostly flat land and two blocks up a steep San Francisco-like hill. We neared our climb when we heard the thunderous roar of trucks approaching like a herd of wild beasts. I turned around and saw three huge flatbeds kicking up clouds of dust. They screeched around the corner and barreled straight toward us. Like frightened chickens, we scattered when the trucks took over the whole road. I ran to the left side, which afforded more space, and so did everyone except Joseph. To my horror, I realized too late that I had neglected the first rule of a parent: protecting my child above all else.

There was no reason to assume that he hadn't scampered out of harm's way. Nevertheless, I tensely watched the truck rush toward us with the relentless charge of an enraged bull. After the first one passed, I could see Joseph safe on the other side, but I still worried about the other two trucks yet to come. On a one-lane road like this, no driver could go safely more than about twenty miles per hour. These trucks, however, seemed to be traveling double that speed. Not that it was unusual to drive so recklessly.

Brazil has among the world's worst fatality rates for traffic accidents. Simply arriving in Maria's hometown from the closest airport requires ten hours of harrowing travel over winding roads, the final two sinew-loosening hours on dirt.

On one trip, we passed three fatal accidents on a single day. After seeing uncovered bodies sprawled out at the side of the road, drivers seemed to reflect for five or ten minutes about refraining from passing on blind curves. When the moment passed, they again stepped on the gas, oblivious to the jolt of reality they had just witnessed. My wife and members of her family routinely click off the names of dozens of people they know who have perished in traffic accidents near their town. I lived in big cities and small towns all over the United States and knew only a handful of people who died in car crashes.

As soon as the last truck passed, I ran to Joseph, grateful that he was unharmed. His main concern was not that he had eluded death by mere inches, but that his sweat pants and socks were full of burrs. We walked to a streetlight, where I could see them and extracted them, sticking my fingers nearly every time.

He told me that I need not worry about him, that he knew how to take care of himself. As a Seattle kid living on a quiet street, he was not prepared for such dangers. Cars in our neighborhood almost never drove aggressively. When Joseph rode his bicycle or skated in the street at home, motorists – already driving twenty-five – invariably slowed down even further.

In all the years I lived in Brazil, I have never seen anyone stopped by police for careless driving. My sister-in-law, however, recounted her own experience.

She was pulled over for driving without a license, but she believed that the real reason was that her husband had refused to lend the car to the police officer. Those who offer their car to the officer or invite him over for a barbeque never get pulled over, whether for lack of a license or dangerous driving. It's more subtle than cash in the palm, but just as effective. My brother-in-law stubbornly refused to lend his car on the principle that the officer ought to buy his own transportation instead of mooching. For good measure, he successfully appealed his wife's ticket, not on the merits of the case, of course, but rather through connections made as a city councilman.

Chapter 27

The End of the Road

Something in the human condition makes us unwilling to accept the end of the road. Our very nature compels us to construct grandiose bridges across rivers, drain swamps, blast tunnels through mountains – and even escape our own planet to set foot on the moon – all in our essential quest to find out what lies beyond. A dead end is simply a challenge to overcome.

Yet, the Pan-American Highway, which stretches nearly thirty thousand miles, from Prudhoe Bay on the frozen northern tip of Alaska to the windswept southern reaches of Tierra del Fuego, reaches an abrupt end at a lonely isolated spot in Panama called the Darien Gap before it starts up again a hundred kilometers away in northern Colombia. That distance could be traversed in an hour on a modern interstate highway in North America. This rugged terrain, however, forces intrepid travelers to hike, paddle in canoes, or find their way with all-terrain vehicles. Few people ever manage to cross overland; most fly instead.

That short stretch of missing highway is all that prevents us from traveling continuously overland between the northern and southern extremes, near the North and South Poles. The highway now unceremoniously dead-ends in the Panamanian town of Yaviza, where the muddy Rio Chucunaque flows into the brown Rio Chico.

I have traveled on well over half of the highway in almost all of the countries it crosses, meandering through misty jungles, day-after-day in parched deserts, and struggling across steep mountaintops through the Andes. I have driven on the highway near its northern terminus in Alaska and reached the end of the road in Argentina near Cape Horn.

Because abysmal transportation is both dangerous and an impediment to economic development, the Colombian and Peruvian governments are allowing private contractors to pave the poorly graded dirt and gravel highway in exchange for collecting tolls on operating concessions.

After seeing so much captivating scenery in so many places from Alaska to Patagonia, the dead end in Panama is a bit of a *denouement*. No sign. No plaque. No monument. It's just like any country road which ends at a river from the bayous of Louisiana to the swampy Pantanal of Brazil.

Unlike Edith Piaf in her famous ballad *Non, Je Ne Regrette Rien*, I do have some regrets in my life, especially as regards the Darien Gap. I had two chances to cross it years ago but decided to skip it. Who goes to Yellowstone and misses Old Faithful or fails to gaze on the Eiffel Tower while in Paris? Sure, a trip to Latin America for most people is complete without venturing to the Darien Gap – most Panamanians haven't even been there – but for the purposes of my own long overland journeys all across the region, it was essential. The Darien Gap was the missing link in the Pan-American Highway, as well as the missing link in my own travels.

The first chance was in late 1982. Shortly before leaving Caracas on my long trek around South America, I flew home to visit my family in Oregon for a couple of weeks. A friend of a friend was piloting a small plane back to the United States and wanted company. Why didn't I go with him? Because it would have taken several days, much longer than the jumbo jet connecting flights from Caracas to Miami to Portland. So, because of my haste, I missed seeing South America, Central America and Mexico up close from a low-flying small aircraft. His proposed route would have skirted right along the Darien Gap.

A second chance came two years later. Upon completion of my odyssey, I decided to fly out of Suriname through Curaçao and Miami to get home. I could have gone overland in a few weeks, but I was weary from being on the road so long, the fleabag hotels, the bumpy bus rides, the toxic food and drink. I just wanted to set foot back home. Besides that, civil wars in El Salvador and Nicaragua made traveling in those countries hazardous.

Three decades after first arriving in Caracas, I journeyed to Panama, finally, to reach the end of the road. I rented a car rather than depend on erratic bus schedules and battled the worst pothole-filled roads I have ever driven, more obstacle course than highway. I can't count the number of times I stopped, sometimes even backed up, just to figure out how to proceed around or through the obstructions. I had to make a Hobson's choice many times, with no acceptable alternatives. Although Yaviza is only three hundred kilometers from Panama City, it takes nearly a full day of nervous driving to get there. After the capital, the road deteriorates as thick, overgrown jungle encroaches on both sides and squeezes two lanes into a single narrow one, like a boa constrictor poised to crush the life from a victim. Horses wandering in the roadway had no fear of cars, nor did sickly dogs, impervious to honking. Although it was ghastly hot, I left my windows open instead of using the car's air conditioning to hear birds chirping and breathe in the luxurious scent of the damp, musty jungle.

Numerous military roadblocks demand identification, plus grilling about destination and reasons for traveling. The commander at each checkpoint was suspicious about why I was headed for Yaviza ("Who travels just to see the end of the road? That makes no sense.") and told me I would be stopped and turned back before reaching Yaviza.

On the outskirts, I was pulled over by the border patrol. The whole region is heavily militarized, and I was accompanied by a soldier as I walked around the town's collection of simple clapboard and adobe houses baking in the equatorial sun. I toured the ruins of Fort San Jeronimo and walked over a narrow footbridge spanning the Rio Chico.

Beyond Yaviza, Darien National Park is sealed off to outsiders after massacres of civilians at the hands of Colombian anti-government guerrillas, *narcotraficantes*, and bandits. The soldier made it clear that I would not be allowed to travel any farther.

The town's hub is its waterfront, a beehive with long motorized dugout canoes – crowded with Indians from outlying villages – swarming in and out. Bunches of plump green bananas were unloaded from boats into a small warehouse near the dock. Surveying this frenetic scene, I pledged to not be deterred. I was going to cross the Darien Gap somehow, somewhere.

It took days to reach another location, a mere twenty miles across the impenetrable jungle, where I intended to enter Colombia on my own two feet. The coastal route used to be infested with Colombian rebels and drug smugglers – guidebooks warn travelers to stay away – but I was assured that the bad elements had been flushed out a couple of years ago and it was safe. Now only one section of that trail remained dangerous.

That required driving nearly a full day to get back to Panama City, and from there, riding a jeep on nauseating curves through the jungle to the Caribbean coast. A small boat took me to Carti Island, where I slept in a hammock on an open deck that shook when waves splashed below, with a view of the ocean and nearby *Guna Yala* islands, better known as San Blas. The communal bathroom was at the end of a wobbly pier missing planks and reminded me of the locals lacking teeth, so I fished a tin can from the trash to use as my urinal at night after the municipal power shut off at 11:30 p.m. The densely populated island's houses are fashioned from slender sticks tied together with twine, with some doors no more than a piece of cloth. Narrow alleys befitting rabbit warrens connected neighbors. The island had a municipal generator and wind turbine, while many of the houses sprouted satellite dishes and solar panels. The residents were quiet and reserved, but late at night the sound of gentle waves disappeared when people revved up noisy gasoline generators and played throbbing music that drowned out the generators.

With little sleep, I rode all of the next day in a thirty-two-foot modern fiberglass boat powered with an outboard engine and topped by a canvas awning to protect against rain or intense sun. The *San Patricio* sliced over the crest of waves, then flew through the air and slapped down with a thud, throwing me and the other passengers up in the air, then back down on our sore rumps. The ocean spray left a fine salty crust on my face, my eyes stinging from the salt water.

The palm-lined San Blas islands were stunning as they glistened in the sunshine, but the ride was mostly tedium and motion sickness interlaced with moments of pure terror, fearing that the next wave could swamp the boat and drown us. The sea alternated from aquamarine to turquoise to deep azure to a foreboding navy blue, depending on the light and angle. Onshore, the towering, jungle-clad coastal range, separating the coast from Yaviza, was forbidding, shrouded in clouds and haze. The boat stopped at several islands, picking up and dropping off Indians, a bit like a rural bus route. The deserted islands and simple villages looked like the ends of the earth, yet some of the women – outfitted in dazzlingly bright dresses and tiny beads wrapped around their legs – spent much of the time chatting on their cell phones in a language I could not understand.

It was dark when we finally reached decrepit Puerto Obaldia near the Colombian border where immigration procedures took an hour; the guards forced us to take everything out of our bags for inspection, and a dog sniffed our bags over and over. It was too late to proceed to Capurganá, Colombia that night, so I would have to wait for morning. The only hotel available had electric outlets exposing bare wires, and there was no shower, just a washbasin. The next day, an immigration official – thick chest hair and a silver cross bursting from his grey nylon shirt unbuttoned halfway down – peered over his reading glasses and informed me that I would not be allowed back into Panama if I stayed less than three days in Colombia. I explained that I had an airplane ticket back to Panama City and only needed one day to hike the trail between La Miel, Panama and Capurganá. He emphasized that if I sneaked into Colombia and back into Panama, I was subject to immediate deportation, five-year expulsion from Panama, and a three thousand-dollar fine.

First Yaviza and now the coastal trail. It seemed that my dream of crossing between Panama and Colombia was vanishing everywhere I looked. But I could at least hike to the border and achieve my goal. Every day, boats carry people back and forth between Puerto Obaldia and La Miel in Panama and Capurganá and Sapzurro in Colombia.

When I boarded the boat, the Panamanian military commander told the captain to let me off in La Miel. But instead of going there directly, the captain steered into the open sea and veered around *Cabo*

Tiburón (Cape Shark), where huge waves crashed thunderously into volcanic rocks. A fellow passenger told me the GPS in his cell phone indicated we were crossing from Central into South America. After about forty-five minutes, we nosed back toward shore and into the port of lovely Capurganá. A dozen passengers disembarked, most of them to wait for the next boat to Turbo, where they would catch buses to Cartagena, Medellin and other parts of Colombia. Clapboard hotels – pastel orange, green and blue – with hammocks on their balconies overlook the waterfront against a backdrop of palms and mountains with lush emerald green vegetation. It was an inviting port-of-call, making me wish I could stay all week. Instead, I could only walk around the dock a few minutes before the boat departed.

During the boat rides and my time in Puerto Obaldia, I bonded with several travelers – fellow free spirits from Estonia, Peru, Cuba, and Holland – the same way I had made friends quickly on the road many years earlier, even though these travelers were the age of my kids.

After Capurganá, I was the sole passenger. The next stop was tiny Sapzurro, where the boat stopped for a half hour. I chatted with Colombian soldiers and friendly locals, who pointed me toward the footpath to La Miel. I sprinted up cement stairs painted red, blue and yellow – the colors of Colombia's flag – climbing the steep hill toward the border, but did not have enough time to reach the top. Instead, I raced back down and hopped on my boat as it pulled out of port.

Back in the ocean, we once again crossed *Cabo Tiburón*. I studied the ferocious waves pounding the volcanic rock and marveled at how one geographical point demarcated the border from one continent to the next.

La Miel was not as seedy as Puerto Obaldia, but was still a letdown after beguiling Capurganá and Sapzurro, where all the buildings seemed freshly painted. Walking along the beach into town from the dock, I passed the military garrison, where I had to check in. The commander in Puerto Obaldia had called and told them to keep an eye on me, so this time two bodyguards accompanied me up the steep mountainside to the border. It took only fifteen minutes to reach the crest of the hill, where harbors and the azure sea lay in either direction. There, I could freely walk back and forth between Panama and Colombia. I gazed at the marvelous views, snapped pictures, chatted with a Colombian soldier and headed back down.

That afternoon I returned to Puerto Obaldia and suffered through another noisy, miserable night in the same shabby hotel in the run-down town to catch my hour-long flight back to Panama City in a twin-engine airplane that fit only about twenty passengers. The hotel's courtyard was filled with Cubans seeking to reach the United States. Many Cubans, Colombians, and other foreigners were stuck in limbo in Puerto Obaldia without proper documentation. Cubans confessed to me that they had bribed officials at the Venezuelan or Ecuadoran consulates in Havana, paying three thousand dollars for a visa. After that, they said they would have to pay bribes every time they crossed another border before trying to sneak into the United States from Mexico. Some planned to stay instead in Panama or Costa Rica.

Following the short flight to Panama City, my feet became blistered while wandering *Casco Viejo*, the well-preserved colonial section. Tourist shops in Panama City sell authentic Panama hats, the easily recognizable elegant white fedoras, but they are made in Ecuador, not Panama. The hat worn by Panamanian men is curious looking: the *sombrero pintado a la pedrá* is rounded, with black bands and a brow curled inward, resembling a swollen lip.

Nearing the end of my trip, I drove to the Caribbean port of Colón to see Gatun Lake and the locks, plus the ruins of Spanish forts at San Lorenzo and Portobelo. On a hot, sticky night, my last before returning to Panama City and a long flight home, I glided alone through an enormous, refreshing pool at the sprawling, five-star Hotel Melia Panama Canal. Floating on my back, I gazed spellbound at the brilliant full moon ringed by clouds. Chirping crickets and cicadas, along with intermittent frightening sounds – the loudest one a spine-tingling cross between a cackle and a howl – erupted from the surrounding jungle. Finally I had found the tropical paradise I was denied when I was unable to stay in Capurganá. Fellow travelers I befriended earlier in the week were off to other adventures staying in low-rent rooms and riding rickety buses, while I was driving a rental car and staying one night in a fancy hotel. I reflected on how much things had changed in some ways, yet stayed the same in others. It struck me that I was lodging in the same hotel, Melia, where I had started my first trip out of Caracas, in Cartagena, three hundred miles across the warm Caribbean and only a few days short of exactly thirty-one years ago. In my room, I switched off the air conditioning, opened the window, and quickly descended into deep slumber, lulled by the gurgling fountain outside, a world away from the pounding loudspeakers all night down the coast in Carti and Puerto Obaldia a few days before.

I had planned on returning to the hotel that afternoon to seek refuge from the blinding tropical sun and oppressive humidity and swim in the enchanting pool. I crossed a single-lane bridge over the Panama Canal, a five-minute trip, to reach San Lorenzo but did not realize I would get stuck on the other side for two hours while the bridge closed for a succession of ships to pass through the locks. Ironically, at the Miraflores Locks near Panama City, the opposite had happened: I had to wait just as long next to empty locks just to see a single behemoth ship pass through, so it did not occur to me that the bridge would close for so long. While waiting, my car got sandwiched in the middle of four vans crammed full of employees wearing red-and-white shirts emblazoned *Panama Canal Company*. As workers piled out of the vans, they cranked up Gloria Gaynor's *I Will Survive*, rather than the ever-present *salsa* or *cumbia*, and broke into feverish dancing. As soon as the gate opened, all semblance of order disappeared as cars, trucks, buses and vans honked and battled for space to pass single file over the bridge.

So, even after upgrading to a rental car and swanky hotel, little had changed from my long trip years ago. I was still trapped by the unpredictable vagaries and chaos of life in Latin America, denied my swim at the Melia on a sweltering afternoon, a fitting end to my extraordinarily long, extraordinary journey.

The Darien Gap

After venturing into the heart of the Darien Gap, I realized that not only is it a daunting, tangible demarcation and impenetrable roadblock between North and South, but it also represents a yawning cultural fissure, a psychological barrier dividing two radically different, and often opposing, worlds.

Closing the circle in my extensive travels, I assumed that my story would be complete, yet in many ways, it remains unfinished. I am not Latin, and as much as I think I know the region, there is even more that I don't know, that however much I understand Latin America, I will never truly comprehend so many of its mysteries and idiosyncrasies.

Furthermore, I came to realize that this same divide exists within Latin American nations, where the wealthy and middle class know little about their countrymen mired in poverty. Brazilian journalist Leandro Beguoci wrote in his blog in January 2014 that news coverage of protests in that country were "simplified, stereotyped" and that "the periphery is still an unknown subject. It is a type of Kazakhstan that speaks Portuguese." If Latins can't even understand what is happening in their own country, how could I?

Latins have an intense love-hate relationship with the United States, as outlined in Chapter 18. They envy the organization, prosperity and open society. At the same time, they resent the lack of respect shown to their traditions, their economic dependency on the United States, and the American consumer culture that encroaches on their own way of life.

Likewise, I realize that I also have a love-hate attitude toward Latin America. I enjoy the warmth and intimacy of interpersonal relationships among Latins, the cohesiveness of family life, and the depth and diversity of cultural traditions. I appreciate the little things, like cozy family restaurants in Latin America where the owner greets each diner individually with a smile, a rarity nowadays in North America.

At the same time, I have no patience for systemic corruption, wanton violence, the utter chaos that reigns in so much of the region, the socio-economic caste system, and the contempt for and exploitation of the poor.

It dawned on me that I have been studying the region unconsciously in the analytical framework of an anthropologist doing field work by living with a tribe and observing language, family life, cultural signals, religious beliefs, superstitions, leadership and power, mating rituals, funerary rites, economic activity, war practices, inter-personal and inter-societal relationships.

More than ever, I am convinced that we must start from a point of mutual respect when dealing with people from other places. Degrading stereotypes only exacerbate resentments. A basic tenet of respect means not telling other people how to run their political or economic systems. It requires truly listening to each other and not just talking past one another, as well as making an earnest effort to coexist. That's a starting and ending point that we must all strive to achieve.

And now, I tip my hat and thank you for accompanying me on this long, incredible journey.

The Culture Vultures

A teenage Argentine girl, arriving as an exchange student to a small town in upstate New York, was greeted festively with a party featuring mariachi music and tacos.

"This American food is very good. What is it?" she asked

Her well-meaning hosts were dumbfounded, thinking that was what people ate in Argentina. Instead, the most popular fare is *parillada*, grilled meat, and Italian food is also quite common.

"What's that music?" she queried.

Again, the Americans scratched their heads. Why did this girl from Latin America not recognize Latin American music?

My friend recounted this story and still found it amusing years later. Mexicans, and only Mexicans, eat tacos and listen to mariachi. Every country has its own distinct foods, music and customs. Argentines listen and dance to melodic tango. Tacos and mariachi are as out of place in Argentina as was the rap soundtrack to the 2013 movie *The Great Gatsby*, which took place in the Jazz Age 1920s, when everybody danced the Charleston.

The Americano, a 1955 movie starring Glenn Ford, shows a Texas rancher taking three Brahman bulls to Brazil to sell them. A scene shows a woman singing in Spanish and dancing the *rumba*, a style popular in Cuba. The singing and dancing were good, but out of place because Brazilians speak Portuguese and do not dance the rumba. The director probably thought that any Latin music would do, and most people watching the movie would never know the difference.

That's akin to playing Edith Piaf as the soundtrack for *Citizen Kane*. Great film. Fantastic music. But a mismatch.

There is no such thing as Latin culture, just like there is no such thing as European culture. Poland, Greece and Belgium are all part of Europe, but have little in common in terms of culture. Language, food, music and habits are unrecognizable from one country to the other.

Styles in Latin America vary widely by country, and even within countries. Brazil is famous for *samba* and *bossa nova*. But my in-laws off in the hinterlands never listened to that. They would occasionally find on the radio, through the scratchy static, *forró* music, distinguished by accordion, triangle, and slapping a two-sided *zabumba* drum, with steps reminiscent of line dancing. Others prefer *frevo* or *sertanejo* duets, among numerous distinct styles. And many Brazilians are keen on mournful ballads from Portugal called *fado* (fate).

Mexico is most closely associated with mariachi, but not everybody enjoys the brass. They might instead listen to *rancheros, jarocho, corridos* (think *La Cucaracha*), or *norteño*. Farther South in Central America, people enjoy *merengue* and *marimba*, depending on region.

In the Spanish-speaking Caribbean, the most popular music is *salsa*, but *mambo, rumba*, and *conga*, among many other styles, are also well known.

Colombia is an interesting intersection of *salsa* on the coast, home-grown *cumbia, vallenato*, and the traditional Andean music popular throughout the region.

Argentina is famous for its *tango*, but Andean and folk music also have large followings.

Most people outside the region know little of the local music, although David Byrne and Paul Simon introduced Brazilian music to a wider audience in the late 1980s and early 1990s.

Caetano Veloso, one of Brazil's most enduring singer-songwriters, once told me: "Paul Simon uses it as a seasoning to his own music. He admires and collaborates. It is wonderful that a poor country has enough music rich enough to interest good musicians."

Lyrics by Veloso himself inspire his listeners. A stately colonial mansion on Avenida Paulista, Sao Paulo's busiest commercial thoroughfare, was about to face a wrecking ball, so a Veloso fan shimmied over the old wrought iron fence and boldly painted one of his popular lyrics, "The power of money rises up and destroys beautiful things," on a wall of the pink manor.

Those words, from Veloso's gracefully soft *Sampa* (which he described to me as a love song to São Paulo) remained affixed more than a year, until the estate was demolished to create yet another glass-and-steel tower in South America's most-populous city.

Veloso sees irony in the graffiti: "That's exactly the kind of beauty being destroyed by the power of money in São Paulo. And yet, those old mansions were built by coffee barons," he said.

Veloso went into exile in 1968 along with his best friend, Gilberto Gil, after their arrest by the military junta which felt threatened by their *tropicalia* movement. The pair lived three years in London. There Gil picked up the rhythms of West Indian and African immigrants and has incorporated those styles into his own repertoire, thereby broadening Brazilian music.

The "queen of *samba*" Beth Carvalho describes the form as "the fountain from which all Brazilian music drinks." She prides herself on discovering and recovering forgotten *sambas* from yesteryear and recording them. This attention has brought some older, neglected talents back from obscurity in their later years.

Marisa Monte is a soprano who grew up idolizing Maria Callas and trained in Italy to sing the classics. But she turned away from opera when she discovered her knack for popular music. "Brazil has a rich, distinctive universe of music. Brazil is a mixture: of rhythms, of ideas, of people, of foods. My work reflects this," she told me.

Monte loves to perform for free. "The price of admission makes the biggest difference. If it's free, the people are a lot more excited. If it's expensive, they're cold. They just pay their money, applaud, then leave," she said. "A free show in Brazil is the most beautiful thing in the world. It's like watching Pelé play."

Saxophonist Ivo Perelman blends Afro-Brazilian *candomblé* chants, the twangs of a *birimbau* – a single-stringed bowlike instrument – and *congas* to create a unique form of jazz.

In Bolivia I met Chilean travelers who snapped up tapes of banned music by Inti-Illimani and smuggled them back home. The group was touring Europe during the 1973 coup; the military dictatorship blocked them from returning for fifteen years and banned their recordings.

The group performs wearing *luchus*, colorful woolen caps common in Andean highlands, playing four-foot-tall wood flutes, large native drums, handheld bells and shells, guitar and *charango*, a stringed instrument made of an armadillo shell.

"Harmony is connected to the natural and the supernatural. When we play, what we are doing is transmitting these sounds. The message is respect, love of nature and cooperation among mankind because this reflects daily life in rural villages," said group leader José Montano. "We are aware that the instruments don't belong to us, rather they belong to a people who have kept them alive for thousand of years to the present time."

The late Mercedes Sosa cut a commanding figure with chiseled features, straight black hair and high cheekbones. Her Indian heritage was reflected in her music, facial features and dress. She was fond of bright, colorful scarves popular in the Andes. When "the voice of the Americas" opened her mouth, out poured the authority of one who suffered repression, poverty and overwhelming sadness. Her talent lay in expressing a song's raw emotions with her powerful, earthy contralto as she pounded a *bombo*, a large Andean drum.

Arrested and banned from performing, Sosa fled to Europe for three years because her song *La Arribeña* ("The Place Up There") was used – without her consent – by Montonero rebels to signal attacks against the military dictatorship. "I never sided with the Montoneros. I don't agree with killing the military or with killing anyone," she told me.

I also met some of the region's finest writers. Gabriel Garcia Marquez, the Nobel prize-winning Colombian author, credits the Latin American environment with influencing him to write "magical realism," a style that is chaotic, bizarre, fertile with detail, harshly critical of governments in the region, and even grotesque in its juxtaposition of the incredible with the everyday. "Surrealism comes from the reality of Latin America," he told me, alluding to poverty and political instability.

I regret that I didn't fulfill my scheduled interview with Jorge Amado, Brazil's greatest novelist in the second half of the twentieth century. He apologized for canceling due to illness and died shortly thereafter.

Recommended Books

Latin America has a multitude of talented writers, among them Jorge Luis Borges and Gabriel Garcia Marquez (I interviewed both), Octavio Paz, Carlos Fuentes, Jorge Amado, Isabel Allende and Mario Vargas Llosa, to name just a few. Rather than discussing the merits of the region's best novelists, for whom excellent translations exist, I am listing some of my favorite books which explain the region:

Brazil on the Rise: Larry Rohter, a correspondent in Brazil for *Newsweek* and the *New York Times,* wrote the definitive book about Brazil by a foreigner.

Distant Neighbors: Alan Riding was a *New York Times* correspondent in Brazil and Mexico and wrote what is widely considered the finest book about Mexico by a foreigner.

In Patagonia: Bruce Chatwin paints a vivid portrait of the desolate lands in southern Argentina and the tough, hidebound people who survive there.

La Capital: Jonathan Kandell, a correspondent for the *Wall Street Journal,* tells the history of Mexico City from the Toltec Indians through modern metropolis.

Our Man is Inside: Diego Asencio, the former U.S. ambassador to Colombia, recounts in painstaking and often whimsical detail his experiences as a hostage of anti-government rebels in Bogotá while profiling both the guerrillas and fellow hostages.

Passage Through El Dorado: Kandell journeys through the hinter lands that the proposed East-West transcontinental highway would traverse, viewing it through the eyes of local people.

The Capital of Hope: Alex Shoumatoff describes how the hypermodern capital of Brasília was conceived and built and what the city has become.

The Children of Sanchez: Anthropologist Oscar Lewis studied a family living in a slum on the outskirts of Mexico City. The book was banned for years in Mexico, proof that it scraped a raw nerve.

The Labyrinth Of Solitude: Octavio Paz masterfully dissects the minds of fellow Mexicans, exposing national neuroses, alienation and solitude.

The Mexicans: Patrick Oster paints enlightening portraits of everyday Mexicans who shatter myths and stereotypes: a fire breather, a peasant, a police officer, a gay man, and others.

The Old Patagonian Express: Paul Theroux whisks the reader along a magical journey by rail starting in the United States and ending in Argentina. It's a light-hearted, sarcastic view of the world seen from a train window.

The Panama Hat Trail: Tom Miller takes the reader on a journey starting from how the straw is cultivated and the hats are constructed until they reach consumers in foreign countries.

The Soccer War: Ryszard Kapuscinski was a correspondent for Poland's news agency when El Salvador invaded neighboring Honduras over a dispute triggered by a soccer game. His stories behind the stories are a masterful oeuvre of reportage spanning the globe.

Tristes Tropiques: A seminal achievement by French anthropologist Claude Levi-Strauss, who lived in Brazil in the 1930s. His descriptions are so detailed and accurate that the places were easily recognizable a half century later. He lived among academics in São Paulo and Indians in remote villages, giving him unparalleled access to Brazilians from all walks of life.

Recommended Movies

Here are some recommended films to better understand Latin America. They are insightful, entertaining and world class:

Black Orpheus (1959): Made by French director Marcel Camus, it has been my favorite since I was a youngster and did not speak a word of Portuguese. Many Brazilians turn their noses up, offended that a foreigner so masterfully interprets their culture for the world. While based on the Greek tragedy Orpheus and Eurydice, the film is quintessentially Brazilian in its depiction of the splendor of Carnival, bittersweet lives of slum residents, local superstitions, heart-pounding Rio scenery, and unforgettable soundtrack.

Bye Bye Brasil (1980): Starring top Brazilian actors, it tells about a traveling circus trying to survive in modern Brazil, where small town residents spurn live entertainment for the mesmerizing TV screen.

Central Station (1998): A spinster takes a young boy to find his family in the hinterlands of northeastern Brazil. The compelling story captured the mood of the national consciousness, while actress Fernanda Montenegro was nominated for an Academy Award.

City of God (2002): The story of slum-dwellers in Rio could easily have fallen into a series of cheap clichés, but the story line was realistic, captivating and fresh.

El Norte (1983): It follows a brother and sister who escape persecution by Guatemala's military rulers during a civil war and flee to El Norte, the United States.

Gabriella (1983): The depiction of cultural clashes, based on a novel by Jorge Amado, features Sonia Braga and the legendary Marcello Mastroianni. Braga also starred in *Kiss of the Spider Woman,* the story of two cellmates in a Brazilian prison under military dictatorship.

Los Olvidados (1952): Spaniard Luis Buñuel directed this gritty masterpiece, a frank, searing look at street kids in Mexico City.

Missing (1982): Costa-Gavras made this drama, based on a true story about American journalist Charles Horman who disappeared during the 1973 coup in Chile. Jack Lemmon plays Horman's father and Sissy Spacek portrays his wife. Similarly, *One Man's War* tells about a family's search for justice after the killing of seventeen-year-old Joelito Filartaga to punish his father for his opposition to the military rule of Paraguayan dictator Alfredo Stroessner.

Pixote (1981): Made by Argentine director Hector Babenco, this is an art-imitates-life-imitates-art story about a boy who yo-yos back and forth between a Brazilian orphanage and the mean streets. Tragically, the movie's youthful star was gunned down by police in 1987.

¡Que Viva México!: Russian director Sergei Eisenstein filmed what resembles a collection of short stories in a brilliant, insightful portrait of life in Mexico from the Maya civilization through the 1930s.

Salvador (1986): This Oliver Stone thriller, shown through the eyes of an American photojournalist played by James Woods, exposes the horrors of a Central American civil war and the tragedies suffered by ordinary people.

The Motorcycle Diaries (2004): A biography directed by Brazil's Walter Salles about the youthful Che Guevara as he traveled around Latin America on a motorcycle in 1952 coincidentally follows much of the same route I traversed three decades later. It features Gael Garcia Bernal, who also starred in the excellent Mexican films *Y Tu Mamá También* and *Amores Perros.*

The Official Story (1985): This Argentine Oscar-winning film stars the iconic Norma Aleandro in a fictional story based on true events about the military dictatorship stealing the babies of political enemies it murdered, and military families raising those children as their own.

ndex

Made in the USA
San Bernardino, CA
01 April 2014